ROUTLEDGE LIBRARY EDITIONS:
KOREAN STUDIES

Volume 6

# RELIGIONS OF OLD KOREA

# RELIGIONS OF OLD KOREA

CHARLES ALLEN CLARK

Routledge
Taylor & Francis Group

LONDON AND NEW YORK

First published in 1932 by F.H. Revell Co., New York
Reissued 1981 by Garland Publishing, Inc.

This edition first published in 2020
by Routledge
2 Park Square, Milton Park, Abingdon, Oxon OX14 4RN

and by Routledge
52 Vanderbilt Avenue, New York, NY 10017

*Routledge is an imprint of the Taylor & Francis Group, an informa business*

*Trademark notice*: Product or corporate names may be trademarks or registered
trademarks, and are used only for identification and explanation without intent to
infringe.

*British Library Cataloguing in Publication Data*
A catalogue record for this book is available from the British Library

ISBN: 978-1-138-38774-4 (Set)
ISBN: 978-0-429-28646-9 (Set) (ebk)
ISBN: 978-0-367-25952-5 (Volume 6) (hbk)
ISBN: 978-0-367-25989-1 (Volume 6) (pbk)
ISBN: 978-0-429-29083-1 (Volume 6) (ebk)

**Publisher's Note**
The publisher has gone to great lengths to ensure the quality of this reprint but
points out that some imperfections in the original copies may be apparent.

**Disclaimer**
The publisher has made every effort to trace copyright holders and would welcome
correspondence from those they have been unable to trace.

# Religions of Old Korea

By
CHARLES ALLEN CLARK, Ph.D., D.D.

千手千眼觀世音菩薩

KWANSEIEUM, GODDESS OF MERCY—BUDDHA OF
THE THOUSAND ARMS AND EYES

# PREFACE

THE lectures herewith were first delivered at Princeton Theological Seminary as the Missionary Lectures of 1921, during the second furlough of the writer. They were further enriched and partly re-written, and delivered again, in 1929, before the Faculty and students of Western Theological Seminary, and the United Presbyterian Seminary of Pittsburgh. Later, they were presented again at the Presbyterian Seminary of Chicago, and two were given at Auburn Seminary, New York. The writer has been urged by many who heard them to have them published for the sake of the wider group which might be profited by them.

The name, "Religions of *Old* Korea," has been advisedly chosen, for there is a new Korea today, and much that was beautiful and charming has now passed away, along with a great deal that was harmful and useless in the old civilization of the people. No book like this can ever again be written about Korea from original sources, for much of the data is passing, or has already passed away. Still, the writer has not felt that his labour was in vain, for we must know the religions which have been in any country, and the way in which those religions psychologically appealed to the people, if we would know how to approach them with a higher religion today.

The religions of China and of Japan, and, to some extent, those of Siberia, have been investigated. Korea, with its "twenty millions of brothers and sisters," lies right in between the three, and constitutes an unworked mine of materials, a virgin field, whose data ought to supplement all that is known of the other fields and integrate it all.

The religions of the various countries of the world are not made-to-order, mechanical things, nor concoctions of witch doctors or priests for their own private profit and benefit. They are the various ways in which men have tried to explain or understand the universe, and the ways by which they have tried to adjust themselves to ultimate reality. Religions grow as men grow; they are living things which develop as they meet felt needs, and die when they fail to meet them. Not only so, religions migrate from one country to another, changing to fit the new environments, sometimes dying off in the original countries from which they came.

Some years ago, the writer evolved a Master's thesis upon the subject of the *Yama Concept, a Study in the Spread of Religious Cult.* Yama is the god of the dead today over the greater part of Asia. It was wonderful, in the course of research on the subject, to see how Yima of ancient Aryan Persia, with his sister, or wife, called " Yimak," changed to Yama of Vedic India, a jolly old King Cole sort of deity, and then to a more grim and terrible being in later Indian history. We saw him pass over into China, becoming " Yenlo " there, with Titsang taking over a part of his functions; then to Yenlo, the horrible spirit of Thibet, pouring molten copper down the throats of opposers. Then came Yumna, of Korea, less obtrusive but all-pervasive, and then the nebulous " Emma-O " of Japan, and there were even indications that the Yome, mentioned by Brinton as the god of the dead in far-off Peru might be a lineal descendant of old Yima, of pre-Zoroaster Aryan day fame.

Japan today presents the picture of a modern nation still holding tenaciously, albeit somewhat precariously, to, what a few generations ago, the world knew as " heathen " religions. How did she get those " heathen " religions, since we know that most of them are not indigenous? What is the connection between the religions of great China, great Siberia and great Japan? Did those religions migrate from one land to another? No one has heretofore made any effort to investigate this matter, although each separate country has been well studied. Possibly a study of the religions of little Korea will help us to understand the matter. In this present generation, Korea, in its cordial reception given to the Christian Gospel, has seemed to show that the people have a distinct " flair " for things religious, to such an extent that some have felt that its new English name, " Chosen " (used in Korea since 1122 B. C.) somehow connects it with that other " Chosen " people at the other end of its continent. Did Koreans always have that flair for religion, and, if so, were they disproportionately responsible for the spread and persistence of these "heathen" religions in this general part of the world? It is questions like these that this book tries to answer. They are things worthy of investigation.

These studies represent twenty-eight years of following a hobby amidst a busy missionary life. The writer has never felt that it was right for him to take missionary time for these researches, and has, at no time, done so, but, in vacation periods, and, in passing by, he has made it a point continuously to ask questions, and note down and tabulate data secured. He has been fortunate in winning the confidence of many of his Korean associates, who have assisted him in his researches, and have brought in bits of data which could not have been secured in any other way. The Koreans are a proud people, of an ancient race, and they will not tell such things as have been gathered here, if they suspect that they are in any way to be the basis of ridicule of their nation or of its culture and civilization. The writer has not needed to make any pretence of seeming to honour their nation. He knows that they have behind them four thousand years and more of history, and that, more than fifteen hundred years ago, they were doing creative work in art, literature and religion, while most of Europe was in darkest ignorance. Some of those ancient works of art have come to light in recent years, and are the equal of those of any land.

The writer has read practically everything that has ever been written upon the religions of Korea, with the exception of those treasures locked up in Chinese books, and, in the text herewith, he has called attention to things said by other writers. By far the greater part of his materials, however, are from his own notebooks, and the references are mainly for corroboration, rather than given as original sources. Either before or after seeing those books, the items quoted have all been verified. As assistance in the matter of method, four courses in Comparative Religion were taken at the University of Chicago during the furlough year 1920.

These studies are sent out, first of all, that the world may know a little more about this people whom the writer loves and honours, secondly that they may be of some assistance, if possible, to those who are seeking to gather and make available information about all of the world's religions, and thirdly in the hope that they may be helpful to junior colleagues in the mission work in Korea, who may come after, and who should know the genius and psychology of the people among whom they have come to work.

Since the delivery of the lectures in 1929, they have been wholly revised and re-written, and much new material added, but the lecture form has been retained, as possibly the most appropriate.

C. A. C.

*Pyengyang, Korea.*

# CONTENTS

I. BUDDHISM . . . . . . . . . 11
Indian Buddhism—Chinese Buddhism—Korean Buddhism: (a) Three Kingdom Age; (b) Koryu Dynasty Period; (c) Yi Dynasty Period.

II. BUDDHISM (*Continued*) . . . . . . . 44
Buildings and Grounds — Images — Ceremonies — Literature, Sacred Books—Sects—Doctrines—The Present Situation.

III. CONFUCIANISM . . . . . . . . . 91
History—Buildings and Physical Equipment—The Great Examinations—Sacrifices and Religious Beliefs—Literature of the Cult—Doctrines—Present Status—Estimate of the Cult.

IV. MISCELLANEOUS CULTS . . . . . . 126
Mohammedanism—Taoism—Japanese Shinto—Pochun Kyo—Kwankong: Cult of the God of War—Choi II: Taichang Cult —Tangoon Kyo.

V. THE CHUNTOKYO CULT . . . . . . 144
History—Ceremonies—Doctrines—Estimate of the Cult.

VI. SHAMANISM . . . . . . . . . 173
History—Importance of the Cult—Buildings—Types of Shamans—Call and Preparation of the Shaman—Organization of the Cult—Kinds of Spirits Worshipped—Apotropæic Rites—Ceremonies and Séances of the Shamans—Doctrines and Morality Teachings—The Future of Shamanism.

VII. FIRST CONTACTS WITH CHRISTIANITY IN OLD KOREA . . . . . . . . . 220

VIII. SUMMARY . . . . . . . . . 256

APPENDICES:
1. THE BIBLE OF THE CHUNTOKYO, "TONG CHUN TAI CHUN" . . . . . . . . . . 258
2. THE BIBLE OF SHAMANISM, "OKJU KYUNG" . . 276
3. THE "ROSARY CLASSIC" . . . . . . . 286
4. BIBLIOGRAPHY . . . . . . . . . 287
5. ANALYZED INDEX . . . . . . . . 291

# ILLUSTRATIONS

FACING
PAGE

KWANSEIEUM, GODDESS OF MERCY, BUDDHA OF THE
THOUSAND ARMS AND LEGS . . . . . . . . Title

A BUDDHIST TEMPLE IN THE MOUNTAINS . . . . 44

THE EUNJIN BUDDHA, THE GREATEST MIRYUCK IN
KOREA . . . . . . . . . . . . . . . 62

KOOKSADANG, NATIONAL SPIRIT SHRINE, SEOUL . . 136

YAKUT SHAMAN OF SIBERIA . . . . . . . . 182

A MOOTANG'S KOOT, SORCERESS IN A TRANCE . . . 212

# I

## BUDDHISM

A COUPLE of years ago, I picked up a folder of the Japanese railway in Korea, and noticed that almost on the front page, in describing for travellers the things worth seeing in Korea, it stated, " Korea is a Buddhist country." A statement like that shows how truly the " wish may be the father of the thought " on the part of the compiler of the folder. It could not but cause a smile to any one who knows the Korea of today. Five hundred years ago, Korea *was* a Buddhist country pre-eminently, and today there are nominally 1,472 temples left, but it certainly is not in any large sense a Buddhist country now. Nevertheless, Buddhism is still a power that has to be reckoned with by any one seeking to do religious work in the country, and it is richly worth our study because of what it has contributed to the culture of the Korean nation all down the ages, and for the revelation that it makes of the psychology and religious genius of the people.

It is curious that up till now there has been almost no research in connection with Korean Buddhism, although that of China and that of Japan are both well known, and would undoubtedly be far better known if the Buddhism of Korea were better understood, especially since Japan received her cult from Korea. Mr. Hulbert, in his *History of Korea*, has incidentally mentioned certain items in its history. Various others, writing in the *Royal Asiatic Society Records*, or in the oldest English magazines in the country such as the *Repository* and the *Review*, have also touched upon it superficially, but no one has tried to study into it more deeply until very recent years.

Madame E. A. Gordon, of Tokio, spent some time investigating the [1] subject in connection with her lifelong study of Buddhism in Japan and elsewhere, and she has written about it in the *Korea*

---

[1] *Korea Branch Royal Asiatic Society Records*, 1914, Vol. V, pp. 1-39.

*Asiatic Society Records* and has a little in her books, the *Symbols of the Way* and *World Healers,* but she was evidently imposed upon greatly by her interpreters, who seem to have sought to tell her what she wanted to find out rather than the facts as they actually were, and her incoherent, illogical presentation makes it difficult to follow her.   Prof. Starr, in his little book, *Korean Buddhism,* suffers under the same difficulties concerning interpreters, and gives largely only what Hulbert and Trollope had already published.   Both Madame Gordon and Prof. Starr also use the Japanese names for everything, so that their books are more or less unintelligible.   About the only real contribution of any value to date is that of Bishop M. N. Trollope, D.D., of the Anglican Church in Korea.   In the *Asiatic Society Records* of 1917,[2] he has, what he modestly calls, an " Introduction to the Study of Buddhism in Corea," which is most illuminating and will always stand as a notable contribution.

What I have to say on the subject has come from some twenty-eight years of occasional study on the matter.   When I first landed in the country, I had for a language teacher a man who had for many years been the abbot of a monastery on the mountain north of Seoul.   He had become a Christian, surrendering his comfortable living, and had come down to Seoul to start life anew.   To make practice conversation, we had to talk about the things which interested us most, so we naturally talked often of Buddhism, and I there acquired my first interest in the subject.   For all my first ten years in Korea, this man was my constant companion wherever I travelled, and he made it his business to search out and pass on to me the sort of information which he knew I wanted to find.   I visited many of the most important monasteries in the country with him, notably on one long walking trip down through the old Silla country around Kyungju, and I saw things there through his initiated eyes.   I have sent him to most of the other large temples of the country which, I did not have time to visit personally, and he has brought back photographs and answers to the long lists of questions which I gave him.

---

[2] *Korea Branch Royal Asiatic Society Records,* 1917, Vol. VIII, p. 1.

I have translated one three hundred page history of Buddhism, the *Poolkyo Yaksa*, written by Kwun Sang No, and have done some work on Yi Neung Ha's encyclopedic *Chosen Poolkyo Tongsa*. In the summer of 1919, Pak Hak Nyun, then President of the Buddhist College in Seoul, came to my study all summer long, four afternoons a week, three hours each time, and answered for me several hundreds of written questions which had emerged in my studies and were troubling me. I found him wonderfully well informed, and secured much data. These are my original sources. I have compared what I found with everything that I could find written on the Buddhism of India, China or Japan, and everything written in the general books on Korea and in the old magazines and *Records* mentioned above. I have mentioned only the most important of these in the Bibliography at the end of the book. Much information was secured in conversation also from the abbots and priests of the many monasteries visited.

I have been several times to Japan and have visited temples there, also made one trip to Peking and saw most of the temples within ten miles of that city, also made two long trips across Manchuria, one of them for a thousand li (330 miles) by cart, visiting shrines along the way. Last year I also visited temples in Shanghai, Singapore, Penang, Rangoon, and crossing India visited the reputed spot where the famous Bodhi tree stood and where one of its descendants stands today. I saw Benares and the recently excavated " Deer Park " of Sarnath, and then visited all of the Buddha museums in the cities of India, and in Paris and London.

The subject of Buddhism is so large that it will be impossible to cover it all in one lecture, so I am going to divide it, taking up first the history, and then, in the second lecture, discussing the doctrines, ceremonies, sects and temples.

### History of Buddhism in General

As to the history of Korean Buddhism, it is necessary that we first go back briefly and show its connection with the whole cult of Buddhism from its inception. The history is continuous all the way from the Bodhi tree out through Kashmir, back into China, then over into Korea, and, incidentally, on over into Japan. For this earlier history, naturally I have no original records, so must borrow. The best short, recent treatise is likely that of Hackmann.[3] I have taken most of my facts on this period from him and Rhys David.[4]

"Buddhism, as everyone knows, came originally from India. Its founder is called 'The Buddha.' That is a title of his rank, like the word 'Christ,' or 'Messiah,' and not his personal name. There had been Buddhas of previous aeons (kalpas), and there is at least one Buddha yet to come, the Messiah Buddha of Mahayana Buddhism, called 'Meitreya' in China and 'Miryuck' in Korea.

"*The* Buddha, *i. e.,* the 'Enlightened One,' was born from an ancient noble Indian family of the Sakyas. From this comes his poetic name 'Sakamuni' ('Saint' or 'Teacher' or 'Ascetic' of the House of Sakya), and also 'Sakayerai' (the 'Coming One' of the House of Sakya), which are his two most widely used names, especially in Korea. His personal name was Siddartha (Korean 'Sidal Taisa'), but, as he renounced that name at the very beginning of his career, he is almost never called that by his followers. There is another name belonging to the family from the earliest times by which he is sometimes known, *i. e.,* 'Gautauma' (Korean 'Godam'). He is sometimes also called the 'World Honoured One' (Korean 'Seichon').

"The father of Gautauma was an Indian nobleman named Suddhodana (Korean 'Chungpan'), who presided over a small district one hundred and thirty miles north of Benares. His capital was Kapilavastu (Korean 'Kapila Kook'). A number of ancient, semi-ruined towns dispute the honour of being Buddha's birthplace, and we cannot positively decide between them, but we are now sure of the general neighbourhood, which was settled by discoveries made in 1896–7. The district was on the borders of British and Nepaulese territory on both sides of the eighty-fourth degree of longitude." (Incidentally it may be said that even as late as the summer of 1928, the newspapers of India, while I was there, were proclaiming the finding of another "stupa" of Asoka

[3] Hackmann, *Buddhism as a Religion.*
[4] Rhys David, *Buddhism*, pp. 1, 5, 25 f., 179.

which purported to upset all of these calculations mentioned by Hackmann.)

" Buddha was not born at the capital. His mother was from the hill country towards the north, and, when the time for her confinement approached, she desired to await the arrival of her firstborn in her childhood home. On the way thither, she was surprised to find that her hour had come. The child was born in the grove of Lumbini (Korean ' Piram Won ') by the side of the road. On the spot where the birth took place, some hundreds of years later, King Asoka raised a memorial tablet with an inscription commemorating the event, and it was that tablet which was discovered in December, 1896, so that both the place and the event are beyond all doubt today.[5] The name of Buddha's mother was ' Maya ' (Korean ' Maya Pooeen '). She died in giving birth to her son. Her sister, Mahaprajapati, also one of Suddhodana's wives, undertook the raising of the child. In later years, she was the first woman allowed in the Order, and it is probably doubtful if women would ever have been admitted if it had not been for her strong pleading and Buddha's duty to her as her foster son.

"All of these events took place about the middle of the sixth century B. C.," the century which produced Socrates and Plato in Greece, Zoroaster in Persia, Laotze and Confucius in China, and the great prophets of the Exile in Israel, one of the great ages of the world for constructive religious progress.

" Gautauma was brought up in the greatest of luxury with crowds of servants attending him, and he was most carefully educated. When very young, he was married. The name of his wife is uncertain." It is given variously as Yasodhara, Bhaddakacca or Gopa. The attendant at the great pyramid-like Buddhagaya temple in 1928 told me that " Gopa " was the name of one of the life-size idols in the corner shrine in the upper terrace. This wife bore one son who was called " Rahula."

" Not long after this event, Gautauma left his home, father, wife and child in order to withdraw into the wilderness. He did this in opposition to the wishes of his family, who did everything possible

---

[5] Rhys David, *Buddhism,* p. 26 f.

to prevent it. It must have been extremely difficult to break all of those ties. He was driven by an overpowering longing to give himself to the problems of human existence, and, for this purpose, he needed to be freed from the bonds of this life.

"Such a mode of action was not entirely uncommon in those days. The religious instinct of India had already produced hermits, ascetics and people of monastic habits. Gautauma sought the usual way to solve the riddle which pressed upon him. He associated with famous anchorites, and sought their advice. It was the accepted opinion of the period that a deeper insight into the meaning of life could be obtained by the help of severe asceticism which would free the soul from physical bondage. Gautauma allowed himself to be driven into this course, but all of his attempts failed to satisfy him. For seven years, he wrestled strenuously, but in vain, until at last he gave up the struggle as a failure.

"Soon after this a great change came over him. As he sat one day under the Bodhi tree, suddenly he received the revelation which he had been seeking, and instantly became a Buddha, an Enlightened One. At that time, he was thirty-six years old. From that day, his whole life was given to the propagation of the Doctrines.

For about forty-five years, he worked among his people, wandering from place to place. "With increasing care, he elaborated his system of thought by means of discussion with foes and friends alike. He won great numbers of adherents, and soon had an inner band of disciples whom he trained and taught. Multitudes of outsiders, who felt that they could not live up to his tenets, at least learned to respect and admire him. He converted his father, wife, son, and other relatives. He travelled over several nearby principalities. Each year, in the rainy season, he went with his disciples to some place where they could settle down and live for three months, and there he gave them special teaching.⁶

"Death found him at his tasks, an old man of eighty, in the year A. D. 477. He died surrounded by his disciples in the city of Kusinagara by the river bank under some blossoming trees. His body was cremated and the relics divided among the princes and

---

⁶ Rhys David, *Buddhism,* p. 57.

noble families." Korean legend says that there were eight million of the little jewel-like relics called "Saree" found in the ashes. "Some of the remains the family of the Sakyas received, and they buried them under a great monument. The place where these relics were buried was found and opened in 1898, the old remains being found entirely untouched."

Multitudinous wild legends have grown up around the Buddha, of Immaculate Conception, when the white elephant came down from the "Tushito" heaven (Korean "Tosul Chun") and entered his mother's side, of the four heavenly Divas (Korean "Sa Chun Wang") and their many miracles, of the fierce battle between them and the Evil One Mara, of the twenty-eight steps taken by Buddha on the day of his birth, of the flowers that bloomed in his footprints and that rained from the heavens, of his miraculous converting of robbers and courtesans and kings and devils wholesale, etc., etc. These are found in the Jataka Tales now published in part in the Sacred Books of the East series. About all that we can rest upon as fact, however, are the statements which we have made above.

During the lifetime of the Buddha, his Doctrine spread over one or two of the nearest kingdoms, Magadha and Kosala particularly. He himself preached often in the market-places of Benares and in the Sarnath Deer Park, just a little way outside of it. After his death, the organization gradually extended its field until it covered the whole of India. Although some of his doctrines, as, for example, his teaching concerning caste, and those concerning the soul, were radically different from the teachings of the Brahmans, there does not seem to have been a very intense antagonism between them. No doubt, by many, Buddhism was thought of simply as another sect of Brahmanism.[7] Through the following centuries, however, they became more and more antagonistic, and it was Brahmanism in its modern form, Hinduism, which finally drove Buddhism entirely out of India, where it no longer exists today. There are Buddhist temples in Ceylon today and in Burmah, and some in the foothills of the Himalayas, but none in India itself.

---

[7] Hackmann, p. 36.

While Buddha lay dying, he is said to have selected Kasyap from among his followers, and to have set him up at Patriarch of the Church.  When Kasyap died, Ananda was chosen, and after him others from generation to generation until Boddhidharma, the twenty-eighth Patriarch, at a time when Buddhism was almost dead in India, crossed over into China in 526 A. D. and, with him, the line of the Patriarchs died out.  After him in China there were five so-called Patriarchs, but they were not widely recognized. The Southern Buddhism of Ceylon has a slightly different line of Patriarchs.[8]

While Buddha was living, his teaching was all given orally. Nothing at all was written.  Whether any existing Buddhist Scriptures date from earlier than 250 B. C. is a great question.  Orthodox Buddhism, however, claims that immediately after the death of Buddha, a Council was called in the nearby Cave of Rajagriha, and that, at that time, the sayings of the Master were written out one by one as they were repeated from memory by Ananda and endorsed as accurate by the Council composed of his near disciples.[9]

Buddha himself opposed asceticism as practised by the Brahmans.  He had tried it himself and found it wanting.  Little by little, however, certain ascetic practices crept into the Order. When these writings were made in the Council in the Cave, all of these ascetic practices were made obligatory.  Even before this, there were many in the Order who did not approve of them. They endeavoured at this time to get the provisions lightened, but their petitions were refused.  Agitation continued, however, and about one hundred years later a second Council is said to have been held at Vaishali, where again all concessions were sternly denied.  The rebels seem by this time to have increased largely in numbers, for they held a separate Council at that time and granted the liberties desired.  This was the first split in the Order.[10]

While Buddha lived, all India was divided into many small independent states just as it was many centuries later when the British took it over.  One hundred and fifty years after Buddha, Alex-

---

[8] Edkins, *Chinese Buddhism*, pp. 60-86; Lloyd, *Creed of Half Japan*, p. 22.
[9] Rockhill, *Life of Buddha*, p. 158.
[10] Hackmann, pp. 37, 39; Lloyd, *Creed of Half Japan*, pp. 24, 25.

ander the Great, by his conquests, stirred the whole west and north of the country. Possibly as a result of this, a great united kingdom was formed under the headship of Chandragupta, a man of low caste, but of great military and administrative gifts.[11] This man had relations, at first antagonistic, later friendly, with Seleucus Nicator, one of the great generals who succeeded to that part of Alexander's kingdom that was nearest to India. To him Seleucus gave one of his daughters in marriage. The Greek historian, Megasthenes, to whom we owe most of our knowledge of India of this period, was sent to Chandragupta by Seleucus.[12]

Chandragupta was not a Buddhist.[13] If anything, he leaned in favour of the Brahmans. His son, Bindusara, who succeeded him, was the one who loaned the elephants to the Persian King to be used against the Greeks under Pyrrhus. He, too, was not a Buddhist, but his son, Asoka (Korean "Aryook" or "Asuta"), who reigned 270–233 B. C., was, in some ways, the founder of Buddhism after Buddha.[14] He has been called the "Apostle Paul of Buddhism." Asoka was an enthusiastic evangelist. He has left innumerable records upon stone pillars and monuments and walls throughout what was his kingdom, and these records, as deciphered today, give us our most accurate information as to the Doctrines and founding of the Buddhist Order.

In his edicts, he claims that Buddhism had spread far beyond the bounds of India. He mentions relations which he had with Antiochus II. of Syria (260–247 B. C.), Ptolemy Philadelphus of Egypt (285–247 B. C.), Antigonatus Gonatas of Macedonia (278–242 B. C.), and many others. While those relations were mainly political, he contrived to recommend his religion to them also. Possibly there were reciprocal benefits along that line. Lloyd and others think that they discern in the Buddhism of the North many traces of Egyptian influence.[15]

With Asoka, the history of Buddhism outside of India begins.

---

[11] Lloyd as above.
[12] *Ibid.*
[13] Rhys David, *Buddhism*, p. 221.
[14] Lloyd, *Creed of Half Japan*, p. 28 f.
[15] Hackmann, *Buddhism as a Religion;* Lloyd, *Shinran and His Work,* p. 76.

After his death, his kingdom disintegrated. For many years, the small kingdoms resulting in North India struggled among themselves for supremacy. During this time, the Greek Bactrian States, successors to Alexander's Empire, were growing. They kept pushing down into India from the Persian side, and, for a time, actually held large sections of Northwest India. Grecian and Indian culture became intimately fused. It is because of this, no doubt, that we find in so much of the art and, to some extent, in the doctrines of Buddhism in China and Korea, features that look as though they must have come from ancient Greece. Even the dress shown in many of the ancient Korean images is Grecian. Note particularly in this line the various bas relief figures in the famous Sukoolam Cave near Kyungju.[16]

This movement of people was stopped by the coming in from the north and northwest of great hordes of Mongolians of the Sakha race, who had been forced on by the restless movements of the Yueh-chi, the progenitors of the Huns of later days. The Sakhas, or Scythians, as they are sometimes called, formed in Northwest India the mighty Kushan or Indo-Scythian Empire whose most noted ruler was Kaniska.

Next after Asoka, Kaniska was the greatest exponent of early Buddhism, a " Wheel King," he is called in the records. In his reign, a wholly new type of Buddhism arose,[17] and, from his time, dates the division of Buddhism into two " Vehicles," the " Hinyana " (Korean " Soseung ") or Smaller Vehicle, and the " Mahayana " or Larger Vehicle (Korean " Taiseung "). The former is the type now found in Ceylon and Burmah, and the latter that found in all Northern Asia, including Korea and Japan. These two Vehicles are so different that they constitute almost two distinct religions.

The great apostle of Kaniska's time was Asvagosha (Korean " Mamyung Chonja "), who wrote the " Kishilon," the "Awakening of Faith," a wonderful book so like some Christian books that some writers have classified it as pseudo-Buddhistic. It has been

[16] Lloyd, *Creed of Half Japan*, p. 82; *Korea Branch Royal Asiatic Society Records*, 1914, p. 20.
[17] Starr, *Korean Buddhism*, p. 51.

translated by Dr. Timothy Richards, of Shanghai. From this time also probably dates the Saddharma Pundarika, the " Lotus Flower Gospel," translated by Richards under the name of the " New Testament of Buddhism." [18] This book is the Bible of more people than any other book in the world, with the exception of the Christian Bible.

The new doctrines which appeared at this time, and which mark off the Mahayana Buddhism sharply from the Buddhism of Ceylon are as follows : [19]

" 1. There was a new conception of an eternal Deity. The Buddha himself had emphatically repudiated the idea that there was an eternal Deity. Now he himself began to be worshipped, was deified.

" 2. The Boddhisattvas, i. e., the Buddhas of second grade, began to be of great importance. These are those persons, souls, who, in their very next incarnation are due to become Buddhas, but who voluntarily defer their own elevation in order that they may assist others in working out their salvation. [20]

" 3. Whereas the old ideal of the Arhat, or disciple, was one who went aside from the world to selfishly work out his own salvation, this new Boddhisattva ideal took its place, and even Arhats aspired to become Boddhisattvas in order to help others rather than for selfish reasons.

" 4. Real prayer began to be offered to the Boddhisattvas, instead of the older plan of trying by self-hypnotism to bring the mind to a state of stagnation. Also the need of faith in the various Boddhisattvas was taught. The cult became practically polytheism.

" 5. Instead of the old idea of Nirvana, where the soul lapsed back into the ocean of life like a ripple upon the ocean's surface, as was said to have been taught by Nagarjuna, there came in the doctrine of the Western Paradise with its multitudinous-storied heavens and equally many horrible hells. No Buddhist in Northern Asia looks forward to Nirvana," though the Koreans know the name " Yulban." They all look forward to going to " Kooknak

---

[18] Published by T. & T. Clark.
[19] Hackmann, p. 51 f.
[20] Richard, *New Testament of Buddhism*, p. 138.

Seikee," to the Western Paradise of Bliss, whither they will journey in the " Panyu Yongsun," the Dragon Boat of Wisdom, which is pictured on the outer walls of most of their temples.

The old idea of transmigration and of the Wheel of Life is not changed. They believe that there are the six grades of living things and that they are all bound to the Wheel. They think that, with every successive birth, they go up or down with the Wheel through the various stages of the heavens, earth or the hells, with no escape until, as Hinyana taught, Nirvana was attained, or, as Mahayana teaches, Paradise is attained, through the merits of some compassionate Boddhisattva. In a temple ten li outside the East Gate of Seoul, I found hanging in front of the incense table of the Buddha a silk ribbon on which some woman had evidently written, or had someone write for her, the words, " Oh, may I die quickly, quickly, and, when I am reborn, be reborn in this world as a man."

Kaniska is said to have called a great Council at Jalandhara in Kashmir, and it is said that there these doctrines were first announced, and three great commentaries in Sanscrit were ordered written.[21]

We do not know the exact dates of Kaniska and Asvagosha, but they are not far from the time when our Lord was teaching in Jerusalem. Everyone has heard of the tradition, which I met a year ago in India, that the Apostle Thomas travelled farther than any others of the Twelve, and that he preached and died in India. The Syriac Church there points out a grave which they insist was his. At this time, apparently, for the first time the doctrine of salvation through the merits of another, i. e., of a Boddhisattva, the doctrine of a great eternal God, the doctrines of Paradise and the hells were taught.[22] There are those like Professor Lloyd, of Tokio, Madame Gordon and others who believe that Christianity touched Buddhism down there on the borders of India or in Kashmir, and that Buddhism borrowed those doctrines from the Christian faith. It is an old controversy as to how far either of these great religions has influenced the other. Estlin Carpenter has

[21] Hackmann, p. 55.
[22] Lloyd, *Creed of Half Japan*, pp. 51 f., 119.

written a whole book[23] in which he draws parallels between the teachings of the two religions. Apparently he thinks that the exchanges were mutual. Some Buddhists have even claimed that Christ during those " silent years " from twelve till His first public appearances, visited India along some of the caravan routes through Damascus, or that at least He knew of Buddhism through teachers who traversed those routes. Of this there is not an atom of proof.

It would not have been at all foreign to the spirit of Buddhism, as shown throughout its history, and as we shall presently show as regards Korean history, if it had absorbed these Christian doctrines. It has always tried to absorb native faiths and not to antagonize them. Japanese Shinto devotees still anathematize Kobo Daisha because in the twelfth century he originated the doctrine of Ryobu or Mixed Buddhism, by which he claimed that the sun goddess Amaterasu was simply Vairochana Buddha under another name, and all of the other Shinto divinities were Buddhas.[24] It has taken Motoori[25] and his successors over a century to fumigate away the traces of Buddhism from their Shinto faith.

Probably no one will ever be able to prove these things, but it is certainly significant that none of these doctrines are even today taught in the Buddhism of Ceylon and Burmah, while, from this time, they suddenly appeared in Northern Buddhism, originating at a point where, if not Thomas, at least the Nestorians, or Magians, or Gnostics or other heretical sects might have met and mingled with Buddhism. It is interesting in the light of this to study the famous Nestorian Stone set up in the city of Sianfu in Western China in the seventh century and discovered a few decades ago. Although called a Christian document, it is a mixture of Christian and Buddhist ideas to such an extent that the Tang Emperor is said to have rebuked the Christian leader King Ching or Adam of that group of people, telling him that the two doctrines must be kept separate.[26] Adam had collaborated with a Buddhist named Prajna in writing it.

---

[23] *Buddhism and Christianity.*
[24] Griffis, *Religions of Japan*, p. 209.
[25] *Ibid.*, p. 91.
[26] Lloyd, *Creed of Half Japan*, p. 203.

In our self-satisfied Occidental way, we take it for granted that all of the interesting part of the world is limited to those few acres which we or our nations occupy. How much time our " Universal " histories in our schools do give today to a few nations who lived in a few square miles between the Mediterranean and the North Sea, or, at the farthest, the Euphrates and the Pillars of Hercules, while we know that great empires rose and fell in other parts of the earth which we seldom even mention.

Particularly we have been accustomed to visualize a great gulf between those Asiatic states that face out upon the Mediterranean and those that face upon the Pacific. There never has been such a gulf.[27] From the earliest times, there has been the closest of land communication and much also by water.[28] Marco Polo was not the first merchant to traverse that territory. Caravans and ships passed back and forth at all times. The people of India are mostly white, Aryans. Modern Comparative Religion has discovered so many similarities in religions founded at great distances from one another where there has been no possibility of intercommunication that it tends to be sceptical of any attempt to attribute too much borrowing of one cult from another. It is worth while, however, to know that there are eminent scholars who have believed that this is one case where the borrowing is so evident that more credence than usual should be given to this theory.

## CHINESE BUDDHISM

Buddhism entered China, not from the south where the Himalayas rear themselves like a great wall, but from the west. Kaniska was an evangelist also. We can believe that his messengers went out to all of the nearby countries and that at least some knowledge of the Law was spread also by the caravans of traders passing here and there. On the borders of his kingdom, Kaniska erected a great image of Buddha which was still standing in the fourth century A. D., according to the report of Fahien, the famous pilgrim who went from China to India then.

The story of Buddhism's entrance into China is quite a romantic

---

[27] *Ibid.*, pp. 37, 59.
[28] Wells, *History of the World.*

one.[29] The Emperor Myungti, of the Han Dynasty, in the year 64 A. D., on several successive nights, had the same dream of a man in golden raiment, holding in his hands a bow and arrows and pointing towards the west. He finally decided to send messengers to the west to seek the man whom he had seen. He selected a company of eighteen ambassadors, who started for India by the western route. On the way, they met two men who came bringing, upon a white horse, certain Scriptures and images and other paraphernalia. They escorted these men back. A temple was given them to live in, and it was called the " White Horse Monastery." Legend tells of the various miracles which these men performed in certifying their faith. They are said to have written or translated certain books, among which, one, the *Sutra of the Forty-two Sections,* still exists. It is a sort of Catechism book.

An old Nestorian tradition (the Nestorians were in China at least as early as the seventh century, as the Nestorian Stone proves) states that these two men were not Buddhists but Christians, disciples of the Apostle Thomas.[30] These men died in 70 A. D.

The next missionaries of Buddhism to China were nearly eighty years later, in 147 A. D., and they were Anshikao, likely a prince from Parthia, and a monk called Lokaraksha. They were followed at intervals by many others. These first two men did a great deal of translation, producing no less than sixty-eight volumes between them. It is interesting to note that none of the Buddhist missionaries of this period came from India proper. Two were from Parthia, three from Thibet, and the others indefinitely described as " from the west." Until 300 A. D. all of the books produced by the Order in China were the work of the foreign missionaries with one exception. Not until 335 A. D. were Chinese citizens openly allowed by their own government to enter the priesthood.[31]

During the fourth century A. D. Buddhism got its first real hold upon China. In that century began the pilgrimages by Chinese to the various shrines and sacred places of India, and these men returned laden with books, relics and sacred pictures. Among the

---

[29] Lloyd, *Creed of Half Japan,* p. 76; Edkins, *Chinese Buddhism,* p. 87 f.
[30] Lloyd, *Creed of Half Japan,* p. 81.
[31] Edkins, *Chinese Buddhism,* p. 89; Lloyd, p. 155.

most famous of these pilgrims were Fahien (399 A. D.), Yuan Chang (630 A. D.), and I Tsing, monks, and the layman Sung Yun. This last one was sent by the Prince of the state of Wei to study and report on Indian Buddhism. These pilgrimages continued through the fifth, sixth and seventh centuries A. D.[32]

Kumarajiva (Korean, Kumarasip) came from India via Turkestan about 400 A. D. He became one of the most famous translators of all of the Buddhists of China. His name as translator is upon great numbers of the books in the Korean temples.

So much for Chinese Buddhism. After the fourth century, it had many ups and downs. At one time, an effort was made to form out of Confucianism, Taoism and Buddhism an amalgamated religion like the Ryobu Buddhism in Japan, but it failed. Some of the Kings persecuted the Church heavily. One King commanded at one time that 120,000 priests demit their ministry and return to private life.[33] Another one similarly sent back 30,000.[34] Buddha's doctrine of celibacy was repugnant to the Chinese, among whom ancestral worship had always been taught. In Thibet, Buddhism got such a foothold that it has dominated the entire life of the nation, public and private, up till today.

In the rest of China, Buddhism is simply one of the " Three Religions," the " three legs of the stool " which all Chinese feel to be indispensable to the stability of the State. The Chinese directs his daily life theoretically by Confucian principles, goes to Taoist temples for charms and magic and fortune-telling, and to the Buddhist temples when he or any of his family dies.[35]

## KOREAN BUDDHIST HISTORY

First let us say a word about Korean history in general and block out the general periods. The Koreans are an ancient people. Legend says that their first king, Tangoon, lived in 2332 B. C., at the same time as the first legendary kings of China. We cannot know that this is true, but we do know that in 1122 B. C., just at

[32] Lloyd, *Creed of Half Japan*, p. 57.
[33] Edkins, *Chinese Buddhism*, p. 122.
[34] *Ibid.*, p. 128; Ross, *Corea: Its History, Customs and Manners*, p. 20.
[35] Soothill, *The Three Religions of China*, p. 5.

the time when Samson was smiting the Philistines, when the ancestors of most Westerners were living a very primitive life in Europe, King (or rather Viscount) Keui or Keuija came from China and set up a kingdom in North Korea. He had been Prime Minister in China under the last King of the Shang Dynasty in the T'sin country. When a usurper overthrew his master, he refused to take office under him, but asked and received permission to emigrate, and he came with five thousand followers to Korea.[86]

From 1122 B. C. to 196 B. C. Keuija's descendants reigned in "Chosen," i. e., in the more civilized northern half of the peninsula.

From 196 B. C. to 57 A. D. there were several small kingdoms or provinces controlled directly from China.

From 57 A. D. till 935 A. D. is called the "Three Kingdom Age," for, at that time, the whole peninsula and likely some of Manchuria was divided among three strong kingdoms, Kogoryu occupying the northern half, Paikchei the southwestern quarter, and Silla the southeastern quarter. After 660, Silla had absorbed the other two kingdoms and ruled alone, but the period to 935 A. D. is all called the "Three Kingdom Age."

From 935 to 1392, the whole peninsula was under the Koryu Dynasty with its capital at Songdo, and, from 1392 till 1910, when the Japanese seized the land, the Yi Dynasty ruled at Seoul.

Buddhism is concerned only with the last three of these periods—the "Three Kingdom Age," the Koryu Period and the Yi Period.

In 372 A. D. Buddhism came to Korea. This was, as my Korean Buddhist history states, the 1323d year since the death of Sakamuni. This would make the birth of Buddha 1031 B. C. Chinese and Japanese Buddhists also set about the same date, 1026 or 1027,[87] while modern investigators are pretty well convinced that the date was 551-560.[88]

A Chinese monk named Soonto was the first missionary.[89] He was sent by Fukien, the King of the Posterior Thsin Dynasty, one

[86] Hulbert, History of Korea, I, p. 6 f.; Gale, "History of Korea," in the Korea Mission Field Magazine, July, 1924, p. 134.
[87] Edkins, Chinese Buddhism, p. 15; Chamberlain, Things Japanese, p. 77.
[88] Encyclopedia of Religious Ethics, Vol. II, p. 881.
[89] Hulbert, History of Korea, I, p. 65; Gordon, World Healers, p. 62.

of the small kingdoms of North China, and came bringing books, images and relics. The " Three Kingdoms " were always at war with one another, and it has been thought that the invitation sent to Fukien was in part a political move against the other two kingdoms, although the glamour of the ceremonials of the Church may have had something to do with it. At any rate, there seems to have been no felt need for his coming among the common people.

Just as the Emperor Myungti welcomed the two travellers with the white horse, so Soosoorim, King of Kogoryu, welcomed Soonto, and built for him two monasteries, one called Sungmoonsa and the other Iboolam. This second temple was put in charge of Ato, who arrived a little later. The King turned over his son to Soonto to be trained and educated.[40]

Paikchei, not to be outdone by Kogoryu, sent for a missionary also, not to a tiny northern principality, but direct to the Emperor of the Eastern Tsin country near Nanking. They asked for a famous teacher named Marananda.[41] Some writers say that this man was a Thibetan, but all of the Korean records say that he was an Indian, so that, even at this early date, 384 A. D., Korea was brought into direct touch with the land of Buddha's birth.

Marananda came, attended by ten priests, either Chinese or Indian. He was given quarters in the palace enclosure and immediately set up temple rooms for worship there. It is not known where the capital of Paikchei was located at that time. One tradition says that it was upon the present site of Seoul, but likely it was somewhat further south.[42]

Silla, the last of the Three Kingdoms, accepted Buddhism forty years later, in 424 A. D., at first with hesitancy,[43] but, in the end, it followed the Law farther than either of the other two. Its first missionary seems to have been " Meukhoja," who, judging from his name, was probably a negro.

By 424 A. D., then, Buddhism, under royal patronage, had taken its place throughout the whole land of Korea. There was little

[40] *Royal Asiatic Society Records,* 1914, p. 14.
[41] Gordon, *World Healers,* p. 64; Hulbert, *History of Korea,* p. 66.
[42] Gordon in *Royal Asiatic Society Records,* 1914, p. 61; Ross, *Corea: Its History, Customs and Manners,* p. 201.
[43] Hulbert, *History of Korea,* I, pp. 75, 76, 80.

opposition to it. A century or so later, when Confucianism became well established, these two cults entered upon a struggle to the death, but, in the beginning there was nothing to oppose it except the degraded Shamanism, spirit worship. In 642 and 649, there was a small flurry of opposition from certain leaders who tried to introduce Taoism, but that was insignificant.

From the beginning, the evangelizing spirit of the Church was very strong. In 545, the King of Paikchei sent missionaries with images and sacred books across to Japan, and urged the adoption of the Doctrine there, and thereafter, for seventy years, this propaganda was kept up.[44] Repeatedly, books and idols were sent over and many of these things are today reckoned among the national treasures of Japan.[45] In 577, the first Korean nun was sent over, and in 584 the first three Japanese women, trained by the Korean nuns, were admitted to the Order. Silla, as well as Paikchei, engaged in this propaganda.[46]

The rulers of all of the Three Kingdoms worked actively for the conversion of their people. Proclamations were sent out urging them to adopt the Law. In 525, the King of Silla passed a law forbidding the killing of animals for food, and commanding that all of the population adopt the Buddhist Eight Commandments.[47] Paikchei did the same. In 599, all of the fishing tackle in the country was confiscated and all imprisoned birds set free. In 536, the King of Silla abdicated, and became a monk, and his wife entered a nunnery. In 573, another Silla queen did the same.[48]

The history of the Three Kingdom Age has been kept with marvellous care for so early a time. Nearly every year is marked by some event of great moment to Buddhism. Perhaps we can grasp these things best if we take them up under topics.

### 1. SACRED RELICS

Relics, particularly those of Buddha himself, are worshipped by Buddhists everywhere. The first of these were brought to Silla

[44] Lloyd, *Creed of Half Japan*, p. 172.
[45] Gordon in *Royal Asiatic Society Records*, 1914, p. 8.
[46] *Poolkyo Yaksa* for most of the facts on this page.
[47] Griffis, *The Hermit Nation*, p. 333.
[48] Hulbert, *History of Korea*, I, pp. 82, 96.

by Kaktuk in 550 A. D.   In 620, others were brought.   In 635, Chachang, the founder of the famous Tongtosa monastery, brought from China a " kasa " cloak and a begging bowl which had been Buddha's own, and also a bone from Buddha's head. These relics are still treasured at the Tongtosa monastery near Fusan.   The bone is enshrined in a globular pagoda back of the main worship hall behind the altar, so that they have never erected any idols in that hall.   In 651, ten more sacred relics were brought from China by one of Chachang's disciples, and, in 852, a tooth of Buddha.   When this last arrived, the King went out in state from his capital to meet it and escort it to its resting-place.

## 2. BUDDHIST BOOKS

The first of these were brought into the country by Soonto and Marananda.   In 566, seventeen hundred more books were sent over by the Emperor of the Thsin Dynasty in China.   From time to time, before and after this, as individuals went on pilgrimages to China to study the Doctrine, they brought back the special books of the sects with which they had affiliated themselves.   In 583, the King sent to the Tang Kingdom in China for a shipment of books. Most of these were in Chinese, but some were in the Sanscrit. Some were written on the famous palm leaves.   We will speak of those in the next lecture.

## 3. PILGRIMAGES

Shortly after Buddhism was first introduced into Korea, Koreans began to make pilgrimages to the great temples and teachers of the law in China.   A well known Chinese book on Buddhism gives the names of six Koreans who, in the latter part of the seventh century, found their way through China to India.[49]   In 583, the son of the King went.   In 596, Payak of Kogoryu went to Mt. Tendai in South China and brought back the tenets of the Tendai Sect.   In 600, Wunkwang brought back the teachings of the Sinin Sect, and, in 634, Myungnang brought more of its rules.   Wunk-

---

[49] Beal, *Life of Hieun Tsang*, p. xxv f.   Most of the facts on this page are from the *Poolkyo Yaksa*.

wang also brought copies of the *Sungsil Non* and the *Nirvana Book*, the sacred writings most used by his sect. In 617, Wunhyo, and, in 669, Wisang went to the land of Tang in China, and brought back many books and relics. These last two were the founders of the Pumusa monastery near Fusan, now one of the five largest in the country. Heikwan, in 625, brought back the teachings of the Samnon Sect from the land of Sui in China. By 625, there were five Buddhist sects in Korea.

Not only were pilgrimages made to China, but also to India itself, both overland through China and by boat along the coast. We have mentioned six of these above. Most of the pilgrims were never heard of again, but some returned, as, for example, Anham, who came back in 620 with three Indians, Pimajinchai, Nongata and Pultadunga. He also brought from India a book called *Kasungman* and many relics. An ancient Korean legend says that Queen Hu, the first queen of the tiny kingdom of Karak in southeast Korea, was the daughter of an Indian King and came to Korea by water. In 695, Pagara, and, in 929, Mahura, both Indians, came to Chosen, and there were many others.

### 4. GREAT MONKS

The greatest priests of the Three Kingdom Period, next after Soonto, Marananda, Ato and Meukhoja, were Wunhyo and Wisang, founders of the great Pumusa monastery, Chachang, founder of the Tongtosa monastery, and Pojo, founder of the Songkwangsa monastery in the old Paikchei territory in the southwest. Pumusa and Tongtosa are in the southeast near Fusan. Wunhyo married a royal princess and became the father of Sulchong, the earliest great Confucian scholar in Korea, inventor of the Nitu system of diacritical marks used in reading the Chinese.[60] Wunhyo himself was a great literary man, at least twelve books having come from his pen. Wuchik, who lived in Silla about 695, was also a famous monk and writer, having produced at least seventeen books besides translations. Tosun, who lived just at the close of this

---

[60] Gale in *Royal Asiatic Society Records*, 1900, p. 6; Hulbert, *History of Korea*, I, p. 119; *Korean Repository*, 1898, p. 47; *Korea Review*, 1901, p. 289. Most of the data on this page comes from the *Poolkyo Yaksa*.

period, and at the beginning of the next, was a famous scholar and prophet.

There were many wonderful things for Buddhism during this period, but there were also some setbacks, as, for example, in 664, when the Silla King forbade for a time all gifts to the monasteries, and, in 805, when the King forbade using silver and gold in decorating the temples, but, in general, the Doctrine had the right of way.[51]

Most of the great monasteries and " universities "[52] that used to stand in Silla and other parts of the country have fallen into decay or have been burned or otherwise destroyed in some of the invasions of the country, that of the Mongols in 1230, that of Hideyoshi and the Japanese in 1592, or that of the Manchus in 1630, but the whole southeast corner, the old Silla land, is full of the ruins of temples, pagodas and monuments. As one travels over it today, he is able to realize just a little the wonders of that ancient time. For a Korean today who knows his country's history, a trip through that territory should be as thrilling as a trip through Palestine is to any Christian.

### THE KORYU PERIOD (935–1392)

Great as was the Three Kingdom Period, the next, that of the Koryu Dynasty, was greater. It was the Golden Age of Buddhism. The first King of the Dynasty was not himself particularly interested in Buddhism, but he thought it wise to use the Order to help establish him on his throne. In one of his early proclamations, he stated that his coming to the throne was due to the favour of the Buddhas. He went out in a royal progress once to welcome a noted priest from India. He is said to have given his own dwelling as a monastery. In 944, he had a picture of the Five Hundred Naheun (Arhats) brought from the land of Tang in China. When he died, he left for the guidance of his successor ten commands, three of which were as follows,—

---

[51] *Poolkyo Yaksa.*
[52] Starr, *Korean Buddhism*, p. 5.

" Protect the Buddhist Doctrine.
Build no more monasteries.
Establish an annual Buddhist festival." [53]

There were some setbacks also in the Koryu Period, as, for
example, in 884, when the people were forbidden to turn any more
dwellings into monasteries, and, in 1168, when another King tried
to get the people to accept Taoism and so complete the " three-
legged stool," Confucianism, Taoism and Buddhism, such as they
had in China. In general, however, the Doctrine had the right of
way over everything.

Just a few instances will show how completely it ruled. In
944, the King went out in state to escort to its resting-place in
a certain temple a Buddhist relic brought from China. At the
same time, he gave seventy thousand bags of rice from the national treasury for the building of new monasteries. In 959, the
King in person went to one of the monasteries and preached a
sermon. In 981, the worship of the spirits of the mountains and
rivers was forbidden as being opposed to the Law. In 987, the
killing of any animals for food during the fifth and ninth months
was forbidden.[54]

In 1006, a great image of Kwanseieun, the goddess of mercy,
was unveiled. It was fifty-six feet high and had been thirty-seven
years in the making.[55] In 1022, and again in 1120 and 1129, certain old musty bones and Buddhist relics were brought from abroad
and installed in state right in the King's palace itself. In 1032,
1049, 1053, 1087, 1090 and 1117, the King fed in the palace enclosure from ten thousand to thirty thousand monks at one time in
feasts. Those figures are no doubt gross exaggerations, but still
the numbers were probably very large.[56]

In 1037, a law was passed *requiring any family having four sons
to dedicate at least one to the priesthood,* and, in 1080, this was
changed to require one son out of three. Nearly every family in

---

[53] Hulbert, *History of Korea,* I, p. 143.
[54] *Poolkyo Yaksa.*
[55] Possibly the Eunjin Buddha, *Royal Asiatic Society Records,* 1900,
V. I, p. 57.
[56] *Poolkyo Yaksa;* also Hulbert, *History of Korea,* I, pp. 165, 173, 176.

the country at one time was furnishing at least one monk.[57] In 1116, there is a record that dancing girls "in clouds" attended the Buddhist feasts. This gives a little idea of the moral state of the nation at that time.[58]

In 1035, the King inaugurated the custom of sending boys through the streets with Scriptures laid open upon little pulpits strapped to their backs in such a way that priests walking just behind them could read the books out loud for the edification of the populace, and to bring blessings upon them. Perhaps this was the origin of the idea of not working for individual conversions, but to simply endeavour to "permeate society with religious ideals." [59]

In 1045, and again in 1054, the reigning Kings took the Fifty Vows of semi-priesthood. In 1048, nine Buddhist festivals were proclaimed as national holidays. Repeatedly, against the protests of the responsible officials in charge, great grants were made from the national treasury for erecting or endowing more and yet more temples. In 1151, a large statue of the goddess of mercy was enshrined in the palace enclosure. In 1197, seven sons of the King became monks at one time. In 1309, the King ordered that the monks no longer bow in salutation to any nobleman or other person other than himself alone, and said that they should not be under the ordinary laws of the land.

Even in 1313, when the Order had passed the zenith of its popularity, ten thousand priests were feasted at one time in the palace grounds. In 1314, an immense library of Buddhist books, 10,800 in number, were bought in Nanking by the King, and the Chinese Emperor added a gift of 4,070 more. Many of these were in the Sanscrit or Thibetan character.[60]

These are samples of the events of this Golden Age of Buddhism. Many of the kings were so taken up with the observances and ceremonies that they had no time whatever to give to the affairs of state. In India, Asoka and Kaniska, who laboured so zealously, are called in the record "Wheel Kings" (Korean—Yoon Wang).

---

[57] *Ibid.*, p. 166; Rockhill, *Life of Buddha*, p. 53.
[58] Hulbert, *History of Korea*, I, pp. 165-180.
[59] Hulbert, *History of Korea*, I, pp. 165-180.
[60] Hulbert, *History of Korea*, I, p. 232.

None of the Korean Kings were given this honour, but many seem to have deserved it.

There are a number of particularly outstanding events of the Koryu Age,—

1. In 928, a full set of the whole Buddhist Mahayana Canon was brought from the land of Tang in China. In 990, certain additions were made to it by books from the Song country, and, in 1056, with yet other books from the Kitan country.[61] Blocks for printing those books were cut. They were all destroyed by the Mongols in their invasion in 1230, but were immediately recut, and the whole set is now preserved at the Haiinsa monastery near Taiku. They constitute the second most perfect set of the Canon in existence, the one in Kioto only surpassing this, and that in Kioto, according to the records, was gotten from Korea in 1408 and in 1421.[62]

2. The second event was the establishment, in 958, of the Buddhist competitive examinations for public office patterned after the Confucian examinations in China. The examinations in Korea before this, from 935 down, had been on the Confucian Classics. Superseding these by Buddhist examinations was a terrible blow to the Confucianists, a blow which they never forgave and which they repaid with interest during the Yi Period. There was friction between these two groups all through the Koryu Period. In 1085, the Buddhist examinations were still further strengthened by being arranged in annual districts and triennial central examinations.[63]

3. The third notable event was when Korea gave back to China the Buddhism which it had temporarily lost. In 958, the Order in China was suffering great persecutions and most all of her books, especially those used by the Tendai Sect, were destroyed. Korea sent back copies of these books and helped to resuscitate the Order in China, so that Korean Buddhists proudly claim that not only Japan but China owes its Buddhism, which it had temporarily lost, to them.

---

[61] *Ibid.*, I, p. 167.
[62] *Poolkyo Yaksa;* Griffis, *The Hermit Nation*, p. 330.
[63] Hulbert, *History of Korea*, I, p. 164.

4. There were fewer pilgrimages during this period perhaps, but still many went, notably Wunheung in 1146 and an Indian called Sillipapila came from there in 938, also Hongpum in the same year and Chikong in 1350, so that contact with India was maintained.[64]

The outstanding priests of this period were,—

1. Chikong, the Indian mentioned above.[65] He was very influential in political matters at the close of the period. When he died, so great was his reputation for piety, his headbone and a tooth were enshrined as sacred relics within the palace of the king. They are now kept in a large pagoda urn in a temple dedicated to his honour twenty miles northeast of Seoul.

2. Naong, a Korean, was the King's Councillor, and one of Korea's really great men.[66]

3. Taiko was said to be the greatest of all the monks of Korea. He went to China in his younger days, and brought back the tenets of the Imjei Sect. He established several temples near Seoul upon the Kwanak and Pukhan mountains. He had so much influence with the King that to him was given the high honour of dining with the King in his private apartments, and he was given full power of appointing all of the abbots in the country, becoming a sort of Pope. The fall of the Koryu Dynasty was due to the wickedness of a monk named Sindon.[67] Because the King would not dismiss Sindon, Taiko resigned his high office, but later, when Sindon was executed, Taiko was recalled.

4. The last of the great monks was Moohak, who was high in favour with the first king of the Yi Dynasty, and helped select the site and lay out the wall of the city of Seoul.[68] The so-called " Peking Pass " northwest of the city is still called by the Koreans " Moohak Chai," or " Moohak's Pass," and the Kooksadang, Na-

---

[64] *Poolkyo Yaksa.*

[65] Trollope in *Royal Asiatic Society Records,* 1917, p. 35; Starr, *Korean Buddhism,* p. 73.

[66] Gale, "History of Korea," *Korea Mission Field Magazine,* 1926, p. 52.

[67] Gale, *Korea in Transition,* p. 80; "History of Korea," *Korea Mission Field Magazine,* 1926, p. 77.

[68] *Royal Asiatic Society Records,* 1902, p. 11.

tional Shrine, on the South Mountain in Seoul, is dedicated to him.[69]

In 1392, Koryu fell, and with it began bad days for the Buddha. During the whole of the Koryu Period, there had been war to the knife between it and Confucianism, and it had shown no mercy. Now no mercy was shown to it because the Confucianists came to power.

## THE YI DYNASTY PERIOD (1392–1910)

The Yi Dynasty, realizing how disastrous Koryu's connection with Buddhism had been, began almost immediately to curb the power of the priests. First of all, it moved the capital from Songdo to Seoul to get away from that Buddhist environment. Later it decreed that no priest or nun should enter the new capital on pain of death.[70] That law stood on the statute books for five hundred years, and even in 1905 was operative, though not very rigidly enforced. Several temples that had already been erected within the city of Seoul were ordered torn down and moved outside the East Gate.

In 1397, the King confiscated the property of a great many monasteries, giving it to his retainers. In 1400, the formal reading of the Buddhist Scriptures in the palace was discontinued. In 1405, the thirteen existing Buddhist sects were ordered to amalgamate into seven. Lands were taken from the weaker monasteries and added to the stronger. The number of monks who could live in any given temple was set by the Government. The temple lands were resurveyed, and redistributed among them. The practice of erecting monasteries near each royal tomb was forbidden (1419), and several already so erected were ordered moved.

In 1422, the seven sects, amalgamated out of thirteen a few years before, were ordered to combine again into just two, the "Sun," or Contemplative, and the "Kyo," or Practical sect. These are the only sects existing even nominally in Korea today, where Japan has more than fifty.[71] Next, the offering of public prayer on

---

[69] *Ibid.*, p. 25.
[70] Hulbert, *History of Korea*, I, p. 319; *Poolkyo Yaksa*.
[71] Hulbert, *History of Korea*, I, p. 319; *Poolkyo Yaksa*.

festival days was forbidden, even on the king's birthday.[72] After 1450, no one could enter the priesthood without a special royal permit, and those priests having families were ordered to demit the ministry, and support their families. Still, in 1465, the temple, Wunkaksa, was erected in the heart of Seoul, and in its grounds was set up the great stone carved pagoda, the finest work of art in all Korea.[73]

In 1474 and 1488, the Dowager Queen tried to resuscitate the Order, but her images were smashed and burned.[74] In 1507, the Buddhist official examinations were abolished and those of the Confucianists substituted. Two monasteries near Seoul, Pongeunsa and Pongchunsa, had been made officially the head temples of the Sun and Kyo sects respectively. This organization was ordered broken up.

In 1512, a great bronze Buddha from Silla was brought to Seoul and melted down to get the metal for the making of arms, an act of vandalism that could hardly have happened in any other age of the country.[75] In 1516, the celebration of death anniversaries at the temples was forbidden. The first and third anniversaries of the death of parents are great days of mourning in Confucianism. Buddhism had usurped those days. Now they were taken back.[76]

In 1549, the Queen Regent again tried desperately to resuscitate the old organization. She restored the examinations, appointed one man as a sort of Pope over all of the monasteries in the country, to be the head of both the Sun and Kyo sects, but she died in 1584, and her Pope was killed and her work wiped out, root and branch. It was the last hopeful attempt ever made.[77]

In 1592, Hideyoshi sent the Japanese, who invaded Korea and laid it waste, from Fusan right up to Pyengyang in the North. A priest called Chunghu, the "Teacher of Sosan," offered his services to the Korean king, and, by his orders, all of the priests in the

[72] Hulbert, *History of Korea*, I, p. 305.
[73] *Royal Asiatic Society Records*, Vol. VI, Pt. II, p. 1.
[74] Hulbert, *History of Korea*, I, p. 322.
[75] *Ibid.*, p. 328.
[76] *Poolkyo Yaksa.*
[77] *Ibid.*

country were organized into military bands.[78] They did not do a great deal of actual fighting, it is said, but they acted as scouts and spies, and helped to stir up and encourage the people to drive out the invaders. After the Japanese were expelled from the country, it was another priest, Yoochang, first lieutenant of Chunghu, who was one of the leading members of the embassy that went to Japan to arrange peace.

In 1636, the Manchus invaded the country and the king fled to Namhan, a mountain fortress fifteen miles south of Seoul, and was guarded there by three thousand military monks.[79]

Just a word as to that in passing. Writers on Korean history and Korean Buddhism have made a great deal of the term "military monks."[80] I think that some of them have used their imagination extensively in the things which they have said concerning them, although Hendrik Hamel, after his captivity in Korea in 1653, does write as though most of the soldiers of his day were religious men.[81] In Japan, there were military monks who were superlative fighters and lived a large part of their time at war. There probably was never anything like this known in Korea.

There were in Korea certain monks who were trained to some extent to use the crude weapons of that day, swords, spears and the bow. They were located at places where they might be needed, e. g., groups at the King's three places of refuge, Pukhan, the North Fortress, Namhan, the South Fortress, and on the island of Kanghwa. There was a group at the Yongchoosa monastery near Soowun, and one in the Pumusa monastery near Fusan, but, in each of the places, there was only a handful of fighting men, largely for defence, never anything like the armies of feudal monks such as were maintained on Mt. Hiezan near Kioto in Japan. These Korean monks were trained somewhat as the militia in America has been trained. It is romantic to think of great strongholds of

---

[78] Hulbert, *History of Korea*, I, p. 402.
[79] Hulbert, *History of Korea*, II, p. 105; H. H. Underwood, *Korea Magazine*, 1918, p. 263.
[80] *Korean Repository*, 1898, p. 304; Trollope in *Royal Asiatic Society Records*, 1917, p. 37; Underwood, *Religions of Eastern Asia*, p. 217.
[81] *Royal Asiatic Society Records*, 1918, p. 132.

military monks, but it does not conform to the facts among the peace-loving folk of Korea.

In 1849, Confucianism had the upper hand, and was persecuting the Order so severely that a number of Buddhist nuns, to show their resentment, went to the sacred grounds of the Confucian College in Seoul, and recited Buddhist prayers there. They were exiled for the sacrilege.

In 1865, the great Regent, father of the late Emperor, gave a feast to two hundred monks within the palace enclosure, the first time that this had happened in about two hundred years. This was the last formal recognition of Buddhism by any Korean ruler.

In 1876, the Shin Sect of Japanese Buddhists decided to open work in Korea.[82] Two years later they took across to their own country a young Korean to train, and, a little later, five more. They built a temple in Wonsan on the northeast coast.

In 1902, all of the Buddhists in the country sent delegates to a Council which decided to organize all of the monasteries of the country under one head temple, with twenty subordinate districts.[83] As none of the existing organizations near Seoul could be accepted as the head one, on account of mutual jealousies, a great new temple called Wunheungsa was erected outside the East Gate, and dedicated with glorious ceremonies. In 1906, it was decided to establish Buddhist primary schools in all of the larger temples of the country, and a higher school in Wunheungsa. This whole project failed, and the property of Wunheungsa had to be sold to pay the mortgages on it.

In 1910, another union was worked out by which all of the monasteries of the country were divided into thirty-two groups, each group under a large temple in its territory, and the representatives of each of the thirty-two groups sat in a General Council in Seoul.[84] A small temple and business office, called Kakhwangsa, was erected in the centre of the city of Seoul, a monthly magazine was started, all of the monasteries were urged to open preaching chapels in their nearby towns, and some of them did so. Litera-

[82] Griffis, *Hermit Nation,* p. 335.
[83] Hulbert, *History of Korea,* II, p. 333; *Korea Review,* 1902, p. 171.
[84] Gordon in *Royal Asiatic Society Records,* 1914, p. 31.

ture of various sorts was prepared for a great forward movement. Primary schools actually were established in many country temples and a college in Seoul.

These plans were irreproachable, but they have not worked out very well. The smaller temples are said not to obey the district head temples, nor do the district head temples always obey the central office. The magazine comes out at irregular intervals. The preaching chapels are empty. In 1924, the college plant was turned over to the Chuntokyo organization mentioned below. There is little vitality in the cult, and it is difficult to galvanize it into life. With the exception of a few heavily endowed temples, the monasteries are very poor, and must be supported by begging. Of course, this was not considered a handicap in the olden days, for it gave greater opportunity to the laity to acquire merit by their gifts. Unfortunately, in these modern days, the laity are not much disposed to win merit in this way, and they are so busy earning a living for themselves that they have little time for the Law. Originally the Order was founded on the idea of poverty, but that was soon changed, as it was for the mediæval Catholic monks, to say that the poverty law simply concerned individuals, who must not own things, but did not refer to the Order as a whole, which might have great wealth.

Tongtosa, probably the largest of the temples today, formerly had as many as two thousand monks, it is said. In 1919, when I visited it, the abbot told me that three years before he had had four hundred, but that the number had shrunk to two hundred and fifty. The others were turning to secular life. As a matter of fact, if one calls unexpectedly at any of the temples, he will find only a small fraction of the priests in residence. The others will be down in the valleys working as farmers or begging.

In 1911, strong efforts were made to amalgamate the Order with one or another of the Japanese Buddhist sects, but they have all failed.[85] Since the Independence Movement of 1919, opposition to amalgamation is still more intense. At one time, the Pochunsa monastery near Nyunbyun had a Japanese abbot, but he has since

[85] *Korea Review*, 1905, p. 150.

retired after twenty years of service there. Recently a Tokio newspaper told of a Korean monk, Kim Teido, who has become abbot of a small temple in Japan, called Bukkokusi, between Osaka and Kioto. There may be other cases of individuals thus exchanged. There are seven Japanese Buddhist sects now working in the country, including at least the Shin, Jodo, Shingon and Zen. The Japanese Government has helped in repairing several of the old monasteries which it considers rightly as national treasures, e. g., Poolkooksa, where is the wonderful Buddha in the Cave, and Haiinsa, where are kept the blocks for printing the Canon, etc. They have also required a complete inventory to be made and filed with the Government of all images, books and relics in each of the temples lest they be stolen by collectors. Many have already been so stolen in the past decades.

The Japanese Government would be very glad to see a revival of Buddhism, partly because that is the " Creed of Half Japan," and partly because it would make a balance perhaps for the Christian Church work. Possibly circumstances may some day bring about a union with the Buddhists of Japan. Unless something of the sort happens, it looks as though Buddhism in Korea would gradually die. Hackmann writes, " The picture of Buddhism which confronts the student in Korea is, on the whole, a very dull and faded one." [86] Still, however, according to the statistics given me by my college president friend, nominally 1,472 and actually 917 monasteries in operation with 6,692 priests and 1,274 nuns, and they report 131,887 adherents, about half as many as the Christian adherent roll of the country. Great numbers of the priests, however, maintain only a nominal connection with the temples, and my friend told me frankly that the adherent roll was largely a guess, since they had no stated weekly meetings in the majority of the temples. Nevertheless, it is a large organization. On certain feast days, even now, thousands of people gather at the larger temples. Most of the worshippers are women. In a recent newspaper, the Government gave the figures of Buddhist adherents as 200,000, but that is probably a good round number for the better figure which my college friend gave me.

---

[86] *Buddhism as a Religion*, p. 257.

The leaders are planning and trying hard, as are the Buddhists in Japan, to adapt their teaching and methods to this new day that has dawned. As a missionary, I cannot but express the hope that they may realize the futility of it all, this fighting for shadows when the great Reality Himself has come. Would that they might see Him as the Desire of all the nations, the one for whom they have been blindly groping, and that they might take Him as the Regenerator of their nation, the Transformer of their social life, and the Saviour of their souls.

# II

## BUDDHISM (Continued)

WE have discussed the history of Buddhism as far as the existing records reveal it. Now I wish to discuss its buildings, images, ceremonies, sects and doctrines.

### 1. Buildings [1]

We have already noted that there were formerly, in the days of Silla, nine great Buddhist "universities." [2] Not one of them is standing today. I visited the ruined site of the one at Poolkooksa near Kyungju in 1919. It must have been a magnificent group of buildings. The stones upon which the supporting pillars rested were still there, great blocks of granite, four foot cubes. The whole institution must have covered as much ground as do many small American colleges. Likely the greater part of it was but one story high, but, judging from the half-ruined temple adjacent to it, it must have been a lofty, stately-looking edifice.

As for temples, there are magnificent ones still standing, some of the buildings coming from thirteen hundred years ago. [3] In all there are nine hundred and seventeen of them, or, if we count all little outlying, semi-abandoned shrines, fourteen hundred and seventy-two. When one speaks of a temple, however, he does not mean a single building, but a great aggregation of buildings, each enshrining its own particular Buddhas. At Tongtosa, for example, there are twenty-one sub-temples, seven located in the thick forests high up on the mountain back of the main site, and the rest in a group together. Very few of these temples are near cities, if we except those by the royal tombs just outside the gates of Seoul. In the olden days, it was the custom to build them far out in the

---

[1] Trollope, *Ibid.*, 1917, pp. 38, 39; Starr, *Korean Buddhism*, p. 90.
[2] Gordon in *Royal Asiatic Society Records*, 1914, p. 24.
[3] Gale in *Royal Asiatic Society Records*, 1922, p. 6.

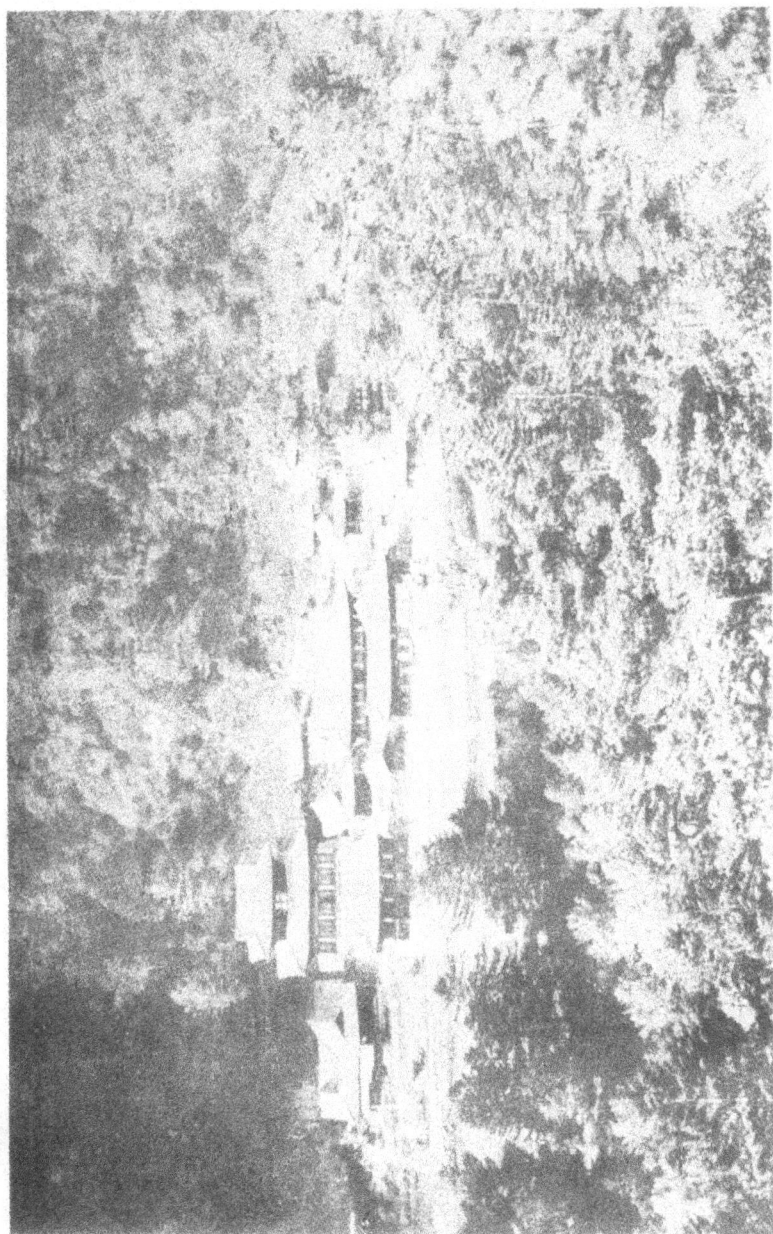

A BUDDHIST TEMPLE IN THE MOUNTAINS

mountains in some more or less inaccessible spot high up among the crags.

Buddhism has always been inclusive rather than exclusive.[4] In each country where it has gone, it has sought not to antagonize the indigenous faiths, but, as far as possible, to absorb them and incorporate them into its own body.[5] We noted yesterday the effort made to amalgamate Confucianism, Taoism and Buddhism in China with Confucius and his leading disciples given places as avatars of Buddhism, and reincarnations of Buddhist deities. In China and Korea, this failed, but, even so, in Korea, Confucius himself has been taken into the Buddhist pantheon as " Yootong Posal." In Japan, it succeeded when Kobo Daishi, in the twelfth century, combined Buddhism and Shinto, forming Ryobu Buddhism.[6]

In Korea, there was less to absorb in the way of religion when the Law first came in, but two elements at least were taken, and, in every group of temples, however small, one will find a separate shrine, or at least an altar to the spirit of the mountain on which the temple stands, and a second one to the spirits of the seven-starred constellation of the North, the Great Bear. In every temple, also, there is a tablet each for the reigning King and Crown Prince where prayers are offered daily.

There are nine hundred and seventeen temples still standing, but those most worth seeing perhaps are located in but four places, southeast Korea, Silla's old stronghold; the Diamond Mountains straight east of Seoul; southwest Korea, Paikchei's former field, and the province of Choongchung, just south of Seoul. In the whole northwest, there are few temples of note left standing now, possibly because of the Mongol and Manchu invasions which swept that part of the country, and in the northeast quarter, also, there are relatively few. It is interesting to note that it is in the northwest corner, where Buddhism is weakest, that Christianity has had its greatest field.

In the Silla field, the largest temples are Tongtosa, where is kept the headbone of Buddha; Haiinsa, where are the blocks for print-

---

[4] Griffis, *Religions of Japan*, p. 203; Martin, *Lore of Cathay*, p. 252.
[5] Underwood, *Religions of the Far East*, p. 193.
[6] Trollope in *Royal Asiatic Society Records*, 1917, p. 15.

ing the Canon, and Pumusa.  Each used to have over one thousand priests.  Haiinsa now has only about forty, and the others less than three hundred each.  In the Diamond Mountains, Yoochumsa, Pyohoonsa, and Changansa are of this class, and, in the southwest, Songkwangsa.

There are scores of interesting temples with fifty to one hundred priests, *c. g.*, Pupchoosa in Choongchung province, Sukwangsa and Sinkeisa in the Diamond Mountains, Wonheungsa near Soowun, Pochunsa near Nyunbyun, etc.

Nunneries are always near monasteries and are usually under their general control.  In Choongchung province, it is said that there are more nunneries than monasteries, and three times as many nuns as priests.

In spite of the repeated actions of the late dynasty in taking property away from the monasteries, many of them are still heavily endowed and well kept up.  It is interesting to note that, though that dynasty claimed to be opposed to Buddhism, over the road approaching many of the temples was erected the Red Gate with its harp-like insignia in the centre above, showing that it was under royal protection.

Not only is this true, but near practically every royal tomb there was a Buddhist temple erected.  Those tombs are located in beautiful valleys, or on hillsides from one to twenty miles outside the capital.  Great forests are planted around them, and special guards watch over them, even though some of the tombs are hundreds of years old.  In 1419, the practice of erecting monasteries near these tombs was forbidden, and some already erected were ordered moved, but it is interesting to note that, even now, wherever you find a tomb, you are pretty sure to find a temple just over the hill where it may be a comfort and yet not interfere with the Poongsoo (Fungsui) of the district.[7]  However wedded to Confucianism a King might be in his life, he liked a touch of Buddhism in his death, at least enough to serve as insurance.

## The Temples Themselves

The architecture, images and pictures in Korean temples always

---

[7] Trollope in *Royal Asiatic Society Records*, 1917, p. 37.

follow certain conventional lines, very much like the temples of China.[8] There are minor variations, but these are relatively small. The Peking, Shanghai, Singapore and Penang temples are all also on about the same model. Those in Japan and Rangoon have images that are almost the same, but the temple buildings and surroundings differ there.

Although nine-tenths of the dwellings of the people of Korea are roofed with thatch, the temple buildings are almost invariably covered with the more expensive, heavy tiled roofs, usually hipped. The ridges and hips are curving as in Chinese buildings, and down the hips in single file are queer little monkey-like figures called " Palkwai," placed there to bring good luck, it is said.

The weight of the buildings is carried entirely on posts, the walls between being of mud and stone, limed on the outside to keep out the rain. The living rooms, like those of all Korean dwellings, are small and full of posts, but the worship rooms are often clear spans of twenty-five to thirty feet wide and fifty to seventy-five feet long with ceilings twenty feet high. The posts are sometimes nearly three feet in diameter. Like all Oriental buildings, they stand in multiple walled enclosures. In China, all temples are said to face south, but, in Korea, any direction will do, even north, though they prefer not to face north, if the lay of the land allows.

As one approaches a temple, he comes first to a massive tiled gate with an inscription over it.[9] At Pongchunsa, sixty li east of Seoul, the legend reads, " Who enters here, leaves the world behind."

A little farther up the road, one comes to a second tiled gate, the " Gate of the Divas, or Four Heavenly Kings," those spiritual attendants who followed after and watched over Gautauma at his birth and throughout his earthly life. They are represented, two on the right and two on the left, sometimes by pictures, sometimes by images. At Tongtosa monastery, they are mighty wooden statues nearly fifteen feet high. Their countenances are fierce. They wear the armour of warriors. One always holds in his hand a spear, one a guitar, one a small tower and the last a snake in one hand and a jewel in the other. Under their feet are life-size

[8] Hackmann, *Buddhism as a Religion,* p. 257.
[9] Starr, *Korean Buddhism,* p. 68.

figures of the opponents of Buddhism upon whom they are trampling.[10]

Passing this gate, one comes next to the two-storied open pavilion, the " Noo." At one side of it or under it, is a great bell, perhaps six or eight feet high and ten inches thick. Korea used to be famous for its bells. Many still existing are wonderful works of art, a dragon at the top serving as a suspending ring and inscriptions being written on the sides, cast with the bell. Some of these bells, more than a thousand years old, carried off to Japan, are counted among the national treasures there.[11] These bells are all struck from without by a log suspended horizontally by two chains.

In the pavilion above, is an immense drum possibly six feet in diameter. Suspended somewhere there or in the inner court is a great brazen gong and a hollow wooden fish. These four articles are used on certain festival days, particularly the fifteenth day of the seventh lunar month, to call to the feast respectively the spirits in the heavens, the spirits of animals, the spirits from the underworld and the spirits of things in the water. In this pavilion on feast days, food is spread for these four classes, or rather, for three of the classes, that for the spirits of the underworld being placed on a stone tablet out in front.

In this pavilion or in the courtyard beyond, full dress dramatic plays representing the scenes in the various heavens and hells are said to be enacted by the priests at certain times. Madame Gordon says that she was told that the whole story of the " Suyooki " novel was enacted at Pongeunsa monastery near Seoul,[12] but I think that her interpreter must have deceived her, for the priests there and elsewhere with whom I have talked said that there was no such thing. These dramatic performances are open air worship services, not unlike the Miracle Plays that used to be given in England some centuries ago.[13]

Passing under, or beside, the pavilion, one comes next to the great guest-room where the worshippers and ordinary guests sleep.

---

[10] Edkins, *Chinese Buddhism*, p. 240.
[11] Cable in *Royal Asiatic Society Records*, 1925, Vol. XVI, p. 1.
[12] Gordon, *Symbols of the Way*, p. 2.
[13] Bates, *English Drama*, p. 35 f.

In the olden days, thousands used to gather at the temples on special days. Madame Gordon has described a recent festival at Tongtosa,[14] where hundreds of worshippers were present. The temples are usually far from any human habitation, so that it was necessary to provide some accommodation for the worshipping guests. In the great, smoky, dirt-floored kitchens, there were big, flat-bottomed, iron rice kettles, sometimes six feet in diameter. There used to be a good deal of rivalry between the Tongtosa monks and those of Pumusa near by. The Tongtosa monks boasted that so many guests came to their temple that they had to have an enormous kettle to make their food, and it was so big that, when the cook wanted to stir the rice, he had to go out into the kettle on a raft. The Pumusa monks retorted by saying that so many guests came to their temple that the iron filings scraped off by the constant opening and shutting of their front gate made a total of a quart a day.

In the guest-room, there is always at least one altar, often in a glass case, usually of Kwanseieum, the goddess of Mercy, in some of her thirty-two forms. Hanging from the ceiling of the room and of the porches in front are many streamers of paper or silk, bearing mottoes written in Sanscrit or Chinese. Inside of the guest-room, there are always many tambourines and jars with Sanscrit writing pasted on the outside, and always the Wheel of Life with Sanscrit writing is pasted in the centre of the ceiling. The intricate, involved wheel seen in Thibet with dragons and other figures writhing in among the spokes [15] is not seen in Korea. Very few of the priests know any Sanscrit, but they can write the mottoes from old copy. They know only by tradition what they mean. In 1891, in a monastery near Seoul, a paper was found dating from 1777 A. D., giving a method for learning the Sanscrit characters. In the olden days, there were great libraries of Sanscrit and Chinese books in the temples for the use of the priests and guests. Now there are only a few, and they are very little read. One finds them all dirty and dog-eared piled around in corners of the room

---

[14] Gordon in *Royal Asiatic Society Records*, 1914, p. 29.
[15] Combes, *Buddhism of Thibet; Korean Repository*, 1897, p. 265, from Courant's *Bibliographie Coreene*.

or on shelves. There used to be even a few books on palm leaves, as in China.

In Buddhism, there are three degrees of incarnation, the lowest called "Arhat" in Southern Buddhism and " Naheun " in Korea, the next called Boddhisattva in the Northern Buddhism and " Posal " in Korea, and the regular Buddhas called " Yerai," which is the " Tathagata " of India. My college Buddhist friend says that between the Naheun and Posal there is a fourth grade, the " Yunkak " or " Pyukji " (possibly Pratyeka) Buddha, who has attained the state in which he observes all of the twelve Nidanas (see below). I have not found any evidence of this grade elsewhere, however. The Boddhisattvas, or Posals, are those who are due in their next rebirth to become Buddhas, but who voluntarily delay their own elevation that they may help others to win their salvation. We shall see all three grades in the temples.

Passing the guest-room, across the courtyard facing inwards and usually much loftier than the other buildings is the Main Worship Hall. In it facing the door is usually a trinity of images, three Buddhas or one Buddha with two Posals, or sometimes a single Buddha or Posal. Miryuck, the Coming Messiah, and Yaksa, the Healer (Indian—Bhaishajyaraja), are usually alone. Sometimes there are four Posals with the Buddha, two on each side, making five images in a row. Often images of Kasyap and Ananda,[16] the two favourite disciples of the Buddha, and first Patriarchs of the Order, stand beyond the Posals to the right and left. When they appear, the Buddha is always Saka.

Behind the images on the wall, is always a painting or a carved medallion, covered with gold, of the same figures that are shown in the images, and many other figures in balanced pairs, other Posals, or Kasyap and Ananda (whether shown in the images or not), or Sariputra and Maudgalyana, and there are usually many angel attendants. In China, Janteng, teacher of Buddha, called " Yunteung " in Korea, appears in these wall pictures, but not in Korea.

Upon the right hand inside wall, as one faces the main images, is usually a large painting covering a large part of that wall and

---

[16] Gordon in *Royal Asiatic Society Records,* 1914, p. 25; Gordon in *Symbols of the Way,* p. 84.

called the " Sinchoongtang." It is supposed to include all of the miscellaneous spirits that worship the Buddha. My college president friend said that possibly it represented some of the Assemblies said to have taken place upon the sacred mountain in Ceylon. This painting is in three strata, and there may be either thirty-nine, one hundred and four or three hundred and ninety faces shown in it. The details are explained in a book called the *Hwaeumkung*. The highest stratum of the picture is presided over by Brahma, called " Pum Wang " in Korea. He sits in the centre of his group. The next stratum below him is under Sakra, called " Suk Wang " in Korea, and the lowest stratum is under Veda, called " Tongjin Posal." He always has wings on his hat, like Mercury of old.

It is curious that among all of the three hundred and ninety faces, all are golden except Brahma, Sakra and Veda, who are white, the Koreans say " because they are Aryan gods." Sometimes this Sinchoontang is divided into two pictures and placed half on each side of the room. Sometimes in the smaller temples, it has only a dozen faces. One finds copies of it unexpectedly in all sorts of places in the apartments of the priests, on the walls at the end of porches or in passageways. In the Sinchoongtang, there is always a picture of " Choo Wang," the kitchen god, borrowed from Taoism in China.[17] He has white bristly whiskers. There is usually a picture of the King of Dragons, borrowed also from the Taoism or Confucianism of China; also, figures representing the spirits or Buddhas of the sun and the moon, and the old man spirit of the mountain on which the temple is built (borrowed from Korean Shamanism). Confucius, canonized as Yootong Posal, is said to be there, and also Anyun, founder of the Confucian Temple in Seoul. He is Kwangchung Posal. Laotze is said to have been included under the name Kaya Kasyap. The four Divas, or Heavenly Kings, always appear in the corners and one or more hideous figures dark red, carrying pitchforks and wrapped around with the coils of a snake.

Next to the Sinchoongtang on the same right hand wall is usually another large painting representing the seven Buddhas of the

---

[17] *Korean Repository*, 1892, p. 203.

seven-starred Great Bear constellation.[18]  This also is from Chinese
Taoism.  In the picture the seven Buddhas usually stand in a row
at the top.  The central figure below may be Saka or it may be
another of the Buddhas called " Chisung Yerai," who always holds
in his hand a small Wheel of Life which looks like a pocket compass.  On his right and left are Ilkwang and Wulkwang Posals,
the Posals of the moon and sun, differentiated by single silver and
gold disks on their crowns.

Next to this picture, still on the right hand wall, is often a picture representing the Ten Kings of Hell.  Sometimes these are not
there but in their separate temple outside.  Whether they are there
or not, there is next to them a smaller picture of Hyun Wang, a
red-faced, fierce-looking individual, who apparently acts as a Pro-
curator, giving a preliminary trial to the dead before they go in
before the Ten Kings of Hell, the Judges of the Buddhist Avernus.

On the left hand wall, at the front facing the Sinchoongtang, is
a large picture showing five or seven ancient Buddhas in a row at
the top.  Usually the picture shows five Buddhas, and is called the
" Kamnotan," after the fourth of the Buddhas in the series, Kamno,
This picture shows graphically the glories of the various heavens
and the tortures of the various hells, or the " twenty-five deaths by
which people may die."  It represents the Buddhas, and particularly Kamno, exhorting the spirits under torment to repent and be
saved from their sad condition.  Demon attendants are seen casting souls into the fire with pitchforks after the fashion of Dante's
Inferno.  At Tongtosa this altar seems little thought of.  It was
locked when I was there.  In the other temples, it seems practically
almost the most important of them all.

Incense is burned daily before the images and pictures, but on
certain days of the year great piles of cooked rice and other grains,
bread, fruit and flowers are brought, and first presented to the
main idols and then stacked in front of the Kamnotan as sacrifices
on behalf of the dead, to rescue them more quickly from their
Purgatory.  Pickle and soup cannot be offered before the main
idols, but I have seen them presented at the Kamnotan.  In China,

[18] Trollope in *Royal Asiatic Society Records*, 1917, p. 15.

only fruit and flowers are said to be offered. These gifts are most common at the New Year's Season. After presentation, they are eaten by the priests. At the side of the Kamnotan, there is often a recess containing hundreds of little tombstone-like tablets of wood, six inches or so high, each bearing the name of some deceased friend. If specially subsidized, the priests will offer food at the Kamnotan and pray daily for these departed ones.

Next to the Kamnotan picture on the left wall is almost invariably a picture of the Shamanistic spirit of the mountain, always shown as an old man, usually seated upon a tiger. Beyond him is almost always an image or picture of the "Lonely Saint," the "Toksungin" or "Laban Chonja." No one knows whom this is intended to represent. Bishop Trollope thinks that it may be Chikai, the founder of the Tendai Sect in China,[19] but every Korean to whom I have spoken has said that it was not so. That guess is as good as any other, however. The Koreans say that he lived before Gautauma and, like Melchisedek, had no beginning and no end, that, when Gautauma came, he gave to that Great One his allegiance. One might hazard another guess that he is that same Janteng of China, Buddha's teacher who is said to be shown in the temples there.

The interior walls and ceiling and exposed beams are all decorated with yellow and red and other colours.[20] In the panels of the walls and ceiling, there are pictures of the various Buddhas or of scenes in Paradise, or sometimes scenes from the famous novel, the *Suyooki,* which we have already mentioned once before. Madame Gordon makes a great deal of this allegorical play in her book *Symbols of the Way.* She says that it is one of the three great Oriental Allegories which rank along with *Pilgrim's Progress* in the West. It was written by the Taoist saint Chiu Chu Chi[21] in the thirteenth century. It tells in allegorical form how the monk Yuan Chang went to India in the sixth century to get the sacred books. He was accompanied by a white horse, a monkey and a pig. They had many weird adventures, shipwrecks, etc. Those scenes

[19] *Royal Asiatic Society Records,* 1917, p. 39.
[20] See article "Architecture," *Encyclopædia Religion and Ethics.*
[21] Gordon, *Symbols of the Way,* pp. 1, 2, 4, 14, etc.

are undoubtedly pictured inside or outside on the walls of many of
the temples, particularly in the little spaces between the rafters and
roof timbers. Suspended from the ceiling or pictured in painting
or carving on the ceiling are dragons, and the mysterious bird,
called "Keumsijo," which devours dragons. Possibly this is the
"roc" or *Arabian Nights* fame. These are all for ornament and
not for worship.

In front of each of the images or pictures on the main altar, is a
shelf or table holding the incense burner and the offerings. There
are also placed the tablets for the King and Crown Prince.

Behind the Main Hall, and nearly always facing at right angles
to it, is the Myungpoochun, or Hall of the Ten Kings of Hell.[22]
In China, there are said to have been eighteen of these Kings or
Judges, but here there are only ten. Usually the Judges are represented by conventional white stone images about four feet high,
either sitting or standing. Behind each on the wall is a large picture showing the tortures in the hell over which he presides, the
hot hell, for example, and the icy hell, the hell where people are
sawn asunder, etc. The fifth King of the ten is Yumna, and he
is really about the only one that receives any attention at all.[23] He
is the Pluto of Korea's Underworld. Everyone in Korea, Buddhist, Confucianist or Shamanist, if compelled to state anything
about the future life, would probably say that the dead go to " Chu
Seung," " that place " to the realm of Yumna, the King.

In this hall, the central presiding figure, greater than any of the
Ten Kings, is Chijang Posal, the Boddhisattva who goes down into
the various hells and pleads with men there to repent. His picture,
so pleading, appears in most of the wall pictures behind the Kings.
He is the Titsang of China, the figure who appeared in the early
ages to take over some of the functions of Yumna when the
Yumna idea first crossed over into China from India. One legend
says that he was once a Brahman maiden in Burmah. Her mother
died and went down to one of the lowest hells. She prayed for the
mother, offering to take her place in hell. Buddha was moved by
her prayer and allowed her to become a Posal, and to give herself

[22] Trollope, *Royal Asiatic Society Records*, 1917, p. 39.
[23] Edkins, *Chinese Buddhism*, pp. 242, 246; Starr, *Korean Buddhism*, p. 80.

wholly to working, not only for her mother, but for other unfortu-
nates bound to the lower parts of the Wheel. This legend is probably one of those rationalizations of an existing procedure which
are continually growing up in connection with religions, but it
makes a pretty story.

In Japan, he is called Jizo Bosatsu, and is the one who receives
and cares for little dead children, and the one to whom mothers
pray.[24] His temples over there have hundreds of little children's
dresses and other garments and toys hanging from their walls and
ceiling. There is nothing like this in Korea. He cares for all of
the dead impartially.

Chijang sits like a Chairman in the Hall of the Kings. Often a
white statue of his mother, possibly that Burmah mother, sits beside him. His statue is yellow or green. Two fierce warrior-like
figures guard the two sides of the door. They are Tongmyung
Chonja and Mooteuk Ki Wang.

In any temple group of any size, there will be a tiny separate
shrine for the Lonely Saint, the Toksungin; also a separate shrine
for the seven Buddhas of the Great Bear constellation;[25] and yet
another for the old man of the mountain sitting on his tiger. In
many places, there is a separate shrine for the Sixteen Naheun,
tiny third-grade Buddhas, with pictures behind each of the images.
In China, there are eighteen of these instead of sixteen. Edkins
says[26] that but sixteen is the number for India and that the last
two were added in China. This shows again how close was the
connection between Korea and India.

In several places in the country, e. g., at Sukwangsa near Wonsan, there are temples containing five hundred of these Naheun, all
sitting around the room on terraces, each on his silken cushion. In
China, they have a five hundred and first one perched up on a
beam, he being one who came late, and was excluded from the
regular company. They do not have this extra one in Korea unless
the Lonely Saint is he. The Koreans say that he is in a class by
himself and was never associated with the five hundred. These

[24] Gordon, *World Healers,* p. 281.
[25] Gordon, *Royal Asiatic Society Records,* 1914, p. 25.
[26] Edkins, *Chinese Buddhism,* p. 249.

five hundred are variously said to represent robber bands or merchant caravans of that number who met the Buddha in his journeys and were at once and thoroughly converted en masse.

In addition to the Main Hall with its Trinity, in large temples, there may be a half dozen or more other Main Halls with other Buddhist Trinities and all of the paraphernalia of the Great Hall. Each will have over its door an inscription indicating which Trinity is there, e. g., " Tai Heung Chun," " Great Hero Temple," always shows that Saka is the central figure. " Keuk Nak Chun " shows that Amida occupies the central seat, this being the " Western Paradise " temple. The " Yonghwa Chun " mark is on the temples of Miryuck, the Messiah Buddha, and " Manwul Chun," " Ten Thousand Months," on that where Yaksa, the Healing Buddha, sits.

In some temples there are no images, but the walls are thickly covered with tiny pictures of Buddhas all just alike and from one to three inches high. These are the " Thousand Buddha " temples. Twenty miles north of Seoul at the Powhangam is a similar " Ten Thousand Buddha " temple. At Yoochumsa, in the Diamond Mountains, there is the famous shrine of the Fifty-Three Buddhas [27] who ages long ago came over the seas in a stone boat which foundered just off the shore. They waded ashore, fought many fearful battles with the dragons of the mountains and were finally enshrined in this monastery which has no other images in its well-kept Main Hall. The fifty-three tiny images of all shapes and sizes are scattered around amongst an imitation forest in a wall cabinet. They do not now seem to total fifty-three, but the priests say that they come and go.

Most of the larger temples have a Hall of Portraits where are kept the portraits of the founders of the given monastery and of other famous priests, as, for example, Moohak, Chikong, Naong, or Chunghu.[28] In nearly every temple, in some of the rooms, is a series of eight pictures, the " Pal Sang," showing the marvellous events of Gautauma's life. At Pupchoosa monastery in Choongchung province, this Pal Sang is shown in statuary. In nearly

---

[27] *Korean Repository,* 1897, p. 321.
[28] Starr, *Korean Buddhism,* p. 91.

every monastery, they also have a " Koopum," or picture of the nine scenes of Paradise; nine, so the Koreans say, in " remembrance of the nine seeds of the lotus." At Yongmoonsa in Yeitchung County in North Kyungsang province, they have one of the revolving bookcases (called Yoonchang) for holding the Canon, though the books themselves are lost. These bookcases are much prized in Japan, and any one giving them a turn acquires as much merit as though he had read many of the books.[29] Prayer-wheels, so common in Thibet and Japan, are not used at all in Korea.[30]

There are apartments for the priests, and always certain rooms set aside for those priests who practice " Chamsun " (Indian— Samadhi), *i. e.,* go apart and sit facing the blank wall for hours and days at a time, trying to bring their minds to a state of total absence of desire, thus acquiring merit and enlightenment.

This completes the usual temple buildings. In the courtyards, there will be many pagodas of from three to seventeen stories high, always an odd number. In past ages, all of the great priests were awarded pagodas, and special posthumous pagoda names.[31] Formerly the soil of India was brought and spread beneath the pagodas before they were set up, but that practice became too great a burden. In many places, there are dolmens near the ruins of temples, but my college president friend and others were positive that it had never had anything to do with Buddhism. Behind most of the temples are long rows of stone vases or urns six feet or so high, called " Poo Too." In them are preserved the cremated remains of notable dead, usually priests. The Buddhists believe that, when a person is cremated, the good in the person is left in the ashes sublimated down in the form of little jewels of various shapes. These jewels are called " Saree." Some people who are cremated leave none, some leave many. Gautauma is said to have left eight million.

All over the country, there are numbers of temples in caves, some natural and some partly artificial, like the one for the Five Hundred Naheun on the Pukhan Mountain north of Seoul. The

[29] Reischauer, *Studies in Japanese Buddhism,* p. 179.
[30] Chamberlain, *Things Japanese,* p. 394.
[31] *Poolkyo Yaksa.*

most famous of these is the one called Sukoolam [32] near Kyungju. Madame Gordon says that that cave was made after the model of the ancient Syrian cave churches, with a covered tunnel first and then a strip of open air and the lofty artificial cave of the church inside. In this cave, there is a wonderful Buddha eleven feet high seated on a pedestal and so placed that the rays of the rising sun just for a few minutes each morning shine through the opening and light its face. The artificially made domed ceiling is perhaps twenty feet high. The astonishing thing in the cave, however, is the sixteen bas relief figures somewhat more than life-size, carved on the circular inner walls. The faces of these figures have a distinctly Jewish cast. Some are men and some are women. One woman seems to be presenting a cup to the next person in the row. Madame Gordon says that it is the Communion chalice. The head covering of the women figures are boat-shaped haloes said to be like those seen in some Syrian temples. At the entrance of the cave on each side are two pairs of stone figures, one pair the conventional distorted demon, but the second pair wear ruffs and cloaks that make one think of the gallant Raleigh. In niches up the walls of the cave are other Buddha figures, an eleven-head Kwanseieum among others. The whole is capped with a stone on which is carved the Wheel of Life. The great Buddha on the pedestal is thought by some to have been the model for the Japanese Buddha at Kamakura. The cave is high up near the mountain top, looking out over the Japan Sea. It was built, so legend says by Meukhoja, the first Buddhist missionary to Silla.

## 2. IMAGES

The images in the Korean temples are beautifully made.[33] They vary in size from a few inches high to sixty feet or more. Some of the Posals are shown in a standing position, but far the greater number are sitting. In the museum in Seoul are shown some images seated upon raised chairs with their knees crossed, but the Koreans say that that type of image likely came from Thibet. Most of the Posals are in red and gold and have crowns upon

---

[32] *Royal Asiatic Society Records,* 1917, p. 19.
[33] Starr, *Korean Buddhism,* p. 85.

their heads, possibly a reminiscence of the fact that Gautauma, before he got the Law, was an Indian Prince.

The attitudes of the Buddhas are particularly three: first that of Witness, in which the left hand lies on the lap palm upward and the right hand hangs over the knee palm down; secondly, the Meditative, in which the hands are both in the lap, palms upward, the right hand on top; or the Teaching attitude, where the Buddha stands with the right hand raised breast high and the left hanging at the side or grasping the robe. Buddha is never shown in Korea with a beard, but sometimes has a painted on mustache.

Monier-Williams [84] describes seven attitudes of Buddha found in Ceylon, the Meditative, Witness, Serpent Canopied, Argumentative, Preaching, Benedictive, Mendicant and Recumbent. Korea has this last in the Pal Sang pictures or images showing his death, but never the serpent canopied, and possibly not the others. The Koreans say that the Buddhas of the Silla Age were largely standing ones, that those of the Koryu Period were either standing or seated, but that those of the Yi Period were all sitting. Madame Gordon and many others have called attention to the Hellenic cast and general style of a great many of the images and pictures.

All of the Buddhas and Posals hold their hands and bodies in certain conventional positions according to rules that originated in Thibet, and they can be identified by these. These forms are described in a book called the *Kyurin Chip*.

Ordinarily, the statues are of bronze, gold plated or of solid gold, but some are of stone or wood painted white or golden, and some are even of iron and left black. The faces are often exquisitely formed and beautiful, expressing sublime peace. The guardian demons at the gates often have distorted, hideous features, but I have never seen a Buddha face that was not attractive.

There are thirty-two "marks of the Buddha" by which a full Buddha statue can be identified, *e. g.*, around the throat are three rings; [85] there is a sort of topknot mark on the very summit of the head called "Yookkei," and another a little farther forward in the hair. In the centre of the forehead is a jewel-like mark, repre-

---

[84] *Buddhism.*
[85] *Royal Asiatic Society Records,* 1914, p. 18.

senting a white hair which Buddha had there. It is called the
Paikho. The hair of the head, called Nakei, looks curly always in
the real Buddha. Some say that the roughness is not to represent
curls but the ragged tufts left when he hacked off his hair with the
sword on that night when he left his father's palace. Both ears
are long and the lobes rest down upon the shoulders. On the breast
of many of the images, the swastika is imprinted.[86] The Koreans
say that it sometimes fades and then comes back again. The
"right revolving" one is used there. The "left revolving" is
used in connection with funerals.

Madame Gordon thought that she had found crosses on the
Buddhas and in the temples,[87] but I think that she was mistaken,
for a noted Korean artist whom I met at Pumusa told me that he
had himself painted the gates at Tongtosa of which she speaks
and that he had not consciously drawn any crosses there.

Sakamuni always has his right shoulder bare, after the manner
of the Hindoos when they start a difficult piece of work. It means
the same as we do when we roll up our sleeves for a hard job. It
shows how determinedly the Buddha set himself to save mankind.

We said a few moments ago that, "in the Main Halls of the
temples, *some one of* the Buddha Trinities were in the central
place." This is true. Buddhism, as we get further into it, seems
not so much a religion as a whole family of religions.

In some of the temples, Sakayerai is the central figure and, at
his left, the place of honour, is Kwanseieum, the goddess of Mercy,
while at his right is Taiseiji, the personification of power. Madame Gordon says that Miryuck sometimes takes Taiseiji's place
in this Trinity, but both my college president friend and the
Pumusa painter whom I consulted said that this was a mistake.

In some temples, there are three Sakayerai images just alike,
each with the right shoulder uncovered. They are the "Three
Aeon Buddhas, of the Past, Present and the Future." [88] In some,
the central image is Vairochana, the "Diamond Buddha," with
Loshana on his left and Sakayerai in third place on his right. This

---

[86] Eitel, *Chinese Buddhism*, p. 337.
[87] *Royal Asiatic Society Records*, 1914, p. 27.
[88] Cf. Candler, *Unveiling of Lhasa*, p. 334.

Trinity is called the " Pup Po Hwa Sin," or the Buddhas of " Law, Compensation and Change."

In many temples, as for example, Pongchunsa, sixty li east of Seoul, there is but a single image of Yaksa, the Healing Buddha (Bhaishajyaraja), or that Buddha with Ilkwang and Wulkwang, the Sun and Moon Buddhas beside him, or possibly that Buddha with Yak Kwang and Yak Sang Posals. In other temples, there is a single image, usually of stone, of Miryuck, the Coming Messiah. He is usually unattended. Sometimes Kwanseieum, the Goddess of Mercy, sits alone upon the altar. We have already spoken of Chijang and his attendants in the Hall of the Kings. In the larger temples like Tongtosa, there are Main Halls for every one of these separate Trinities or combinations. At Tongtosa is a Miryuck Buddha within its Hall, of which Madame Gordon speaks. Her " helpful " interpreter told her that there had been a miracle in the case of that Buddha, that the people in the temple had risen one morning and found the Buddha pushing his way up through the soil full blown and ready to be worshipped. The abbot of the monastery told me that there used to be a boulder there, and that they hired stone-cutters to carve it and then built a temple over it and dedicated it !

If the right shoulder of the Buddha is bare, or, if there be statues or pictures of Kasyap and Ananda, one can be sure that the image is Sakayerai. If the two hands are placed together to form a letter "A," it is Vairochana. Chijang is usually shaven like a monk and carries a jewel and staff. Sometimes he has over his head a sort of green shawl. Kwanseieum has another tiny Buddha, Chunkwang Yerai on her head, her mother, or holds in her hand a bottle. Taiseiji also has a bottle, the Kamno, or " Bottle of Gracious Dew." Kwanseieum usually has her right hand up and the left in her lap with the palm upwards. She appears also in thirty forms. A common one is that of the " Thousand hands and thousand eyes," where a forest of hands, fanlike, surround her with an eye in the palm of each hand. This is to indicate Omnipotence and Omniscience. She is shown also with 84,000 arms to show her power. Often she has forty-two arms, bristling from her, twenty-one on a side. Sometimes she has eleven faces, as in the Kyungju

Sukoolam Cave, three side by side, front, right and left facing, then three above, and three above that, and then one and one. Sometimes she is shown like Aphrodite, arising out of the sea. The " White Buddha " outside the Northwest Gate of Seoul is of this type, the " Haisoo " Kwaneum. In Thibet and in Japan, she is sometimes shown holding a child in her arms,[30] looking very much like the Virgin Mary, but she is not shown that way in Korea. Moonsoo Posal (Manjusri) nearly always sits upon a tiger, and Pohien Posal (Samantbhadra) rides upon an elephant. Miryuck is shown sometimes with an extraordinarily long right arm, which Madame Gordon thinks a coincidence at least of the " strong hand and outstretched arm of Jehovah." [40]

Always behind the images on the main altars on the wall there are pictures showing the same figures as the images and also other similar figures. There may be but three images on the altar, but in the painting there will be those and then the Posals in pairs, all, except Chijang, in red and gold like the Indian Prince. The common pairs are Kwamseieum-Taiseiji, Moonsoo-Pohien, Chijang-Cheiwhakara, Ilkwang-Wulkwang, Brahma-Sakra.[41] Whenever these last two appear here also, their faces are white. Pupki Posal is the only image on the altar of the Pyohoonsa monastery in the Diamond Mountains, a standing figure.

The colours in all of the wall pictures are very gaudy, and, at first sight, are so different from Western art that they are not attractive, but, when one gets accustomed to them, they are not at all unpleasing.

In addition to the wall pictures within the temples, unlike the temples of China and Japan, the outer walls are also simply covered with paintings, sometimes showing scenes in Paradise with dancing angels and redeemed spirits, sometimes scenes from the Suyooki novel mentioned above. One curious picture recurs over and over again. It shows the " Panyu Yongsun," or " Dragon Boat of Wisdom," just starting off laden with the redeemed going to the Western Paradise. Amida Buddha is Captain. In No

[39] Edkins, *Chinese Buddhism*, p. 246; Armstrong, *Buddhism and Buddhists in Japan*, p. 21; Martin, *Lore of Cathay*, p. 254.
[40] Gordon, *Royal Asiatic Society Records*, 1914, p. 10.
[41] Trollope in *Royal Asiatic Society Records*, 1917, p. 32.

THE EUNJIN BUDDHA—THE GREATEST MIRYUCK
IN KOREA

Wang Yerai is pilot. Many people are shown seated in the boat, and others are shown just failing to catch it. Chijang Posal is shown exhorting the passengers to persevere to the end. Evidently Buddhism has its Noah also.

There are no live animals kept in Korea temples such as the snakes in the Penang Snake Temple, or the giant turtles in the Golden Lotus Temple there, or like the fish in the Rangoon Pool beneath the Shwe Dagon Pagoda. No white horses are cared for as they are in China, perhaps in memory of those white horse messengers to Han Myungti. There are no Buddhas who act as guardians of special trades or crafts, as in Japan, no special Buddha that brings riches, no Buddha that looks over the affairs of literature, none that presides over rivers or other places.

There are no Butsudan, or Buddha shelves, in Korea as there are in Japan in most of their private dwellings. A few wealthy Koreans have little semi-private temples adjacent to their homes or within their own yards, sometimes with a single priest hangeron, always present, or coming occasionally from a nearby temple. There are no Buddhist shrines in homes, even such as those in China. It evidently was not a home cult. All worship was in the temple and largely by proxy through the ministrations of the priests. Occasionally a family will have a Buddhist book, either for reading or which they hold as a sacred relic or something of a fetich. From having such in their possession, they are said to acquire merit.

All over the country among the mountains, often far from the temples, sometimes in connection with them, are great stone faces or heads called Miryucks,[42] some carved in bas relief on the cliffs, some full statues standing alone, some partly on the cliff and partly free. The great statue of Eunjin near Kongju in the old Paikchei field is the finest of these.[43] It stands sixty-five feet high. Thirty miles north of Seoul in a grove near Paju are two gigantic stone Miryucks, partly carved on the cliff, with the heads and shoulders free showing above the trees.[44] In the Diamond Mountains is one face cut on a cliff sixty feet high, and there are scores of smaller

---

[42] Underwood, *Religions of Eastern Asia*, p. 102.
[43] Jones, *Royal Asiatic Society Records*, 1900, p. 53.
[44] *Korean Repository*, 1892, p. 19.

ones in every part of the land. The "White Buddha" outside of the gate of Seoul is very well known.

All of these stone images are popularly called Miryucks, *i. e.,* by the same name as that given to the Messiah Buddha whom all North Asia is expecting soon to come. Likely there was originally, before Buddhism came into the country, a cult of worship of these images, many of which then existed, and the name was similar to "Miryuck." When Buddhism came, in its usual manner, it simply absorbed the cult, putting the Buddha name to the stones, and then gradually creating many more like stone artificially. Really very few of these images are Buddhas. Most of them are images of Kwenseieum, the Goddess of Mercy. The Eunjin "Buddha," and the "White Buddha" near Seoul are both "Haisoo Kwaneum," or "Kwaneum of the Sea Water." Most of these are more or less reverenced by passersby. Possibly they used to have ministering priests in olden days. Many do not have them today.

On account of the multitudes of these Miryucks, Madame Gordon says that she was told that Miryuck was the most worshipped Buddha in Korea, as Amida holds first place in Japan, and Kwanseieum in China.[45] Koreans all tell me that this is a mistake. In Korea also, Amida holds unquestioned first place in all Buddhist ceremonies and prayers. Next after him comes Kwanseieum and then perhaps Chijang. Miryuck is relatively little thought of and few prayers are offered to him. In China, there are many places where one idol is worshipped to the exclusion of all the others, as, for example, Kwanyin on the island of Pootoo. As has been noted above, in certain of the Korean temples they have one Buddha and at certain places another as the central figure on their altars, but there are no large places where only one image is shown as the single patron deity of the district. So much, then, for the physical properties of the cult.

### 3. CEREMONIES OF BUDDHISM

*1. The Ceremony of Installing the Images and Sacred Pictures*

The images are always hollow, and there is usually a small door

---

[45] Gordon, *Royal Asiatic Society Records,* 1914, p. 10.

in the back. When the image has been constructed and is ready for dedication, cloth or other materials are taken and more or less rudely fashioned into the shapes of the vitals of the human body, and their several names are written on them in Chinese letters. When the dedicatory ceremony is held, these articles are passed into the image's interior from the back and sealed there with accompanying ceremonies. Last of all, the pupils are added to the eyes, and the dedication is complete.[46] In China, it is said that sometimes a live mouse is sealed in the image so that its life may pass into the image and give it a dynamic urge.[47]

When a Sinchoongtang, or any of the similar paintings, are dedicated and made ready to receive the prayers of the faithful, the same articles are prepared and placed in a wallet similar to those which Koreans all carry at their belts. During the ceremony of dedication, the wallet is hung on a nail just above the picture. Until this is done, the picture is not worshipped.

This is about all that there is to the consecration of the images. It is said that sometimes when temples are repaired and the Buddhas disturbed and discommoded, after the repairs are completed the images are taken out in the yard and carried seven steps, east, south, west and north, and restored to the altars. These twenty-eight steps are in remembrance of the twenty-eight which Buddha took on the very day of his birth. Back in the sixteenth century, sometimes the images were taken out and carried in public processions. Members of the Japanese Embassy at that time are said to have been shocked at seeing a standing Buddha so carried.[48] Such processions ceased two hundred years ago when Buddhism was disestablished.

### 2. The Ceremony of Initiation of Priests and of Members

(a) For Laymen.

There is no such ceremony as baptism to signalize entering the Buddhist fold. Members simply present themselves at the temples

---

[46] Edkins, *Chinese Buddhism*, pp. 51, 52; Tyler, *Primitive Culture*, II, p. 178.

[47] *Encyclopædia of Religion and Ethics*, VII, p. 126.

[48] *Korean Repository*, 1896, p. 50.

and agree to keep the first five of the Buddhist " Ten Commandments." The Koreans make a regular Torso Pentalogue out of those Five, calling them respectively, " Sasil, Tooto, Saeum, Mangu, and Pooreumjoo," or, to translate, " Not to kill any living thing, not to steal, not to commit impurity of any kind, not to lie and not to drink wine."

The remaining five of the Ten Commandments are binding only upon the priests and nuns. They read, (6) Not to sleep or sit on a high, broad bed, i. e., not to be lazy, (7) Not to possess gold, silver or jewels, (8) Not to take part in singing, dancing or theatrical performances, (9) Not to use flowers or perfume for personal adornment, and (10) Not to eat at unseasonable hours, i. e., be greedy.

Sometimes in the Koryu days, devout laymen took three more of these along with the first five, making eight in all. These were called the Palkwanchai. My college president friend says that the extra three were numbers six, seven and eight. Others say that they were numbers eight, nine and ten.[49]

In Japan, the Shingon Sect, at least, has a sort of baptism ceremony with water in which the five grains are mingled.[50] This is not known in Korea, though the " Tageui Mool," the water that has been on the altar before the images, is sometimes drunk by the worshippers, and sometimes sprinkled on the ground to sanctify it. We shall note later how the Chuntokyo devotees also drink the water that has been upon their altar during their services. The priests wash themselves before entering the temples to perform their ministry, but simply for cleanliness' sake. It is not a ceremonial.

(b) For Priests and Nuns.[51]

For these professional workers, there are several grades of initiation. Upon assuming the whole Ten Commandments, a young boy was admitted to the Order as an acolyte. He was called by the Indian name, " Shami," which has been taken into the Korean language along with the word " Shramana " or " Biku "

---

[49] Hackmann, *Buddhism as a Religion*, p. 22.
[50] Lloyd, *Creed of Half Japan*, p. 115.
[51] Rhys David, *Buddhism*, pp. 140, 159.

for priest, and " Bikuni " for nun, and " Upasaka " for devout layman.

A layman wishing to become a semi-professional priest could do so by taking a certain Fifty Vows called the " Posalkei." Two at least of the Kings of Korea (in 1045 and 1054) did this. A regular priest has to be over twenty years of age, and takes two hundred and fifty vows. A " Bikuni " or nun is compelled to take five hundred vows. Priestly ordination is called " receiving the fire " (pool tatta). When these vows are taken by the priests and nuns, a bit of candle wick soaked in grease is laid on the inner side of the left arm just below the elbow, and set on fire.[52] It inflicts a burn and leaves a scar, so that they can never disavow having followed this vocation.[53] In China, this burning is done on the top of the head.[54]

Formerly ordinations could be held only at Tongtosa and Haiinsa monasteries in the south, as they alone had " Keitan," altars, but now they are held in all of the larger temples, especially the thirty-two head temples mentioned in the last lecture. The altar of Tongtosa is not a complicated three-story construction such as they have in Japan, but simply a long, narrow shelf affair of black wood extending clear across the building. It is about four feet high, and has several narrow shelves one above the other stepped back, and, upon these, tablets are placed and various ornaments. No one ascends the altar as in Japan. They simply stand in front of it.

Directly in front of the altar at Tongtosa, a filmy curtain of some red material hangs from the lofty ceiling, and beyond that is a great audience chamber where sermons are delivered at times to several hundreds of people at once. Near the curtain is a curious pulpit flat-topped with a low rail six inches high around the back and two sides. It looks like any ordinary pulpit except for the rail The abbot told me that the speaker in their meetings always sat cross-legged on top of that pulpit, instead of standing

---

[52] Griffis, *The Hermit Nation*, p. 335; *Royal Asiatic Society Records*, 1918, p. 138.

[53] DeGroot, *Religion of China*, p. 170.

[54] Giles, *Civilization of China*, p. 56; *Encyclopædia of Religion and Ethics*, III, p. 553.

behind it as Westerners do. As the audience sits on the floor and the speaker also, unless the latter's seat is elevated, most of them cannot see him. Madame Gordon speaks of the wonderful "Empty Altar" of Tongtosa, and tells how it was never used for any purpose except when the invisible Buddha himself descended to speak to his people.[55] It is another pretty story, but the abbot said that he was the only one who ever sat there. Interpreters are sometimes too "helpful" altogether.

Formerly at least ten priests had to be present when an acolyte (Shami) was ordained. Now three or four are sufficient. Now they quite often wait for priest ordinations until there are a large number to be taken in, thirty if possible, but even that is not required. These ordinations occur only once in two or three years nowadays, as relatively few people are entering the Order. It occurs most often on Buddha's birthday, the eighth day of the fourth lunar month. No spectators are allowed. At the ceremony, three older priests preside, one as Chairman (Hwasangsa), one on his left as First Assistant (Kalmasa), and the other on his right as the (Kyosoosa) Exhorter, this last being evidently the one giving the pastoral charge. Seven "Chinsa," or witnessing priests take part, and there are about ten Ilyu, or serving men. The two hundred and fifty vows are asked, and made and the arm-burning seals it all. The newly-ordained priest assumes the "kasa" robe, a sort of toga that covers all of the body except the right shoulder and arm. This toga is made of about one hundred and twenty-five tiny bits of cloth, and usually has the names of the Four Heavenly Kings or Divas on the corners. The cloth is purposely torn into these small bits and sewn together again, so as to deprive it of all commercial value, and keep up the appearance of complete poverty even when the kasa is new.[56] It is always worn during ceremonies and worship services and may be worn at all times. It is usually red or yellowish in colour, but may be blue, and the ribbons may be multi-coloured.

The only knowledge absolutely required of one who would be a priest today is the ability to repeat the Sikkyung or grace at

---

[55] *Royal Asiatic Society Records,* 1914, p. 28.
[56] Rhys David, *Buddhism,* p. 156.

meals,[57] the Chunsoo, or the morning and evening prayer dharani sentences and the Songchoo, which are certain general prayer sentences in Sanscrit.

In the modern schools an effort is made to give a great deal more of training than this, and priests are now graded into eight classes according to their education. Those educated in the formal Buddhist schools of today, primary, through secondary to college, eight years in all, at graduation become " Taisa," or " Great Teacher." Two years later, if they have done well, they are promoted to " Choongtuk," or " Medium Merit." Two years still later again, they become " Taituk," " Great Merit," and finally two years later, " Taikyosa," which might be something like Doctor of Divinity. Those who have not taken the formal course but have studied privately and in summer schools and the like, after ten years of supervised study become " Taisun," then " Choongtuk," then " Sunsa," and lastly " Taisunsa," these terms being translatable literally with much the same words as the above four, but representing a slightly lesser degree of standing. The above is the ideal scheme, but, as a matter of fact, there is a good deal of chaos in the grading practically.

When a priest is ordained, he is said to leave the active work-a-day world entirely. He drops his citizen name, and adopts the name of Buddha. If one meets a priest on the road and asks his name, he will answer, " I am Saka," i. e., " I am Buddha." If you want his citizen name, you must ask particularly for it (Sokineui Irhom). It is a pretty custom said to have been introduced by Doan, a famous Chinese monk in the state of Wei in the sixth century.

The priests are supposed to be strict vegetarians, as the Order has required that ever since the beginning. Some do practise it, but my college president friend said that they were allowed to eat meat when very hungry if they had not seen or heard the animal being killed. He called attention to the legend that Buddha himself died from eating boar's flesh. He said that the story of that incident was in a book called *Sunchon Chulhak,* or " Philosophy of the Sun Sect."

---

[57] *Korea Magazine,* 1917, p. 217.

The priests are recruited largely from indigent families living near the temples. Boys are taken into the temples and girls into the nunneries in childhood and at first act simply as servants. As they get older, they begin to study and finally qualify. The modern schools try to shorten that period and some few candidates come from those who have simply studied in the schools.

### 3. Prayer

Nine-tenths of the services in the temples consist simply of repetitions of the Sanscrit formulæ called Dharani, *e. g.,* "Soori, soori, maha soori, soori soori sabaha, Namu Ami Ta Pool, Namu Ami Ta Pool," or "Yook cha tai myung wang Chin Un, Om mani pan mi hom," or "O choori choori Chun jei sabaha," etc. None of these formulæ are retained by the priests as private secrets of the craft as in Thibet. Any one may buy the little *Chunsoo Kyung* book containing a thousand of these, and he may recite them at will. Of the meaning of most of the formulæ, the ordinary priest or devotee has no idea whatever. If he did, they might help him to really worship. For example, that last one, "Om mani pan mi hom," has been translated by some who claim to know as, "Oh, thou god that dwellest in the lotus flower, help!" Buddha is quite commonly shown seated upon a lotus flower or holding one in his hand. All down the ages, that cry has gone up from all over northern Asia. Sven Hedin [58] says that he found the words everywhere in the lama country in Thibet, carved on pillars and boulders by the wayside, and on banners in the temples. He heard it sung and chanted by priests and laymen all over the land. The old priest in Kipling's *Kim* story went along the road mumbling this prayer to himself in his great Search. It is used as a charm and written on talismans, "Oh, thou god that dwelleth in the lotus flower, help!" My old abbot language teacher of whom I spoke at the beginning of these lectures had lived in the temples from childhood, and first taught me the formula twenty-five years ago, but he himself did not know the meaning then, though he had used that prayer tens of thousands of times.

---

[58] *Trans-Himalaya,* pp. 305, 366.

Most of the prayers of Buddhism are recitations like this, but the human heart hungers for something more than this, even though they will expressly disavow it in words. My college president friend said that, as a matter of fact, after the formulæ have been repeated a few times, direct petitions and prayers to Amida or Kwanseieum are offered which are not very different from Christian prayers. They call these free prayers Chookwun.

Laymen, as a general thing, do not pray a great deal in Buddhism. The priest is provided to do that for them. They learn a few of the dharani sentences sometimes and repeat those. Bishop Trollope quotes a note at the end of a Buddhist book written in 1796 where it reads, "Any monk or layman, male or female, who is not sufficiently educated to recite this (Chinese) Classic, may acquire equivalent merit by reciting the spell, ' Om oryouni sabaha, Om haritarisari sooroji samiriji pilsayei sabaha, Om horohoro saya molkyei sabaha,' " a meaningless series of Sanscrit syllables.[59]

The priests do not make any special prayers for their own cleansing before they offer the prayers for the people.

The priests and nuns carry rosaries much like those of the Roman Catholics and for the same purpose. Usually there are 108 beads upon the rosary which is hung around their necks.[60] Sometimes a hand rosary with but twenty-one beads is used, or one with very large beads, seven in all. Occasionally in paying a special vow, a rosary of one thousand beads is used. In China, they have eighty-one beads, but never in Korea. The Mohammedans use ninety-nine to show the ninety-nine beautiful names of Allah.[61] The Shivaites of India use thirty-two.[62] What the special significance of the 108 beads may be we do not know. The Koreans have many fanciful rationalizations of the custom. They say that they refer to the twenty-eight stars of the four quarters of the heaven added to the twelve feast days and certain other numbers. See the translation of the Rosary Classic in Appendix III.

[59] *Bookman,* 1922, Sept., p. 1.
[60] Rhys David, *Buddhism,* p. 209; Armstrong, *Buddhism and Buddhists in Japan,* p. 27.
[61] Candler, *Unveiling of Lhasa,* p. 348.
[62] Monier-Williams, *Brahmanism and Hinduism,* p. 67.

The priest's prayer day begins with four A. M. and closes with
nine P. M. There are special prayers at those two times and at
nine A. M., four and six P. M. They also have grace at meals.

In the ancient Silla days, there were great convocations for
study and prayer held from time to time under the patronage of
the kings. One of these was called the " Paikchwagot," or Hundred Seat Lecture, because just one hundred scholars participated
actively, though any one might come and listen, and multitudes did.
A little later, in the Koryu time, the P'al Kwan Chai festival,
where laymen gathered to assume or renew the Eight Vows, was
popular.

Always in the rainy season the priests have taken time for retirement and prayer and study of the ceremonies and Scriptures.
Usually these periods of retirement have lasted seven, twenty-one,
forty-nine or ninety days. Special lecturers have come and explained the books. These Classes are kept up even today whenever
as many as thirty people have been willing to meet. They are now
called " Tochang " or " Sallim." They are even now great times
of revival when the priests renew their vows, and again receive the
arm-burning to seal the new consecration. Often one sees a dozen
to twenty of these burn-scars on a man's arm marking the seasons
of blessing.

Occasionally, when devotees pay particularly for it, prayers will
be held in the temple or in private homes continuously for seven
days or thirty days, day and night, without stopping, and tradition
records how one famous priest with thirty-two of his friends engaged in a ten-thousand-day prayer, serving in relays, several
working simultaneously. At the end of the time, so the record
states, Buddha came in his Dragon Ship of Wisdom and took them
all off to the Western Land of Bliss. After such a siege, they
were no doubt ready to go.

In the prayer sentences used in invoking Loshana of the Vairochana Trinity, Koreans use the word "Abarahakka," [63] as do the
Japanese of the Shingon Sect. Prof. Lloyd, of Tokio, says that
the same syllables were used in the early centuries after Christ by

---

[63] *Creed of Half Japan,* p. 38.

the Gnostics in Egypt in invoking the central Deity of their queer pantheon. He believes that many of the teachings of this sect (Shingon) came from Egypt, not from India, both nations having had the Five Deities, a central one and four lesser ones grouped around it forming a "Diamond World of Light." In each, there is the doctrine of emanations. The other word, "Caulaucau," which Lloyd found in this cult and in the Gnostic teaching is not known in Korea.

### 4. Preaching

Formerly there was little formal preaching in the temples, at least for the past hundred years or so, and little expounding of their Scriptures except in the summer "Sallim," retirement seasons. Now they are establishing preaching chapels in many of the larger towns after the model of the Christian churches, and, in some of the temples themselves the pavilions have been arranged for preaching rooms. At Tongtosa monastery, they say that they have preaching regularly on the first and fifteenth of every month. In the city of Seoul, they have it regularly on the Christian Sunday.

### 5. Marriage

The priests, being ostensibly celibates, and teaching that same state as the ideal, naturally have not performed wedding ceremonies even for laymen. During the last few years, however, in an effort to imitate the Christians, and keep up with the rapidly moving times, the Buddhists in the central Kakhwangsa temple in Seoul have held several public weddings. It is an innovation, however, which is not likely to spread, as public opinion is against it.

We said that the priests are ostensibly celibates. No doubt many of them are, and for strictly religious reasons, as also many refrain rigidly from wine and meat, but the majority of them have always lived openly or secretly pretty much as the layman do, having families and children secretly down in the lowlands beneath the monasteries. Until recently, their marriages were not recognized as legal. They were simply common law arrangements. Now the

Japanese Government allows them to register their wives legally just as the Shin Sect does in Japan.

### 6. Funerals

Throughout Asia, the people turn to Confucius or Laotze to tell them how to live and to Buddha to look after them when they come to die. As noted above, practically all of the people in Korea, even Confucianist scholars, expect after death more or less clearly to go to "Chu Seung," "that place," to King Yumna. Up till the end of the Koryu Dynasty, all Korean funerals were in the hands of the priests, but the Yi Dynasty kings stopped that, and, in 1516, even forbade the people going to the temples to celebrate death anniversaries of parents and others. Today the priests seldom go to private houses for funerals, but the bereaved go to the temples, and pay special fees for having special offerings and prayers made for their dead, before the Kamno altar of which we spoke a little while ago. Especially on the fifteenth of the seventh lunar month and at the Korean New Year's this is done. At the funerals, lotus flags such as are carried in funerals in China are not used, but there are many black lotus flowers used to decorate the Kamnotan at the central Kakhwangsa Temple in Seoul.

Koreans do not use coffins as do the Chinese. They take a thick plank and bind the bodies to it with long bolts of cloth tied around and around both body and plank. Underneath the head of the body, they bore seven holes partly through the plank arranged like the seven stars of the Great Bear Constellation, possibly in honour of the seven Buddhas said to rule there. Even non-Buddhists, however, follow this custom, so that it is probably older than Buddhism in Korea. "Tabi," the Indian word for funeral, has been taken over into Korean, and the priests in conducting the funerals use a book called *Tabi Moon,* prepared by the priest Naong when his mother died.

Cremation has been the most approved method of disposal of the dead among Buddhists, especially since 681 A. D., when the first Korean King ordered his body to be so treated.[64] The Japanese

---

[64] Hulbert, *History of Korea,* I, p. 167.

have now built modern crematories in various places in the country near the large cities, but all down the centuries all cremation has been in the hands of the priests, and it is carried out in the open air. It is called "Fire Burial." In the far mountains, it is done on great pyres of wood. Near the city, charcoal is used. Priests are usually cremated in a sitting position,[65] but laymen are placed lying down. The fire is lighted after a special ceremonial manner from five separate places. The ashes are afterwards carefully searched to find the "Saree," or little jewel-like relics said to represent the sublimated goodness of the person deceased.[66] The rest of the remains are not preserved except in the case of distinguished persons whose ashes are kept in great mortuary urns in the temple grounds.

After death, prayer is offered at the temple at regular intervals consecutively to each of the Ten Kings—Judges of the Lower World, one king each day being honoured on the seventh, fourteenth, twenty-first, twenty-eighth, thirty-fifth, forty-second, forty-ninth and one hundredth day after death, and on the first and third anniversaries of that day.

## 7. *Festivals and Special Days*

All devout Buddhists observe to some extent the first and fifteenth day of each month,[67] and during the whole of the fifth and ninth lunar months they are particularly faithful to their religious duties. In some of the temples, the first and fifteenth of every month are special days, and, in some parts of the country, in order to compete with the Christians, the Buddhists have of recent years actually been keeping the Christian Sunday and holding services similar to the Christians' services.

The fifteenth day of the seventh lunar month is the day for feeding the hungry spirits. This festival lasts from the evening of the fourteenth to the sixteenth. The spirits are all summoned by the great bell, the drum, the gong and the wooden fish and food is spread in the pavilion or on the stone table out in front for them.

---

[65] Hackmann, *Buddhism as a Religion*, p. 118.
[66] Starr, *Korean Buddhism*, p. 56.
[67] Ross, *Corea: Its History, Customs and Manners*, p. 356.

There is a similar ceremony on the fifteenth day of the eighth month, though not quite so elaborate. Buddhists do not now go as the Confucianists do on the fifteenth day of the eighth month, or of any other month, to spread food in front of the graves.

Buddha's birthday, the eighth day of the fourth lunar month, and his death day, the nineteenth of the second lunar month, are also special days, also the times of eclipses of the sun and moon, the Buddhas residing in them being particularly worshipped at that time. For very devout believers, nearly every day of the month is a special day, e. g., the fifteenth for Amida, the eighteenth for Chijang, the twenty-third for Taiseiji, the twenty-fourth for Kwanseieum, and the thirtieth for Sakayerai.

At any time when any devotee will pay for it, special ceremonies and dramatic plays, called Yochap, will be given in the temple courtyards. Great Buddha paintings similar to the Sinchoongtang, twenty feet high and wide or larger, are suspended perpendicularly from bamboo frames at one side of the inner courtyard, and the plays were performed before them with appropriate prayers and actions.[68] It has been claimed that general dramas were given in this way, but that is a mistake.

## 8. Music

Unless the banging of gongs and the booming of the drums be so counted, we may say that music was little used in the ancient temples, nor is it used to any extent now. The prayer formulæ are recited in a sort of singsong tone, but there is no musical accompaniment. A sort of clarionet, called the Hoisuk, is sometimes used in the temples, but not in the regular services. I saw a small cottage organ in the priests' rooms at Tongtosa, and a larger one at the central, Kakhwangsa, temple in Seoul. In the public services, the priests do all of the talking and reciting. There is no reciting in concert and no congregational singing of any sort.

## 9. Fasting and Feasting

By Buddha's Law there should be but one or, at most, two

---

[68] Starr, *Korean Buddhism,* p. 94. See picture.

meals a day for priests particularly, and nothing eaten after noonday, the whole afternoon being given to meditation and study and prayer. As a matter of fact, few Koreans observe this. On the first and fifteenth days of the first, fifth and ninth lunar months, all who have any pretensions to faithfulness, do observe a fast, but there is little of asceticism in Korea at any time.

Each priest is allowed to possess four dishes for eating. They are called Parotai. They nest one into the other. This is in memory of the time when each of the Four Divas brought to Buddha a bowl of rice. He knew that if he took one bowl from any of them, the others would be broken-hearted, so he took all four and pressed them together so that by a miracle they became one, with just the rims of the four showing at the top.[69] The Korean dishes, as they nest together, give this appearance. Chinese monks, like those of ancient India, are allowed but one bowl each, it is said.

Of course, no women live in the temples. The younger priests act as cooks, and serve the meals to the others after first spreading the tables before the altars. Madame Gordon tells of the priests of Tongtosa who spread the food before the Buddhas, and says that they had white paper bound over their lips and, like the lepers of Israel, cried " Unclean."[70] This is another one of those stories kindly furnished to her by the interpreter. The abbot told me that, if the men ever did wear white paper like that, and he did not act as though he had ever seen it, it was for sanitary reasons only, similar to the custom of barbers in the East, and not for any other reason.

## 10. Begging

One hardly thinks of begging as a ceremony, but such it was in Buddha's original Law. He required even the wealthiest of his followers to practise it. Sometimes they did not actually eat what they gathered, but they had to gather it. I have seen in the Japanese quarter of Korean cities, well-dressed Japanese men and

---

[69] Rockhill, *Life of Buddha*, p. 34.
[70] *Royal Asiatic Society Records*, 1914, p. 28.

women going from house to house in winter evenings begging as a religious act of devotion. Possibly they were gathering money for the poor, but they were beating lightly on gongs to call people out.

Most of the support of the Korean monasteries today comes from endowment fields and forests, with the few sporadic gifts and fees, but that is usually insufficient, so that most of the priests do more or less of begging, especially in the Fall just after the harvest. One sees them going through the villages from house to house, a priest and an acolyte. The priest wears a toadstool-like hat with five corners, the hat lifted up off his head on a framework several inches high. The acolyte wears a peaked cloth cap not very different from the head-covering of some Catholic nuns. They stop at every house and beat on a brass gong, singing all the while some sort of a monotonous sing-song prayer or petition. The small boy, being free to enter even the women's apartments of the houses, circulates around and stirs up the household, if they do not show a desire to come out. When a gift is forthcoming, a blessing is called down upon the house. If it does not come, there is apt to be a curse. Orientals are so much afraid of curses that they usually give a penny or two to get rid of the pair. The aggregate of the collections must be quite considerable. In the Fall, they are often given grain by the farmers, and carry it in bags on their backs as they go on their rounds.

## 11. Practice of Magic

The priests do not like to advertise the fact that they descend to magic, to fortune-telling, crystal-gazing and the like, but many of them unquestionably do. They have a book on crystal-gazing called the *Yoji Kyung,* and the *Milkyo Chip* directs them how to make the various charms. At many of the temples near Seoul one can buy charm papers a foot or so square for pasting on one's front door as protection against all sorts of evil spirits. These are all printed with a certain sort of red mineral ink called Choosa, a colour which gives them much power against the spirits. The charms not only protect against spirits and diseases from without, but they insure domestic tranquillity, obedience of one's daughter-in-law, the birth of many sons and increases in wealth. Similar red-printed charms are folded and carried in men's wallets, as talismans. Sometimes these charms are made of wood with the name of the Great Bear Constellation (Chilsung) carved on them. These are tied on children's belts as protection against evils. In some of the temples the paper charms printed from the wooden blocks are burned and the ashes dropped into water. Devotees are assured that if they will repeat the " Namu Ami Ta Pool " formula while they drink this ash water, that they will be transported to Paradise. Sometimes to exorcise evil spirits, the patients are taken before the Sinchoontang and prayers are offered there and the magic dharani formulæ are read.

All of these ceremonies and magical acts are probably not true Buddhism, but represent an edging over into the Shamanistic field. We shall see in studying the works of the Shamans how they use many Buddhistic images and concepts and formulæ in their frankly demonistic cult. Where the two cults touch, there is apt to be a tendency to overlap. Good Buddhists do not approve of these activities which we have just mentioned, but they do exist.

### 4. LITERATURE OF THE CULT

The literature of Buddhism is immense. As we have already noted, none of it was produced before Buddha's death. Orthodox Buddhism says that the Scriptures were put into writing immediately after Buddha's death at a Council in the Cave of Rajagriha. Many writers doubt whether any writings were collected previous to the time of Asoka, but there are some scholars who accept the orthodox story.

The Canon of the Hinyana, Southern Buddhism, is in the Pali language and is a closed Canon to which no new books have been added for ages. In bulk it comprises not more than twice the size of our Christian Bible.

The Canon of Mahayana, Northern Buddhism, is in Sanscrit or Chinese. It has not yet been closed and its books number thousands. Bunyio Nanjo, of Japan, has compiled a Catalogue of them with just the name and a brief word of description of each, and it makes a very large volume. There are blocks at the Haiinsa monastery for printing 6,791 volumes of 1,512 sets, and the total number of the pages about a foot square is 81,258. Every book that one picks up, whether produced a thousand years ago or ten years ago, has the heading " Pool Sul," " Buddha said," or the other common formula given by Ananda, " Thus have I heard " (" Yu si amoon, ilsi pool ichai "). Half of the books will have on them the name of Kumarajiva, the translator, who lived in China in the fourth century. It is absolutely impossible to even guess what books have some degree of authority and which are productions of writers of no standing. There are a few standard Classics, of course. Some books run to eighty or even a hundred volumes in a set, as, for example, the *Hwaeumkyung,* so often found in the temples. The Pongeunsa monastery, just outside of Seoul, has the blocks for printing this one set of books.

In 1898, Bunyio Nanjo discovered in a monastery near Seoul a Buddhist book written in Sanscrit on palm leaves like those books in China, six leaves in all.[n]

No Buddhist ever seriously tries to master any large portion of this vast library. Each takes one or more books or sets from the mass and bases his Gospel on that, disregarding the rest. The *Awakening of Faith,* by Asvagosha, mentioned in the previous lecture, and the *Lotus Flower Gospel* (Saddharma Pundarika), called *Hwaeumkyung* above, are found in most of the temples.

Some sects, like the Zen in China, try to get along without any books or with very few, confining themselves to meditation instead of to book study. Boddhidharma, the twenty-eighth and last of the active Patriarchs of the Order in China, when he arrived there in the sixth century, became so bewildered with the immense mass of literature that had grown up, much of it mutually contradictory, that he swept it all away and declared that Buddhism could not be learned from books, but must be gotten by introspection and prayer. For the last ten years of his life, he exemplified his own teaching by sitting continuously all that time facing a blank wall

---

[n] *Korean Repository,* 1898, p. 293.

" until his legs rotted off," and he " cut off his eyelids to prevent himself from going to sleep," when drowsy. He is known to the Koreans as the " Wall-Gazing Brahman." [72]

Printing from movable type was invented in Korea two hundred years before Europe invented it. [73] The Japanese are known to have adopted it from the Koreans in the twelfth century when a copy of the Buddhist Canon printed from wooden blocks was sent to them. There is a Korean book extant which dates authentically from 1317, at least one hundred years before Europe had printing. Most of the Buddhist books, even up till today, are printed from wooden plates upon which the letters are cut so as to stand out in half relief. The ink is smeared on by hand and then the paper laid over it and pressed down by hand.

Madame Gordon speaks of the " Five Classics." The most used sets seem to be the *Kishilon, i. e., Awakening of Faith,* and the *Lotus Flower Gospel* mentioned above, the *Puphwakyung, Amita Kyung, Keumkang Kyung,* or *Diamond Classic,* and the *Neungeum Kyung.* There is the *Chijang* book also that is quite popular. Which five of these make *the* Five Classics, I do not know, nor did my college president friend know. Possibly this is another case of the " helpfulness " of the interpreter.

Practically all of the Korean Buddhist literature is in the Chinese. Professor Starr reports that the *Suyooki* novel mentioned above had been translated into the Korean easy alphabet script, but my college president friend says that it is not so. Bishop Trollope also denies Starr's statements. [74] Here again is the difficulty in working through interpreters. The *P'al Sang* (*Biography of Buddha*) and a few small books to be used as propaganda are in the alphabet script, but that is all. Even their new magazine is largely in the Chinese or Mixed Script.

In 1456, King Seijo, grandson of the King Seijong who invented that alphabet script, had thirteen of the Buddhist Scriptures translated into the new writings and published, but of these

---

[72] Edkins, *Chinese Buddhism,* p. 102.
[73] Griffis, *The Hermit Nation,* p. 67; *Korean Repository,* 1897, p. 259. Also 1898, p. 57.
[74] *Bookman,* 1922, Sept., p. 1.

there are only six extant today, the *Wonkak Myung, Amita Kyung, Neungeum Kyung, Puphwa Kyung, Yunka Chip* and *Wurim Kyung.* Even these are seldom seen. They cannot be bought in any store in Seoul. In fact, there are few Buddhist books of any sort purchasable at any store. Any one wishing copies of the books must order them specially made. For a copy of the *Milkyo Chip,* the central temple officials in Seoul asked about $50 gold.

The Koreans do not reverence every wee bit of paper with writing on it as the Chinese used to do, but the devout ones believe that the possession of a Buddhist book brings merit, and the helping in the distribution of such books still more merit.

### 5. THE SECTS OF BUDDHISM

The various sects of Korean Buddhism all originally came from China, pilgrims going there as detailed above and bringing back the tenets and literature of the various organizations. There is no record, however, of there ever having been any organic connection as to government between the Order in the two countries, nor is there any connection whatever today. The Buddhist system left to itself is somewhat congregational anyway, each monastery and its monks largely managing their own affairs.

The Korean records say that Soonto, who first brought the Law to Korea in 372 A. D., brought the Hinyana (Soseung), and often in their books, or conversation, the priests will designate some doctrine as " Hinyana." [75] Apparently this is simply a matter of ignorance of what Hinyana is. Apparently they conceive of that word as the name for things heretical. Their doctrines are all of them really Mahayana.

Korean Buddhism strongly influenced Japanese Buddhism for seventy years during the sixth century A. D., but there has been no organic connection since. The lamas from Thibet have recently visited Korea on two occasions, about 1910 and 1917, and the system of manual gestures used in prayer, and the attitudes of the images in the temples are said to come from Thibet, but there is no other connection there.

---

[75] *Poolkyo Yaksa.*

Various Indians have visited Korea, or have lived there in ages past, as we have noted in the historical survey. In 1912, a famous Buddhist from Ceylon, Dharmapala, visited Seoul and presented the central temple with a bone from the Buddha's body enclosed in a golden casket. It is shown to the faithful with great ceremony on just one day during the year in the Spring. Korea has, however, no organic connection with India.

Originally, as we have noted, thirteen sects were brought from China.[70] Of some of these only the names remain. They are the " Chokei, Chongi, Pupsang, Tendai, Hwaeum, Tongmoon, Chaeum, Choongto, Sinin, Siheung, Imjei, and Chunto Soja sects." We have noted how one of the Yi Dynasty kings forced the thirteen to amalgamate into seven and later another king forced the seven to amalgamate into two, the Sun and the Kyo: the Contemplative and Practical. Nominally these two sects exist today. Practically there is but one sect, a combination of the two. My college president friend says that the practices of the modern sect are largely influenced by the Imjei Sect ideas, possibly because the influence of the great priest, Taiko, mentioned in the history, is so recent.

The highest kind of Buddhist practice in the country today is known as " Chamsun " (Indian Samadhi). It consists in going into a bare, empty room, and sitting down facing a blank wall, and trying to bring one's mind into a state of absolute quiescence. Certain formulæ called " Hwatoo " are sometimes used to assist in this, or to serve as points of departure, in the beginning of the Chamsun periods. Some of these are, " Buddha's substance is in all animate and inanimate creation except in the dog;" " If there were no ears, would there be no sound?" etc. My old language teacher abbot used the former of these Hwatoo in his great Search for enlightenment up till he found his enlightenment in Christ.

An acolyte is sometimes set down before a pinhole in a paper window through which he can see some large object outside, such as a cow or big rock. He is told to concentrate his mind on that

[70] Rhys David, *Buddhism,* p. 218.

object and that, once he gives it his full, steady attention, the object will suddenly come bouncing right in through that pinhole.

It is not the intention of these exercises that the person should think out solutions to them as problems. They are given simply as aids in getting a grip on one's own mind, to fix it intently upon something until by auto-intoxication or self-hypnotism the mind becomes absolutely quiescent and without desire. When one reaches that stage, so they say, the individual will at once become enlightened as to all knowledge and become a Buddha.

The men who practise Chamsun are the only true Buddhists, and are the " Sun " sect as far as there is any separate sect. The asceticism which they practise is the only voluntary form practised in Korea. They allow themselves but one suit of clothes, and, though they wash that one from time to time, they wear it until it literally falls into shreds, thus showing how oblivious they are to the things of this world.

There is no mutilating of the body as a religious exercise by any one. In the olden days, when everyone had a topknot, the priests alone went with shaven heads, but there were no queer tonsures. There is no such think as long fastings, as wearing of chains or thorns as penance. Monks are never walled up for life in stone cells as they sometimes are in Thibet. There are very few hermit monks. There was one a few years ago near Wonsan. His disciple took him supplies once a year. Other than that, he never saw or spoke to any one.

The Chamsun monks are honoured by everyone. Any temple that has one or two of them is sure to be well supported, for the people believe that in ministering to them they themselves share in the merits of the holy men. My college president friend said that, out of the 7,700 priests in the country, less than three hundred practise Chamsun.

In the olden days, priests were required to be always on pilgrimages, and were never allowed to remain more than three months in one temple. There is no such rule now. The priests move about a good deal, but only as their duties require, or the possibilities of subsistence in one place or another seem better. There never were laborious pilgrimages on hands and knees, or

" inching along " measuring one's length on the ground, or any of the similar exercises so common in India. The Koreans call that sort of thing " Kohaing wayto," but they do not practise it.[77]

## 6. Doctrines of Korean Buddhism

The Doctrines of Buddhism in Korea are the same as those of the Mahayana everywhere, those doctrines adopted back in Kaniska's time, which we have mentioned in the previous lecture. Here, as everywhere, we hear of the Four Noble Truths (Korean—Sachei), and the Eight-fold Path (Korean—P'al Chung Moon), and the twelve Nidanas (Korean—Sip Ee Inyun), the Six Paramitas (Korean—Yookto), and the Three Refuges (Korean—Sam Kwee). They talk of Karma (Korean—Haingpup) and the Five Skandas (Korean—Ochoong), of the great ocean of life and death (Korean—Saingsa Taihai) and of transmigration (Korean—Yoonhoi). It is doubtful if the Koreans have added anything of special value to the Buddhist thought of the world. They are not particularly given to philosophizing as the people of India are said to be. Of the Japanese, Chamberlain says, " The complicated metaphysics of Buddhism have awakened little interest in the Japanese nation. The Japanese have never been to the trouble to translate the Buddhist Canon into their own language. The priests use the Chinese version. The laity use no version at all nowadays, though they seem to have been more given to searching the Scriptures a few hundred years ago." [78] In spite of the great vogue which Buddhism had during the Koryu Period, I think that this is a fair characterization of Korea also, though no one can possibly tell how much of the existing literature was actually created by Koreans and how much has value. It is all marked " Pool Sul," " Budda said." We have noted the many books written by such men as Wunhyo. Possibly some day those books may be found and opened up to the world to see what their contribution actually is. Today it is the practical features of the cult certainly more than the philosophical that attract attention. In the college in Seoul, while it was running, the students studied West-

[77] Trollope in *Royal Asiatic Society Records*, 1917, p. 25.
[78] *Things Japanese*, p. 79.

ern philosophy, and, in talking with some of them, they insisted upon using the phrase " In nai Chun," " Man is God (or heaven)." We shall see that phrase appearing prominently under the Chuntokyo cult later. Evidently the teachers were inculcating a sort of pantheistic idea of philosophy. With the Korean language in its present chaotic state of change, it is impossible to judge what they meant by such phrases.

Buddhism, like all of the cults of India in Buddha's day and later—the Jains, the Sankya philosophers, the Krishna cults, and Rama cults and all of the rest—looked upon life as essentially an evil thing. All men, demons and even the gods themselves were bound to the Wheel of Life, ascending or descending in successive rebirths, according to an exact system of retribution, exactly according to the Karma merit accumulated in the various previous lives. Down through the hells or up through the multitudinous heavens, it was all one. They were all on the Wheel, and salvation consisted in anything that might give release from the Wheel into a state of peace.

The ordinary method of escape from the Wheel was asceticism, by crucifying the body. Buddha tried that method and rejected it. When his vision came under the Bodhi tree, he grasped the truth of the Four Noble Statements, and out of them came all of the other categories. How his various lists are related to one another, no one clearly knows, but the order suggested by Dr. Eustace Hayden, of the University of Chicago, seems as coherent as any, and we give that here,—

" Evidently the Eight-Fold Path was his starting-point in securing release from the Wheel."[79] This involved,—

"(1) Right views (Korean—Chung Kyun), *i. e.,* freedom from illusions and superstitions.

"(2) Right aspirations (Korean—Chung Sayoo), *i. e.,* desire to attain salvation. Desire to live in love with all men. Desire to serve all living things.

"(3) Right speech (Korean—Chungu) *i. e.,* that which is kind,

---

[79] Cf. Menzies, *History of Religion*, p. 371.

frank and truthful. No abuse, or angry word. No slander or gossip. No impure or bitter word.

"(4) Right conduct (Korean—Chung Up), *i. e.*, peaceful, honest and pure. This includes the Ten Commandments.

"(5) Right livelihood (Korean—Chung Sin), *i. e.*, one must earn a living without hurting any live thing.

"(6) Right effort (Korean—Chung Chung), *i. e.*, self-discipline, self-control.

"(7) Right mindfulness (Korean—Chung Yum), *i. e.*, be not weary in well doing.

"(8) Right rapture (Korean—Chung Myung), *i. e.*, meditation upon the transitoriness of life, the frailty of men, the sorrows of existence, and the certainty of the end to it all.

" The Four Noble Truths really constitute an elaboration of the first item of the Eight-Fold Path, *i. e.*, an explanation of 'Right Views.' The first of these Truths was that all life is suffering. (Korean—Kochei).

" The second Truth was that this suffering was due to desire (Korean—Chuichei).

" The third Truth was that the way to release was by getting rid of desire (Korean—Myulchei).

" The fourth Truth was that one could rid himself of desire by following the Eight-Fold Path (Korean—Tochei).

" The Twelve Nidanas are to some extent another statement of the same thing. They are like the spokes of a wheel. As long as they are all there, the wheel must continue to go around and around, eternally. Once extinguish desire, and the wheel disappears. These Nidanas might be translated as follows,—

" Ignorance produces synthesis.
Synthesis produces cognition.
Cognition produces name and form.
Name and form produce the sixfold sphere.
The sixfold sphere produces contact.
Contact produces feeling.
Feeling produces craving.
Craving produces grasping.

> Grasping produces renewed existence.
> Renewed existence produces birth.
> Birth produces old age, death, grief, lamentations, distress, melancholy and despair."

This all sounds like gibberish from Alice in Wonderland, but likely there is some idea behind it of desire as the root of all the world's ills.

Buddha, while alive, refused to discuss those metaphysical questions which were so dear to the Brahmans and Sankhya philosophers of his day.[80] "Is the world finite or not? Had it a beginning, and will it have an end? Is there a God? Is personality eternal?" None of these questions had any interest for him. He was entirely practical. He saw a world full of suffering. How could that situation be cured? Nothing else interested him.

Nirvana has been said by some writers to mean annihilation. Others indignantly repudiate that idea. Apparently, Buddha thought of it simply as a state of release from the Wheel, of peace after the long ages of racking on the Wheel. He was satisfied with that. He clearly denied the existence of a Personal God as we know Him. He had no teaching of a Paradise, as we think of it. Release from torture on the Wheel was the practical, immediate thing for him, and it filled his whole horizon.

We have seen above how more than half of the Buddhists of Asia refused for long to be satisfied with this barren idea of life, of the soul, of God and of the future life. As early as the time of Christ or perhaps earlier, Buddha himself was deified by the Mahayana. Amida, the Saviour Buddha, Kwanseieum, the male-female, father-mother Goddess of Mercy, Miryuck, the Messiah to come, and all of the other Posals came to be worshipped. We have a doctrine of salvation by the merits of another, Amida. We have eighteen chief Paradises and perhaps a million in all, and as many corresponding hells.[81] Gautauma was seeking a human salvation, so had no need of prayer. Today millions of Asia on occasion pray to him, or have prayed to him in times past, " Om mani

---

[80] Rhys David, *Buddhism,* p. 87.
[81] Eitel, *Chinese Buddhism,* p. 205.

pan mi hum," "O thou god that dwellest in the lotus flower, help!"

I have verified the fact that men like my college president friend know these various categories mentioned above. Most of the priests, however, are densely ignorant of them, and could not by any possibility be made to understand them. Again and again, as I have visited the temples, I have been exasperated by this ignorance. Often the priests have not known the correct names even of the images upon their own altars. The Koreans are not the only Buddhists who are thus ignorant. Giles writes, "There are no educated priests now in China." [82] Knox writes the same of Japan. [83] In all of these countries, there are no doubt some men who can talk intelligently of the deeper doctrines of the Law, Certainly there are not great numbers of them.

Buddha's sun seems to be setting in Korea. Korea owes it a debt of gratitude. It came to Korea in 372 A. D., and was vastly superior to the degraded spirit worship and Shamanism which it found. It gave Korea a moral code, more or less defective and yet infinitely better than nothing. [84] It has collaborated with Confucianism all down the ages, giving "sanctions" to make even Confucian ethics operative. It gave education of a sort and stood for education always. It has always had faults, glaring ones, but it also had a great contribution to make to Korean life and culture in those dim ages of the past. Its sun rose in 372. It reached its zenith in the Koryu Age. It has steadily gone down ever since. Buddhism seems to have no message for the present age. Efforts will be made to keep it alive. It will not die all at once, but "Ichabod" seems to have been written over it, and it must go.

As the sun of Buddhism sets, it should be a joy to all lovers of Korea that a greater Sun of Righteousness has arisen to give light suitable to this new day. May the Buddhists themselves soon come to see that a Messiah greater than Miryuck has come, a Saviour more real than Amida, a compassionate Friend Who loves more than Kwanseieum or Chijang, and Who has power far

---

[82] *Civilization of China*, p. 49.
[83] *Japanese Life in Town and Country*, p. 64.
[84] Martin, *Lore of Cathay*, p. 253.

beyond all that of Taiseiji! Christianity coming now can thank Buddhism for making all of these ideas familiar to the whole people, and for making it easy for them to receive them. May the whole land accept this new, true statement of those ideas as eagerly as it did the Buddhism in the Koryu Age, and may the whole people become one in serving Christ, our King!

## III

## CONFUCIANISM

CONFUCIANISM came to Korea in 1122 B. C. That seems a strange statement to make when we know that Confucius himself was not born until five hundred years after that, nevertheless the statement is true. Confucianism is far older than Confucius. He himself claimed to be only an editor and compiler in connection with all of his books except the one, *Spring and Autumn*. No doubt he was far more creative in his work than he, in his modesty, was willing to admit. He did edit largely the poems and history and the like of the previous ages, but he first took them into his own mind and rethought and corrected them, and then practically recoined them all. Even though he may not have made many changes in them, the very fact of his having sorted out, expurgated and rearranged the ancient writings to suit the conditions of his own times, rejecting the useless and irrelevant, makes him a great creator.

Korea, after 550 B. C., received his finished work, and all down the centuries Koreans have looked to him more than to any other as their living Master. " Japan has always been at heart Buddhist and never took to Confucianism thoroughly." [1] The Chinese themselves say that during the later centuries the Koreans followed the Master more completely than they themselves have.[2] True as this is for Confucianism after 550 B. C., it is true also of the Confucianism brought into Korea by its founder Keuija in 1122 B. C.

Viscount Keui, or Keuija, was a great man even while he lived in China. He was Prime Minister under the last Emperor of the Shang Dynasty there. When the usurper seized the throne and

---

[1] Gale, "History of Korea," in the *Korea Mission Field Magazine*, April, 1925; *Presentation of Christianity in Confucian Lands*, p. 23.
[2] *Royal Asiatic Society Records*, 1900, p. 1; Gale, "History of Korea," in *Korea Mission Field Magazine*, 1924, p. 202.

killed his King, he could have continued in his position, but the Chinese principles of propriety forbade. He had already made a name in Chinese literature for himself, having written a book called the *Hongpum* which is said to be the one incorporated by Confucius in his Classic, the *Shuking,* the Canon of History, one of the Five Great Classics of China.[8]

The old histories say that, when Keuija came to Korea, he brought with him the two books *Sijun* and *Sojun.*[4] These two words may possibly be interpreted to mean " poetry and history." The famous works which bear those names were not written until centuries later in China. No doubt the Korean historians, in this account, mean that Keuija brought over the aphorisms, proverbs, principles and other original data from which in later days those Classics were written. Among the five thousand followers who came with Keuija, were men qualified to teach those principles.

The records also say that Keuija " brought the science of manners, music, medicine, sorcery and incantation." With him also were men able to teach useful trades, silk culture and weaving being specifically mentioned. Keuija brought or invented a short but effective penal code which prescribed the death penalty for murder and fines for other offences such as theft or brawling. There were laws for the dividing of all farm lands equitably, laws regarding marriage and slavery, and requirements that both men and women should work industriously.[5] He is said to have given five other laws which are not specifically defined. Possibly they were the " Laws of the Five Relations "[6] which Confucius later made the basis of his whole system.

In any event, we know that away back in the dawn of history Korea received from China priceless information and truth which otherwise she might have had to evolve through the toil and suffering of centuries. The credit is mutual, China's for sending and Korea's for accepting in so docile a manner. There is no record of war or other violent opposition to Keuija's taking the headship

---

[8] *Presentation of Christianity in Confucian Lands,* p. 72.
[4] Hulbert, *History of Korea,* I, p. 4 f.
[5] *Ibid.,* I, p. 8 f.
[6] *Korean Repository,* 1895, p. 97.

of the country. All of the relics of that age point to a civilization very wonderful as compared with that of Manchuria or Japan at that time. The great wall, which Keuija built around his capital, Pyengyang, at that time, is still standing, five miles in length, though it has crumbled down and shows now only as a mound. The traces of streets, parallel to the river and right angled ones across them used to show in parts of the area enclosed by the wall. A well which he is said to have dug is still used, rivalling Jacob's in antiquity. A large grave outside the city to the north in a beautiful grove is said to be his, and ancestral worship is offered there. To make the nature of his people less turbulent, he is said to have planted the gentle willow trees along the river front, and in all Korean literature Pyengyang is known as the "Willow Capital."

On a tablet in front of that ancient grave, a stone which was erected in 1613 A. D., are these words, "God (Heaven) did not permit Keuija to be killed (by Moowang the usurper in China) because he reserved him to preach religion to us, and to bring the people to the ways of civilization." [7] The religion that he taught was Confucianism at least in embryo. It is not claimed that all Koreans were full-fledged Confucianists from 1122 B. C. The developed cult probably did not come in until the second century A. D., or later, possibly much later, as shown in the history below, but the beginnings were there.

I would like to take up this study under some seven heads, the history, buildings, ceremonies and beliefs, the examinations, the doctrines and present status of the cult.

## I. HISTORY

There is little of even reasonably acceptable legend for the Dynasty which Keuija established, and which held the throne until 196 B. C. There is a tradition that Keuija's son erected an ancestral tablet house; that in 773 B. C., for a time sorcery and incantation were forbidden; that, in 702 B. C., a sorceress who deceived the people was executed; that, in 670 B. C., the King ordered the con-

---

[7] Gale, "History of Korea," in *Korea Mission Field Magazine*, July, 1924, p. 138.

struction of a building of five hundred " kan " (a kan is seven feet square) as an asylum for widows and orphans and childless aged persons.[8] These stories are of doubtful value.

In 147 A. D., in the more dependable history of Silla, we have a note that the King put to death a number of scholars who had opposed his usurping the throne, and among them a noted scholar named Ko Pok Chang.[9] Evidently there were scholars in those days, and, as Buddhism did not appear until 372 A. D., those scholars must have been Confucian. The King before that, in 134 A. D., was a famous road builder, a form of activity which Confucius highly praised. In the record of the introduction of Buddhism in 372 A. D., there is a note that, at the same time Confucianism received a great impetus, a school for studying the Classics being founded that year, and a small Confucian temple being erected.[10]

In 417 A. D., ox-carts were introduced into Silla from China;[11] in 479, a horse relay system; and general markets all over the country; in 503, plowing with oxen was begun, and the barbarian custom of burying servants alive with dead masters was stopped. All of these things point to something more than a barbarian civilization. During all of these years from 196 B. C., the country was always more or less bound to China. The old capital, Nangnang, founded 50 B. C., has just been unearthed a little way down the river from Pyengyang.

It is interesting to note in the early history of both Korea and China that the first heroes were all Sages, inventors of things useful to men, such as letters, the plows, the practice of medicine, the boat or the wagon; or else reformers and administrators. The great generals and mighty warriors seem to be the product of a later age.[12]

In 503, the Kingdom of Silla adopted that Chinese form of its name to take the place of its native name which was similar, but pronounced " Suyabul." Confucianism was making progress, for

[8] Hulbert, *History of Korea*, I, p. 11 f.
[9] *Ibid.*, p. 54 f.
[10] *Royal Asiatic Society Records*, 1900, p. 4; *Korea Review*, 1901, p. 56; *Korean Repository*, 1892, p. 101.
[11] Hulbert, *History of Korea*, I, pp. 70, 75, 77.
[12] Gale in *Korean Repository*, 1895, p. 13.

we find that in that year the Confucian custom of wearing mourning for a parent for three years was introduced.  In 514 A. D., the Chinese custom of conferring posthumous titles upon kings was adopted by Silla, and ten years later by Paikchei.

In 543, the Silla King ordered the great scholar Kimgu Chilbu to compile the history of his country.[13]  This was two hundred years before the earliest history was written in Japan, and this history was not a collection of myths and legends, but a proper one made up from the Government Annals, which a certain amount of knowledge of the Chinese characters had enabled the officials to keep before that.  Japan probably received Confucianism from Korea at about this time, though it is not clearly known.  They did not do much with it until the tenth century.[14]

In 599, the first history of the northern kingdom, Kogoryu, was written in five volumes by order of the King by Yi Moon Jin, a doctor of the College of Literati.  The later history, *Sam Keuk Sageui*, states that Yi had available one hundred books of Annals called the *Yugeui* or *Book of Remembrance*.  In 664, Silla is said to have erected an ancestral tablet house for its kings.  In 700 A. D., Sulchong, the famous Confucian scholar, son of the great monk, Wunhyo, invented the Nitu system of simplified spelling for Chinese characters.  We have a record for that year that states, " Silla imported from China pictures of Confucius and paid increasing attention to that cult.[15]

In 896, Choi Chi Wun, a noted Korean scholar, who had gone to China, and passed the highest examinations there, returned and took office under the King of Silla.  In 953 A. D., the great scholar, Sam Geui, a Chinese, came to Korea and took office under the fourth king of Koryu.[16]  It was through his influence that the Confucian Examinations, patterned after those in China, were introduced, or possibly better organized.  There is one legend that they were actually introduced two hundred years before.[17]

[13] Hulbert, *History of Korea*, I, p. 81 f.
[14] Griffis, *Religions of Japan*, pp. 107, 108.
[15] Hulbert, *History of Korea*, I, p. 119.
[16] Gale, " History of Korea," in *Korea Mission Field Magazine*, Nov., 1925; Hulbert, *History of Korea*, I, pp. 146, 147.
[17] *Royal Asiatic Society Records*, Vol. XIII, 1922, p. 9.

This was the greatest step for Confucianism up to this time, 953 A. D.

There was a slight setback under the next King, who was intensely taken up with Buddhism, but, in 976, the examinations were renewed, and a great impetus given to the study of the Classics. The King in person examined the papers of the candidates of that year. In 983, the custom of having the King personally plow a furrow in the Spring time, symbolically sharing the toil of his people, was initiated. This custom was kept up till about twenty-five years ago. In 991, the first national " Sajik " shrine was set up in Songdo similar to the " Temple of Prayer " in Peking.[18]

Confucianism received a great impetus again about the year 1000, when an envoy brought from China a picture of the Sage and a picture of his shrine in China, also the history of the seventy-two disciples of the Sage whose tablets are kept in the Confucian temples in Peking. The record for that year states, " The students of the Confucian schools were encouraged with gifts of clothes and food, and several were sent to China to pursue their studies." Evidently there were Confucian secondary schools at that time. The Bureau of History was recognized in that year, and the annals put into better shape.

In 1084, Confucianism received a terrible blow in the abolition of the annual Examinations and the substitution of others based upon the Buddhist Classics. From time to time until the end of the dynasty, the war between these two religions was on, the kings quite generally siding with the Buddhists.

In 1145, the *Sam Kook Sa,* or *History of the Three Kingdom Age,* was written by Kim Pu Sik, one of the greatest scholars of Korea, a devout Confucianist.[19] He based the history upon previously written royal annals. Practically every history of Korea written since then has been based upon this one, so Kim Pu Sik is the father of authentic Korean history.

In 1351, another Korean, Yi Sak, passed with honour the great

[18] Gale, " History of Korea," in *Korea Mission Field Magazine,* Nov., 1925.
[19] Hulbert, *History of Korea,* I, p. 177.

Examinations in China and returned and memorialized the King upon certain matters.[20]

One of the first acts of the Yi Dynasty, when it secured the throne in 1392, was to order the casting of a great font of metal type of the Chinese characters for the purpose of printing the Classics. This was in 1400 A. D. Before this, there had been printing from wooden plates for two hundred years. At about this time, the Buddhist Examinations were abolished and the Confucian Classics reinstated in their place.

In 1420, the King recognized the foundation of the Confucian Temple which had been privately brought about thirteen years before, and he invited thirteen of the best scholars of his realm to pursue their studies there.[21] This institution was patterned after that in Peking. It was not a school in which students took courses and after a time graduated, but rather an Academy of Learning in the French sense, where the masters gathered and, as the spirit moved them, engaged in debates and discussions about the Classics, or searched them to increase their own mastery of them.

In 1441, the Confucian scholar, King Sejong, invented the Korean alphabet, which is one of the most perfect in all the world.[22] It has but twenty-six letters, and will write every sound of the English letters except " th " and " f." It has an additional sound, similar to the German unlaut " U." Many of the Confucian books were published in this script when it came out, and the Classics were brought to the masses. This is the script which has been used by the Christian missionaries since they entered the country, and has been one of the human elements that has made possible the rapid growth of the Christian Church. The characters are wonderfully easy to acquire. School children get them in a few days. The old Confucian scholars viewed them with scorn. " Why," they said, " the miserable characters are so easy that a woman can learn them in a month! " The people even up till today still cling to the Chinese characters and, since the entrance of the Japanese,

---

[20] *Ibid.*, p. 239.

[21] Gale, " History of Korea," in *Korea Mission Field Magazine,* 1926, p. 200.

[22] Hulbert, *History of Korea,* I, p. 307; *Royal Asiatic Society Records,* 1912, p. 13.

have trended still further that way, because of national pride sacrificing one of the most useful vehicles of popular education ever invented in any land.

In 1472, the King ordered that, whenever a scholar committed a crime, he was not to be tried by the ordinary courts, but the Confucian College, his peers, were to try him.[23] It is interesting to compare this action with that mentioned in the first lecture where the King gave even greater privileges in this line to the Buddhist priests.

In 1494, Korea came under a profligate king who expelled all of the scholars from the Confucian College, and filled the buildings with dancing girls and sorceresses. He soon died and the former conditions were restored.

In 1518, Cho Kwang Jo, called the "Confucius of Korea," became advisor to the king. Great quantities of Confucian literature were produced under his direction and distributing depots were provided by the King all through the country. The famous decennial examinations were also established at this time.[24]

In 1538, the history of the Dynasty was written up to date by Confucian scholars, and the next year the *Okpyun*, the Korean-Chinese dictionary, was compiled by them. This latter achievement also had a great deal to do with the extension of education among the masses.

In 1623, ancestral sacrifices were instituted by the Government at the ancient grave of Keuija near Pyengyang. In 1625, the King decreed that the children of concubines might aspire to passing the Examinations and to securing of official positions.[25] This was a revolutionary decision, as these men, many of them the brightest minds in the land and the best scholars, had before been denied this privilege. It very greatly increased the number of active exponents of Confucianism.

In 1659, while "offering sacrifices to Heaven," as the records state, the King caught cold and died. Evidently at that time the Confucian practice of offering sacrifices to Heaven either

[23] Hulbert, *History of Korea*, I, p. 319.
[24] *Ibid.*, I, p. 329.
[25] *Ibid.*, II, p. 80.

on the mountain, or at the national Sajik shrine, was well established.

In 1792, ancestral sacrifices began to be offered by the Government at the tombs of Tangoon (first founder of Korea 2332 B. C.), Suro (founder of the Kingdom of Karak, predecessor of Silla), and Taijo, the founder of the Yi Dynasty.[26] In that year, new type were cast, and great numbers of the Classics printed and circulated by the Government. In 1805, complaint was made that the officials did not attend to their duties because they were spending all of their time in the study of the Sacred Books. Confucianism must have reached its highest point of popularity at about that time. After that, corruption seems to have begun to creep in, insomuch that gifts properly placed were said to insure one passing the Examinations. This undermined confidence in them and destroyed enthusiasm for them.

The first treaty with an outside nation was made in 1876 and the " Hermit Nation " began to be opened to the world. It soon began to be evident that a knowledge of the Chinese Classics was not the best preparation for efficient service in official positions in this modern age. In 1895, the year called " Kapo Nyun " in the Chinese cycle, the great Examinations were abolished, and the glory of Confucianism began to pass away. Since then, it has steadily diminished as a formal cult, as we shall see a little further on in our discussion.

## II. BUILDINGS AND OTHER PHYSICAL EQUIPMENT

The buildings of the Confucian College or Temple inside the northeast gate of Seoul are almost without exception the finest real Korean buildings in all Korea, not even excepting the palaces of the King. They are larger and much finer than those of the Confucian Temple in the city of Peking.[27] The grounds around them are spacious. Ancient trees of great size are dotted through them. Most of the buildings are set on high foundations six feet or thereabouts above the ground, and the foundations are all of smooth white cut stone, most restful to the eye. The roofs are of

---

[26] Hulbert, *History of Korea*, II, p. 188.
[27] Gale in *Korea Magazine*, 1917, p. 300.

tile, some of them the ordinary black sort, and some of the blue porcelain-like kind which used to be used only on royal buildings. The hips and ridges of the roof curve as in Chinese buildings, and they are whitened with lime so that the effect is heightened. The wooden posts on which the buildings rest are two feet or more in diameter, and, for the main temple, they are fifteen feet or more high.

The Main Worship Hall of the institution is possibly thirty by eighty feet. In it there is nothing but a row of lacquered chairs, the seats a little higher than ordinary chairs. The centre one facing the entrance door has standing on it Confucius' tablet and is slightly larger than the others. The ten others hold the tablets of his first disciples. On ordinary days, these tablets are covered with lacquered boxes, but on worship days, the boxes are taken off, and food is spread before each tablet on small, table-like altars. The tablets are of wood and are perhaps eighteen inches high, five wide and one inch thick. The whole wall towards the south is composed of movable doors which can be taken out, throwing everything open.

At right angles with the front of this Main Hall, extending southward and forming with it a large court, are two Auxiliary Halls each about twelve feet wide and possibly one hundred and twenty feet long. In these Halls are the tablets of all of the rest of the Sages of this " National Temple of Fame," 116 Chinese and sixteen Koreans being honoured by having their names placed there.

The whole Confucian College grounds are roughly a square. This first court is in the southeast quarter.[28] The southwest quarter is filled with a great number of lower but strongly built, tile-roofed buildings, some for storing the paraphernalia of the cult, but most of them as apartments (Myungyoontang) for the three hundred " Chinsa " (Literati) who used to live there on the king's bounty, giving themselves to study, or to supervising the great Examinations, or to preparing for greater fields of usefulness.

---

[28] *Royal Asiatic Society Records,* Vol. II, Part I, p. 14.

The northeast quarter of the square is taken by another great court in which there is a lecture hall (Taisung Chun) where the "Yoorim," or Literati, periodically gathered to listen to expositions of the Classics, or to engage in debates about them.

The northwest quarter of the square is a great grassy enclosure containing one immense tiled roof building, one of the Examination Halls used up until 1895. The other Examination Hall is in the grounds of the West Palace at the other end of the city. All of the buildings of this institution are in good condition today, after more than three hundred years of service, except the Examination Hall, which has now only the posts and roof left standing.

As has been said above, this institution was not a school in the modern sense. It was rather a Standardization Bureau for the Classics. It is called "Sung Kyoon Kwan," or "Moon Myo," the Temple of Letters. Anyo,[29] one of the Sages whose tablet is in the Halls, was most responsible for its establishment. He lived in old Silla about 1000 A. D., and was a Councillor of State to one of the earlier Kings of the Koryu Dynasty. Being very much worried over the decadence of learning in his native land, he went to China and brought back seventy-two portraits of the Sages whose tablets are in the Peking Temple. He also brought the musical instruments and vessels used in China. Temporarily, with his own funds, he set up the College in the capital, and he presented to the temple one hundred of his own slaves as attendants. Many years later, the Government recognized the institution as a national affair and Anyo as its first President. He was not elevated to the rank of Sage until A. D. 1314, when his tablet was placed in one of the lateral halls.

The present site was chosen in 1398, shortly after the founding of the Yi Dynasty. In 1400, the first buildings burned down, possibly taking with them the seventy-two portraits, for there are none now in the Main Hall. The Halls were rebuilt in 1407, and, as we have noted above, the King took special cognizance of them in 1420. In 1592, when the Japanese ravaged the country from

[29] *Korean Repository*, 1895, p. 183.

south to north, they again burned the temple. It was rebuilt in 1601 and those buildings are standing today.

In China, the great tablet of Confucius stands in the central place in his temple and his four main disciples' tablets are placed two on each side of his. They are never represented by images. There are just the simple tablets. These disciples are called by the Koreans "Maing, Sa, Chang, and An." The Chinese names in China are "Mencius, Szu tsu, Ts'eng tsu and Yuen tsu." The same tablets have the same places in Korea. In China, other tablets are added to make a total of seventy-two arranged half on each side of the Master. Sometimes there are said to be five hundred tablets there.[30] In Korea, there are one hundred and thirty-two, not counting Confucius' own. Of these, as has been said, one hundred and sixteen are of the great Sages of China and only sixteen are the great men of Korea itself.[31] In the main hall there are ten Tablets besides that of Confucius, this being the same as in Peking. The rest are in the eastern and western galleries extending out in front.[32]

In the eastern gallery, there are seventy-six tablets, of which sixty-eight are Chinese and eight Korean. Of the Chinese, fifty tablets are for men of the ancient Chow Dynasty, six for scholars of the Han, one from Tang and eleven from Song.

The Koreans in this gallery are (1) Sulchong of Silla, son of the monk, Wunhyo, and inventor of the Nitu system of simplified writing for Chinese characters, and counted as the father of Confucianism in Korea, (2) Anyo, of the Koryu Age, founder of the College, (3) Kim Kwang Pil, who was banished for too plain speaking to the King, and then executed in banishment, but, after his death, raised to the rank of Premier, (4) Cho Kwang Jo, called the "Confucius of Korea" because of his learning and piety (he also was banished once, but recalled and made Premier), (5) Yi Kwang, (6) Yi I, (7) Kim Chang Saing, a man of Kwangju, and (8) Song Choon II. The last six of these men were canonized during the Yi Dynasty Period.

---

[30] Underwood, *Religions of Eastern Asia*, p. 161.
[31] *Korean Repository*, 1898, p. 143.
[32] *Royal Asiatic Society Records*, 1900, p. 13.

In the western gallery, there are fifty-five tablets, forty-seven to Chinese and eight to Koreans. The Chinese tablets are for thirty-four men of the Chow Dynasty, six from the Han, one from Chin, five from Song and one from the Mongol Period.

The Koreans of this gallery are (1) Choi Chi Won,[33] the scholar who went to China about the year 1000 A. D., and passed with honour the highest Examinations there, and then won fame as a military and literary man there before returning to his home in Silla, (2) Chung Mong Ju, a man from the southeast who was Premier in the Koryu time. He was murdered by some of his political opponents on a stone bridge at Songdo, and the Koreans point out a red stain in the stones today as being the mark of his blood. (3) Chung Yu Chang was a schoolmate of Kim Kwang Pil and was Minister of the Right, i. e., Vice-Premier, at one time, (4) Song Si Yul, (5) Kim In Hoo, (6) Sung Hon, (7) Paik In Gul and (8) Yi Yun Jo. The last six of these also were canonized during the Yi Period. For many generations past no new names have been added to this Hall of Fame.

So much, then, for the central temple in Seoul.

When the Yi Dynasty came into power in 1392, it established a small Confucian Temple in every one of the three hundred and sixty or so county seats of the country.[34] Each of these temples (called "Haing Kyo") was patterned after the central temple. In each there were tablets at least for Confucius and his four main disciples. Usually there were more, though none had as many as for the central College. Over the road leading up to each of these temples the "Red Gate" with its harplike ornament in the middle of the lintel was placed to show that it was under royal patronage and a part of the established state cult. Each temple had endowment lands near it given by the Government. Always on some hill near by was one of the "high altars" where on occasion offerings were made to Heaven and to Earth. The first official act of any magistrate in the olden days, when he assumed his post, was to go to the Haingkyo and bow and worship the tablets, and then go to a similar shrine near by, called the

---

[33] *Ibid.*, 1903, Vol. III, p. 1.
[34] *Korean Repository*, 1892, p. 169.

" Kaiksa," where the ancestors of the ruling royal family were commemorated.

Yet again, in addition to the county seat Haingkyo, there were great numbers of more local temples called " Suwons," possibly as many as one hundred in all the land, erected by villages or communities in honour of local Confucian scholars whom the villages, after their death, felt worthy of a wider ancestor worship than that of their immediate families.[35] In connection with these temples and the county seat temples, there were usually quiet rooms where the Literati could gather and study or debate, just as they did in the main Lecture Hall in Seoul. In the county seat temples, the genealogical records of all of the gentry of the county were preserved, and they kept the strictest censorship lest any commoner should try to " crash the gate " and set himself up for gentry. As a matter of fact, however, it was always an aristocracy of learning, and any son of a commoner who could win in the Examinations could establish himself and his family as gentry in a few decades.

The only remaining physical properties of the cult are the altars which we will speak of in connection with the sacrifices.

### III.  The Great Examinations

No discussion of Confucianism is intelligible without some knowledge at least of the Examinations which validated it from an economic standpoint, and provided the cult with whatever in the way of priesthood it might be said to have. We have noted already how the moment that the Examinations were abolished, the cult began to die as though the cord of life had been cut there.

The Examinations, as we have said, were brought from China by Sam Geui in 953 A. D. Hulbert believes that he found traces of them earlier even, in 789 A. D.[36]  In any event, they were the centre of the life of the nation from 953 until that sorrowful year " Kaponyun," 1895.

The full story of the Examinations has been written by Hulbert

[35] Gale, " History of Korea," in *Korea Mission Field Magazine*, 1926, p. 221.
[36] *Royal Asiatic Society Records*, Vol. XIII, p. 11.

in the thirteenth volume of the *Royal Asiatic Society Records*. I will just mention some of the points briefly, which I have discovered through personal research.

The study of the Classics began, of course, back in the little villages where in tens of thousands of little schools, one aged Literatus for teacher and five to twenty pupils sat on the floor rocking back and forth, singing the characters at the top of their voices from six A. M. till sundown; where each pupil got his quite literal baptism of indelible ink as he learned to manipulate the inkstone and handle the horsehair brush.

From these schools came swarms of young men or older men to the great provincial examinations held on the twentieth day of the eighth lunar month in every year that had an " intercalary " month, *i. e.*, every third year. This was called the " Kamsi " or " Chosi " examination. One thousand men [37] were selected in this examination from the whole nation, a certain percentage from each of the thirteen provinces and about five hundred from Seoul. Any man who desired might take the examination in Seoul, but most went to their own provincial head cities.

The year after this first examination, on the same day, the thousand men assembled in Seoul, and took their second examination called the " Hoisi." The best two hundred men in this examination were promoted here and given the name of " Chinsa." Of the total body of Chinsa in existence at any one time, three hundred lived always at the Confucian Temple, and were supported by Government funds. Since there were always many times three hundred of these men, the particular assignment to be in the temple quarters was much coveted. Of course, the ranks of the three hundred were being continually decimated as men were promoted to public office. The choosing of these doubly lucky men was in the hands of the Paikkwan, or one hundred highest officers of state, who nominated officials. The formal appointment, after the nomination, was by the King.

The highest examination of all was called the Taikwa, and was offered perhaps ten times a year, every time that there was a royal

---

[37] *Korea Magazine*, 1918, p. 64.

birthday to be celebrated, or other happy occasion. Candidates could take the examination whenever it was offered, even though they had already failed a dozen times. Those who passed this examination were given the rank of " Choosa," and were eligible to office in any of the nine upper grades of the public service as fast as they demonstrated their practical ability.

Besides these literary examinations, there were parallel ones all along the line for military honours, the first examination leading to the degree of " Sundal " instead of Chinsa. These were called Mookwa examinations, while the literary were Moonkwa. The Mookwa degrees were not so prized as the Moonkwa, but they also led directly to public office. As all magistrates were changed every three years or oftener, the chances of promotion were always good. Some counties would not accept as a magistrate a man born of a concubine.

There were nine types of matter upon which the examinations were given, including poetry, narrative, letter writing, and other compositions of various sorts.

In China, the contestants were locked in tiny brick cells, each man by himself, but, in Korea, they wrote out in the open, grassy courtyard. The greatest precautions were taken to prevent cheating. The compositions when completed were copied by official scribes so that the examiners might not recognize the handwriting and display favouritism. Noms de plume were affixed and the papers were thrown over a high wall to the examiners so that they could not see the throwers and make any guess of those interested in the papers.

These provisions were very fine in theory and might have guaranteed exact impartiality, but humanity is frail and it must be confessed that, especially in the latter days, a round sum of money properly placed would help cover many mistakes on a paper and win the coveted parchment. One of the ignorant coolies in our village in Seoul when we landed was a Sundal, although he could hardly write his own name in Chinese. He paid nearly twenty-five good American dollars' value for the honour. Because of this corruption, all down the ages there were scholars who refused to take any of the examinations. Upon occasion, these men were summoned by the King and assigned to public office just upon the general knowledge of their superlative qualifications.[88]

### IV. Sacrifices and Religious Beliefs

As noted above, Confucianism had many economic accompaniments. Skill in the cult practically guaranteed a good livelihood as well as various worldly honours such as men covet. It was, however, far more than a mere employment agency device. The things that made it live and gave it its amazing vitality all down the centuries were the moral and religious phases of the matter. Nearly everything ever written by the scholars, from the first primer in the village school to the theses in the Taikwa examinations, was composed of more or less stereotyped moral maxims or their explication. These were not mere copybook maxims either. They established universally known standards of behaviour by which the actions of all men, but especially of all educated men, were judged. The rules of " Yay," decorum or propriety, were fixed. Certain things were not done in polite society. The rules may have been superficial in some ways, but they were wonderfully effective.

The " sanctions " behind these rules came from the religious beliefs of the people which headed up in the various sacrifices to Heaven, to Earth, to ancestors, etc. The greatest of all of these sacrifices were those performed in the Confucian Temple in Seoul, or those at the national " Sajik " shrine.

### 1. *The Confucian Temple Sacrifices* [89]

The great ceremonies in the Sungkyoonkwan came twice a year in the second and eighth lunar months. At that time, all of the Literati of the land, who could possibly be present, came to the temple. There are no separate priests in Confucianism. Every scholar who has passed the examinations has learned the rules of ceremony, and is more or less competent to lead the services. At the great temple, however, either the King in person, or the President of the college acted as chief priest so far as there was one.

---

[88] *Korea Magazine,* 1917, p. 262.
[89] Gale in *Korea Magazine,* 1917, p. 302.

Everyone present wore the old court dress which Korea adopted when the revered Mings of China ruled Korea, the reddish robe, and belt with eyes before and behind, the thick-soled Chinese cloth shoes, and the round-topped cap with "ears" coming out from behind almost like the wings of an aeroplane.

Out in the great courtyard before the Main Hall, on the right and left were set up the framework for holding the foot long bells, about ten on each frame. These bells were of slightly different sizes and made a sort of harmony when they were struck to indicate the various items of the ceremony as it progressed. The great wide doors of the central hall were thrown open. The covers on the tablets were removed, and before each tablet in curious-shaped brazen vessels were placed raw beef and pork, uncooked rice, fruits, wine and flowers. Everything is uncooked in this sacrifice, as that is held to be more honouring than cooked things.[40] There was no provision for burning the offerings in the central temple, or for burning great bales of silk, etc., as was done in Peking.

When all was set, the President alone, representing the nation and particularly the King,[41] went into the hall, prostrated himself before the tablets one after another, and offered praise. Most of his words were, of course, addressed to Confucius' tablet. Usually the prayers used were taken from certain standard printed books of prayers, but some freedom was allowed for new petitions. In general, the prayers were like this one, which is said to have been used in China.[42]

"Great art Thou, O perfect Sage! Thy virtue is full, Thy Doctrine complete. Among mortal men, there has not been Thine equal. All Kings honour Thee. Thy statutes and laws have come gloriously down. Thou art the pattern in this Imperial School. Reverentially have the sacrificial vessels been set out. Full of awe, we sound the drums and bells. I, the Emperor, offer a sacrifice to the Philosopher Confucius, the Ancient Teacher, the Perfect Sage, and say: 'O Teacher in virtue equal to Heaven and Earth, whose doctrines embrace the past and the present, in reverent

---

[40] *Korea Magazine*, 1917, p. 547.
[41] Jones, *Korea, the Land and the People*, p. 56.
[42] Underwood, *Religions of Eastern Asia*, p. 160.

observance of the old statutes, with victims, silks, liquor and fruits, I carefully offer sacrifices to Thee. Mayst Thou enjoy the sacrifices! ' "

### 2. Ceremonies at the National Sajik Shrine [43]

Fully on an equality with this ceremony and possibly surpassing it was the worship at the Sajik Shrine, inside the northwest gate of Seoul. Here there were ceremonies somewhat like those in Peking where worship was offered to Father Heaven and Mother Earth, looked upon as being the progenitors of all mankind. At this shrine, there were no buildings that had a part in the ceremonies. There were just twin altars in the open air in a lovely wooded park. Each altar was about twenty feet square, faced all around with smooth cut stone, but filled in with earth on top. [44] Here each year at the same time as the Confucian sacrifices, the King personally went, put on the ceremonial priest dress with its breastplate not unlike that of the priests in Israel, and, as the sacrifices were burned upon the altar, offered prayers on behalf of the nation.

The sacrifices offered were cattle, sheep (brought from China, since there are no sheep in Korea), [45] pigs and chickens. Only the best of each sort could be offered, animals without blemish, and they each had to be of a single colour, not striped or speckled. The killing was always done in advance by the low caste butchers. It is said that at times while the sacrifice to Heaven was burned, that to Earth was simply buried in the soft earth of the top of the altar. [46] Three times in history white horses are spoken of as offerings in connection with worship like this. [47] In 1630, the Manchu ambassadors demanded that the Korean King with his own hand sacrifice a white horse to Heaven and a black cow to Earth to make binding the peace treaty which he had concluded with them. The Koreans say that this sacrifice came from the Chow Dynasty in

[43] Korean Repository, 1895, p. 184.
[44] Royal Asiatic Society Records, 1902, p. 14.
[45] Ross, Corea: Its History, Customs and Manners, p. 71; Mrs. Bishop, Korea and Her Neighbours, pp. 78, 188.
[46] Underwood, Religions of Eastern Asia, p. 116.
[47] Hulbert, History of Korea, I, pp. 102, 110.

China, so it is called " Choorei." Heaven was particularly worshipped in the Spring time and Earth only in the Fall.

### 3. Ceremonies at the " Temple of Heaven "

Until 1895, when Korea became wholly independent from China, the Sajik Shrine was the only place where Heaven and Earth were fully worshipped. When the King became an Emperor, he erected on the grounds of the South Detached Palace a nine-storied pagoda and white stone pavilion just like those in the " Temple of Heaven " in the city of Peking, and, for a few years, he worshipped there twice a year, and prayed to Heaven and Earth as in the Sajik Shrine, offering the same sacrifices. That was a very late development, however, and did not last long.

### 4. Special Altars

In the northern part of the city of Seoul was the Taibotan altar where prayers were made for the lamented Ming Dynasty of China which had been so kind to Korea during its period of dominance there.[48] In times of drought, or of national calamity of other sorts, special worship was felt to be desirable, and there were four special altars for that, north, east, south and west of the city where " Kiochei," or Rain Ceremony Prayers, were offered and sacrifices made. Outside the east gate was the field where once a year the King went in the Spring, and plowed a furrow with his own hand to thereby share symbolically in the toils of his people. At that place, sacrifices were offered to Sillongsi,[49] the " Spirit Farmer," the mythical individual who in far-off China five thousand years ago was supposed to have originated the art of farming. In each of these places, the worship was similar to that in the Sajik Shrine, and was conducted either by the King in person, or by some one from the Confucian College sent by him.

Near the palace in Seoul was a great building called " Pongsansi " where the sun, moon, stars, and the spirits of the winds, mountains, rivers, etc., were honoured. Far up in the north is the

[48] *Royal Asiatic Society Records,* 1900, p. 12.
[49] *Korea Magasine,* 1917, p. 52.

Great White Mountain, Paiktoosan.  Once a year, envoys were
sent to offer there worship to the spirit of the whole land.  In
every Confucian temple compound was a small shrine to the
" Pookeuntang," the presiding spirit of the site upon which the
temple was built and of the district.  Even the most devout Confucian scholars felt that it was not out of order, in fact, that it
was quite appropriate to honour this spirit since they were his
guests upon the site, and he the lord of the soil.

### 5. Temporary Sacrifices

We have mentioned the Kiochei, Rain Ceremonies, on the four
altars, in time of drought, or of other national calamity.  In addition to these, if the distress was acute, the King would order
Nochei, or Road Ceremonies, where sections of the main roads
were fenced off for a few hours in the city or country, temporary
altars erected, and prayers made, like those of the Kiochei.  Sometimes there were similar ceremonies in the open plains near villages, sometimes even on the hills nearby, where Heaven was
worshipped.  These were called " Chunchei."  In China, only the
Emperor was authorized to offer prayers to Heaven.  The common people offered theirs to their ancestors.[50]  In Korea, throughout its history, this worship has been offered in every county seat,
either by the magistrate, or by his representative.

### 6. Sacrifices in the Country Districts

Alongside of every Confucian temple in the county seats, on the
nearest hilltop, was a " high altar," much like those at the Sajik
Shrine in Seoul, and blood offerings were presented at least twice
a year by the literati, the flesh of pigs or fowls being offered in
brazen dishes, uncooked, and rice and flowers being placed beside
them.  These offerings were not burned.  In the Chunchei Ceremonies mentioned a moment ago, even Village Elders were allowed
to preside and offer the same sacrifices and supplications.  For
those less skilled, there were special Books of Forms to be used,
but usually also one or more free prayers were allowed for special

---

[50] Martin, Lore of Cathay, p. 78; Presentation of Christianity in Confucian
Lands, p. 67.

things desired.  Possibly this village worship was Shamanistic.
See the discussion of that below.

All over Korea, there were shrines to the mythical Dragons, and
Confucianism comprehended that in its cult.  That verges so
closely upon Shamanism, however, that I have left it for that
lecture.  They believed intensely in the laws of " Poongsoo "
(Chinese Fungsui), the Science of Wind and Water, but that too
I have passed on to the later discussion.  They believed in the
mythical Kirins, or unicorns, which appeared to indicate the birth
of great men.  The phoenix also was thought to be endowed with
great powers and the turtles from the cracks in their shells could
tell the future.  These last three beliefs were not matters of worship, however, but rather superstitions, more or less innocuous.

### 7. Ancestral Worship

This is so well known in China that it need not delay us long,
as it follows exactly the same rules in Korea as elsewhere.  As a
matter of fact, however, it is the most vital thing in the whole cult
of Confucianism.  The scholars and the people shared more or less
actively in all of the worship described in the previous sections,
and gave it more or less of their interest, but none of it gripped
them as did the ancestral worship of their own households and
hereditary clan headquarters.  Every boy must marry as early as
humanly possible in order that he and his fathers might surely
have a son to worship and care for their sacred tablets.  The house
or clan that had and worshipped five generations of tablets scarcely
needed any other patent of nobility.  There never were any " god-
shelves " of Buddhism such as they have in nearly every house in
the rest of the Japanese Empire, but no house of any social standing in Korea lacked its small tablet house back in the yard, or its
tablet cabinet on its porch, or in some of the apartments.

The first thing after the death of a man's father or his mother,
a small paper three inches by eight folded in a certain way and
bearing the name of the deceased was taken and pasted on the wall
to temporarily receive one of the three spirits of the departed.
Then messengers were sent out far into the forest to find a chest-
nut tree in some place " where the sound of the crowing of a cock

has never been heard." The whole tree was cut down and from it a piece perhaps two and one-half inches by eight for the tablet and another one half as large for the base was taken. The tablet was sawed down its length to make two flat pieces the full width of the piece. Where the two pieces of the wood overlaid with their flat sides together between them a recess was made half an inch deep and wide and four inches long, and in that recess, the name of the deceased was written. A hole the full size of the end of the tablet was cut in the base piece. When the two flat pieces of the tablet were held together and all set in the base, the tablet was clamped together perpendicularly as one piece. The name was again written on the outside of the tablet, which was sometimes painted for that purpose white on its front face, and sometimes lacquered. A tiny hole, the size of a knitting needle, was then bored through the whole tablet from right to left, through the inner recess. This was to make an opening by which the spirit might come out and " eat of the essence of the food " during the times of sacrifice.

Koreans believe that everyone has three souls. At the funeral time, one soul stays in the dead body and goes into the grave; one goes into the prepared tablet, and the last one goes off to the realm of the shades or to " Yumna, the King " in " Chu Seung," " that place," as taught by the Buddhists. The funeral ceremonies include a lot of exorcising of spirits and the like which are more a proper part of the Shamanistic worship and will be treated there. They show how intertwined the various religions of the country have become. It is difficult, as we have already seen in connection with Buddhism, to tell at times where one religion leaves off and another begins. Confucianism in China, according to DeGroot, busies itself to a large extent with the Kwei and the Shen, the evil spirits and the good, but it might be debated as to whether they have any proper place in a discussion of Confucianism, or whether they are not extraneous matter from the degraded and all-pervading Taoism there which have adhered to the higher cult.

At the grave, and in the home, the spirits are formally exorcised. The grave itself is sought and found according to the rules of Poongsoo (Fungsui), and its exact location, facing and depth decided with meticulous exactness. After the burial, the soul that is to go into the tablet is lighted back with torches to the home, lest it lose its way, and the sacrifices begin before it and are continued until it becomes the sixth oldest tablet extant, *i. e.*, after some hundred and fifty years, when it is taken out and buried before its appropriate grave, since only five tablets are kept at a time, in one household. The great worship days are the first and third anniversaries of the death, when all of the clan members gather and there is much weeping and wailing. Devout families worship regularly twice a month, and some even every day for the first three years. After that, the Korean New Year's time and the anniversary days are celebrated with offerings in the home, and the fifteenth day of the eighth lunar month with offerings made on the stone tables before the graves. In all of these cases, cooked rice and other foods, including wine, are spread out as for a feast, and then the worshipper prostrates himself and mourns the departure of the deceased, and offers petitions for favours. Formerly only uncooked rice was used, but now it is cooked. After the ceremony it is eaten by the family.

Near Chairyong a few years ago, one devout son worshipped daily at his father's grave for ten years. He always stepped in the same places as he approached it, and placed his feet, knees and head in the same places so that holes were dug there and visitors from a distance came to see and admire his filial piety. In the olden days, there used to be hundreds of stories [51] like that, of sons who cut off their fingers and made soup from them to feed their aged parents; of others who always laid down for a time in the evening in their parents' beds in order that any possible existing vermin might first bite them and get so satiated that later they would not bite the parents; of sons who erected booths beside their parents' graves and never left them during the first three years of their mourning, etc. Behaviour of this sort was so praised that it helped to tighten the hold which ancestral worship in general had upon the people.

The worship of Heaven and Earth, and this ancestral worship

---

[51] *Oryoon Haingsil,* book entire.

are the only two elements in Confucianism worthy of being called "religious" in the ordinary sense of the term. Confucius does not seem to have had any enthusiasm for the latter. He did not begin to offer worship to his own father until half through his career. Without question, one of the greatest things that has kept the ancestral worship alive has been its connection with the system of caste. The Hoi Polloi kept no ancestral tablets. Having them was a sign of belonging to the gentry of the land. Whatever may have been the cause of the cult in the beginning, however, it is the one thing today that is vital in Confucianism. Just a few years ago a cultured young Korean back from an American college[52] wrote a passionate appeal to the missionaries and other Christian workers of the land urging that the worshipping of the tablets be permitted to Christians in order that opposition to the Gospel on the part of many of the cleanest people in the land might be overcome and the people won to Christ.

The whole question as to whether this bowing to the tablets is worship or not has been debated again and again. Even as old a missionary as Dr. W. A. P. Martin, of China, believed[53] that it was not opposed to the worship of God. Many Christians in Japan bow regularly before the tablets, explaining that while bowing they pray to God, and not to the spirit in the tablet! At the dedication of the great Shinto Shrine in Seoul in 1928, for days before, the newspapers were full of laboured arguments to prove that such bowing was in no way different from the ordinary giving of honour to a living parent or ruler, and that Christians could take part in the exercises without compromising their religion. It was interesting to notice how those same newspapers, after having in the editorial columns proved to their own satisfaction that the bowing was not worship, in the other columns would announce gravely that the "worship" would take place at certain designated times and places, showing that subconsciously they always accepted it as real worship themselves. If it were not real worship, I doubt if it would have had the vitality that it has had as a religion.

----

[52] Y. T. Pyun, *My Attitude Towards Ancestral Worship.*
[53] *Lore of Cathay,* p. 275.

In Korea, the best Christians have been practically unanimous in considering the bowing as real worship and they have endured multitudinous persecutions and hardships rather than take any part in it, or continue holding their tablets after their conversion. It is still one of their greatest difficulties.[54]

## V. LITERATURE OF CONFUCIANISM

As in China, the Bibles of Confucianism are the five *Kyung* or canonical books and the four *Su* or books of lesser distinction. Education used to consist in mastering these books verbatim to the last jot and tittle. If a student could memorize them all, his chances in the examinations were very good. These books are already available for Western scholars in Legge's translations in China. They are the fundamental basis of Confucianism everywhere.

Next after the Classics themselves come the great Commentaries. The Korean scholars, like most of those of China and Japan, have almost universally adopted the interpretations of Chuja (called Chusius or Chuhi in China). Every scholar has these and they used to study them exhaustively.

Based upon these books, and partaking of their ethical spirit and religious viewpoint, there are thousands of other books in Korea. Unfortunately, most of them were not published for general distribution, but were sent out in semi-private editions to friends, and they are very difficult to secure. Few of them have up till now been translated. Dr. Gale, in his *History of Korea*,[55] translates some of the finest gems from them, just short passages which nevertheless breathe the spirit of humble devout faith in an overruling Providence, *e. g.*, Kim Chang Up (1685 A. D.) writes, " Chun is not the blue sky, but God Who resides in the heart and is to be feared." In his translations, Dr. Gale usually uses the word " God " for " Chun," the word usually translated " Heaven." It is doubtful if that is fully justified, though this quotation seems to favour it. " Chun " never has for a Confucianist the full content of meaning which the word " God " carries in English. How-

---

[54] Underwood, *Religions of Eastern Asia*, p. 163.
[55] Also *Korea Magazine*, 1917, pp. 204, 347, 549, and 1919, p. 159.

ever, there is no doubt that the word also means to them a lot more than simply the blue sky, or an absolutely material Heaven above. They are not very clear in what they mean by " Chun," but they certainly visualize somewhat of personality there.

There are, as has been noted, many Books of Forms and Prayers formed more or less upon Chinese models, which are considered as a direct part of the literature of Confucianism. All of these books are in some way a part of the cult, but the nine Classical books and Chuja's commentaries are probably the only ones that speak with real authority concerning it.

## VI. THE DOCTRINES OF THE CULT

The doctrines of Confucianism in Korea are all practically the same as those in China as interpreted by Chuja in the twelfth century A. D. For the broad outlines of the cult, Chuja made no changes. The Nine Books are concerned mainly with the " Oryoon " or Five Relations among men; that of kings to subjects, parents to children, brothers to brothers, husbands to wives, and friends to friends.[56] Confucius' great general principle for governing those relations was that of each doing his own duty in his own place. His greatest word is duty. When asked as to how one should requite an enemy, he is said to have replied, " Requite an enemy with justice." That is his general attitude towards all of the relations; justice, not love. Mooti, who lived shortly after Confucius, advocated love as the best principle of life. Mencius, following the Master, opposed that teaching as " soft pedagogy."

As for the philosophical doctrines behind Confucianism, in adopting Chuja's interpretations, Korea took up with something quite different apparently from what Confucius himself taught. Confucius himself was not over-enthusiastic about the gods or anything supernatural. He told his disciples to have as little to do with such things as possible. However, he does not seem to have been actively opposed to them.

Chuja is a straight out materialist. Griffis writes of his in-

---

[56] Underwood, *Religions of Eastern Asia*, p. 3; *Korean Repository*, 1895, p. 98.

fluence in Japan, " Chuhi's Confucianism in Japan was a full-
blown system of pantheistic rationalism." [57]   Legge has argued
vigorously for a primitive monotheism in China back in the dim
ages before the " days of Kings Yo and Sun " (as the Koreans
say in speaking of that age), and there is a good deal of evidence
for it.  The worship of God by Tangoon on the high altar on the
island of Kanghwa, of which we speak in a later lecture, points to
much the same thing in Korea.  If there was such a hazy idea
abroad in the land, Chuja scattered it.  " It is Chuhi's interpretation of the Classics which more than any other influence has
given Confucianism the reputation of being wholly materialistic
or practically atheistic." [58]

Giles has pointed out [59] that in the age of Confucius there were
a number of philosophers who had theories of the original nature
of man; Kao stating that at birth man was neither good or bad by
nature; Hsun Tzu saying that at birth man is positively evil;
Yang Hsiung that he is neither wholly good or wholly evil, but a
mixture of both, the development in either direction depending
wholly on environment, and Confucius insisting that at birth man
is wholly good.  Chuja pushed Confucius' thought on this matter
to the limit.  He taught that there was no personal God, no original sin and very little sin of any sort, except as there might be
breaches of the laws of decorum and propriety.  Of course, he
therefore had no doctrine of atonement, and no need of sacrifices
as expiation or anything after the manner of atonement.  Of the
future life, he wrote, " Hon Pi Paik San," " Spirit escapes, soul
scatters," and that is a most common proverb in Korea, seeming
to imply annihilation at death.  He did teach "Ai In Yuk Ee,"
" Think of others before oneself," and many other admirable
things in morals, but he identified man with the universe and made
the cosmic spirit in the universe the only real god, so that his
influence was strongly against anything that looked to a supernatural religion.

Fortunately, in Korea, Buddhism and the all-pervading Spirit-

---

[57] *Religions of Japan,* p. 136.
[58] *Presentation of Christianity in Confucian Lands,* p. 66.
[59] Giles, *Civilization of China,* p. 134 f.

ism that headed up in Shamanism was always present and kept even the Confucian scholars subconsciously conscious of a world beyond that of the senses. " Chun Lee Ku Yuk," " Opposing Heaven is sin," was one of their phrases that show a consciousness of something more than an impersonal, material world, especially, if we translate " Chun " as " God." Their definition of " sin " was fairly liberal to themselves, but still the right idea was there as a principle. " Where is there a man without sin? " was a common question among them. They would argue to show that there is no future life for any one, yet always visualized some sort of a hazy existence [60] like the ancient Hebrew idea of Sheol or the Greek idea of the realm of the shades, else they could not have had ancestral worship. Buddhism helped there also in crystallizing an idea of which they could not get free. The people commonly said that at death they all went to " Chu Seung," " that place," to Yumna, the Pluto of the Buddhist and Pre-Buddhist world of the dead. Chinese Buddhism said much about Kwei and Shen, the good and evil spirits. Shamanism, followed by the women folks of those Confucian scholars, talked almost entirely about " Kwisin," and that kept vivid the idea of a spirit world, as did the dragon worship, and the ideas about Kirins and phoenixes, and other mythical beings.

Douglass says of China [61] what was undoubtedly true to some extent of Korea, " The worship of spirits (in the Confucian ceremonies) takes the shape rather of respectful recognition of their existence than of devotional address to the Godhead. Prayer is unnecessary because heaven does not actively interfere with the soul of man. It has endowed him at birth with goodness which may, if he will, become his nature, and his true destiny will thus be realized, but all of this is to be accomplished by his own efforts. One of their common sayings is, ' The Sage is the equal of Heaven (Chun).' " Yet so inveterate is the thinking habit of man that, as my Buddhist college president said of the believers of his cult, after the Confucianists have finished the formal ceremonies and prayer sentences, they usually go on with a few words or un-

[60] Ross, *Corea: Its History, Customs and Manners*, p. 357.
[61] *Confucianism and Taoism.*

expressed longings of genuine heart prayer. " The best literati say grace before they eat their meals, thus, ' We offer thanks to Thee, Great Giver of food,' at the same time placing a spoonful of rice beside the dish." [62]

A Korean follower of the Chuntokyo cult quoted in the *Bookman Magazine* [63] makes a comparison of Christianity and Confucianism which is interesting. He says that the latter holds to rules of morality while the former depends on faith; the latter thinks of evolution and development, while the former thinks of creation; the latter sees with the eyes of this world, the former of the future world; the latter has no idea of a resurrection, while the former is waiting for one; the latter thinks only of personal sins, the former of congenital, original sin; the latter teaches love to others within a limited sphere while the Christian, " like Mooti of old," teaches a love that is limitless.

How much Korean Confucianism may have added to the doctrines of the cult beyond what was passed on to them by China we cannot know until there are scholars who can read the literature of the two countries understandingly and who may have the proper scientific training to make valid comparisons. Knowing the Koreans' intellectual capacity in other lines, and their intense application to the study of this cult, it is hardly thinkable that they have not made worthwhile contributions. There may even be, buried away in that literature of which we have spoken, whole schools of thought that would have been as powerful as Chuja's thought if the country had been in intellectual contact with other outside nations. Japan does not seem to have developed such schools. Chamberlain says [64] of them, " No Japanese has ever developed a system of Confucian thought. They were only expositors. There are not even any commentaries that are worth reading. They have simply reprinted the Classics and texts of Chuhi. At present the Confucian Classics are wholly neglected. The Confucian temple in Tokio has been turned into an Educational Museum." Nitobe might claim that Bushido was a system of

---

[62] *Korea Magazine*, 1917, p. 217.
[63] *Bookman, June,* 1924, p. 1 f.
[64] *Things Japanese*, p. 103.

thought that was basically Confucian, but he and Chamberlain would probably not agree upon Bushido.

Taken all in all, then, in spite of the Chuja interpretation of the Canonical Books, the cult in Korea seems not to have gone excessively far in the direction of materialism, and certainly the ethical rules of the organization were wholly admirable.

## VII. Present Status of the Cult

As an organized religion, Confucianism in Korea is practically finished, even more so than the cult of Buddhism. When the great Examinations were cut off in 1895, all incentive to study the Classics automatically vanished. Official position no longer depended upon one's knowledge of Chinese poetry.

The next great blow came from the modern schools that were founded first by the missionaries and later by the Korean Government and now on a far wider scale by the Japanese Government. In the old village schools, about the only two subjects taught were the Classics, or the Chinese characters in them, and a little mathematics. They scarcely paid any attention even to their own marvellous alphabet script of which we have spoken. All of this was worth while when it led straight on to official positions and a livelihood, or at least to a high place of honour in the community. The modern world felt that it needed a different type of graduate, and, to make room for the modern studies with all of the sciences, the Chinese characters and even the Classics themselves have been gradually forced into the background. In the Mission and Church schools, their place is wholly taken by the Bible and other Christian books on ethics and kindred subjects. In the Japanese Government schools, their place is taken by " Soosinsu " books of ethics based upon the Educational Rescript written by the Meiji Emperor. The average college graduate today cannot read freely more than a few hundred characters, and the thought-world in which he lives is as alien from that of his cultured grandfather as is that of our day from that of Moses.

This ruthless scrapping of old thoughts and customs probably had to come, and for the populace as a whole this will be a more comfortable material world because the scrapping has come about, but to one who loves the Orient and these beautiful fragile things of the spirit which were produced in the ages past, it cannot but bring a feeling of sadness. That exquisite wielding of the inspired scholar's brush, those delicate shadings of thought and nuances given in the poems, those esoteric allusions and philosophic spider-web spinnings can never be produced in the present bangety-bang world atmosphere. It takes time to do those things, time for broodings of spirit, for reading, for conversing, for intense think-ing. This age is too busy to read, or think, or for spiritual cre-ation. One pays a price for progress.

The next great blow to the cult came in the progressive hypothecation of its physical properties by the Japanese Govern-ment. Most of the county seat temples have already been turned into village schools, or gaols, or police stations, except where the local Literati were able and willing to buy them in and maintain them. It is doubtful if any of the old Suwons exist in the country villages. The Temple of Heaven grounds in Seoul are now used for the Government's foreign hotel, and its guests play around on the white pavilion which was formerly only a place of worship. Even the great Sajik Shrine is now deserted, or used for a public park. The other altars around the capital are almost forgotten, and students of an agricultural academy somewhat appropriately now plow Spring furrows where the King used to do it in memory of Sillongsi.

In the great temple in Seoul, the sacrifices of the second and eighth months still go on, but, as it is now thirty-five years since the great Examinations were abolished, the real literati who may attend are all sixty years old, or older. Kim Yoon Sik was the last President of the College, an aged patriarch more than eighty years old when I knew him well, some ten years or so ago. He had held every high office in the kingdom in past decades and was a famous scholar and writer. His wife and daughter, with his consent, became baptized members of the Central Presbyterian Church while the old gentleman was still living, and several younger members of the household were in the Sunday School.

In 1919, when the Independence Movement was on, the old gen-tleman and Mr. Yi, the Vice-President of the College, united in an open petition asking the Governor-General to gather up all of his Japanese fellow-citizens and go back to their home country, giving Korea its freedom. As a penalty, both scholars were deposed from their high offices in the temple, and there were no others worthy to take their places.

In the Japanese Government newspaper of January 16, 1930, there is a news item which states, " It is reported that the number of Confucian believers scattered throughout Chosen is some five hundred thousand, and the Government General is setting on foot a plan for the encouragement of Confucianism and its culture. The plan has now definite prospect of realization, definite decision is shortly to be reached. It is understood that the Government General is planning to establish an Institute styled Myungryoon Hakwon in the former Confucian Institute, with the scholars in Chosen, at an estimated cost of Y24,000."

This is interesting, but will probably be futile. In any event, what is established will not be the old Confucian Temple, for the old style scholars are gone. There are very few scholars in Korea today, Korean or Japanese, who can read freely the Chinese books which the old Chinsas used to feed upon. It is interesting that they are retaining for the name of the new Institute the same name that used to be applied to the Chinsa's living quarters in the southwest quarter of the temple grounds, but even that will not bring the old Chinsas or any one like them back to share in their labours.

One thing only of the old cult is still vitally active, *i. e.,* the worship of the ancestral tablets in private homes and the spirits themselves at the graves, of which we have already spoken. Even that, however, is being progressively neglected and possibly after another decade or two may be a thing of the past. One still sees crowds of people going out in the Fall to worship at the graves, but the whole population does not go as in former days. In the *Korea Magazine* for December, 1917, is an article on " Korea's Receding Pantheon " which pictures well how these things are going.[65]

## VIII. ESTIMATE OF THE CULT

In 1895, Baron Yun Chi Ho, one of the Korean Christians best

---

[65] P. 542.

known in America, writing for the *Korean Repository Magazine* [66]
gave a terrific indictment of the faults and weaknesses of Confucianism, seven points, largely true. Briefly they are as follows:
(1) Confucianism enfeebles and gradually destroys the faculty of
faith. It is an agnostic system. (2) It nourishes pride, tells men
that they are naturally good, overlooks the distinction between
moral and mental. (3) Knowing no ideal higher than a man, it is
unable to produce a godly or god-like person. Its followers may
be moral, but never spiritual. (4) It encourages selfishness. It
never says, go and teach. It always says, come and learn. (5) It
exalts filial piety to the position of the highest virtue, but saps the
foundations of morality by classifying women with menials and
slaves. (6) It aims to make people good through legislation. (7)
It makes men hunger for office that they may be in a position to
squeeze and hurt others.

I wonder if Baron Yun would write like that today, with the
greater breadth of view and wider culture that these additional
thirty-five years have brought to him.

While much that he says was true, yet Korea owes an enormous
debt to Confucius. Buddhism gave to Korea conceptions of a
supernatural God or gods, the idea of a Saviour, of a future world,
of faith and the like, but its ethical system was weak. Confucius
gave it an integrated plan of morality. Its ethical scheme at its
best is far below that of Christianity, and so many of Baron Yun's
criticisms are largely true, but it is not quite fair to compare Confucianism with the better thing that has come after. It should be
compared with what was in the country before it came, and what
is in those parts of the country where it did not touch. Looked at
in that way, the cult is not so open to question.

Undoubtedly Confucianism gave to the nation certain fundamental ideas and ideals of right and justice and truth which have
become a part of their very bone and sinew, ideas upon which
Christianity can build with a knowledge that they will hold. The
idea of filial piety has perhaps been over-emphasized a little, but
it makes almost an ideal preparation for receiving the idea of a

---

[66] P. 401.

Father God. There is a fair amount of honesty and business morality among the people. Certainly Confucianism, with its intensive training in ethics, was more responsible for that than any of the other cults. It stood for scholarship and a rich culture, and Korea is the better for that. It emphasized always the idea of the superior man or the gentle man, and encouraged men to aim at becoming such. There was sexual immorality in Korea in the olden days, and society winked at the having of concubines, but the Confucian system, until 1625, did not allow the son of a concubine to take its great examinations, and even up till today, the children of a concubine are treated like servants and do not inherit the father's property if there are children of the real wife. There was much injustice by officials, especially during the last one hundred years or so, but the moral sense of the people trained under Confucianism would stand only up to a certain point, when they would rise up and eject the oppressor and the higher officials allowed public opinion to rule and did not return the culprit to his post.

Confucianism as a cult has passed now, or is almost passed away. The great question of the day is as to what will take its place. With all of its faults, certainly Confucianism is vastly better than crass atheism such as has come to many of the peoples of Asia. Confucianism's greatest fault perhaps may be described by the French proverb, " The good is the enemy of the best." Its ethics are good. Many other things in it are good, but they are not enough. The Christian Gospel can meet every need that the ancient cult ever met, and go far beyond them, too. It can stand the fierce light of a searching scientific age. May Korea see that, and in its time of need turn to the satisfying Gospel of the Christ!

# IV

## MISCELLANEOUS CULTS

KOREA is not as rich in cults as some of the countries of the world, but it has had a goodly share of them and slight contacts with a number outside of Korea. I would like in this period to take up particularly the Pochunkyo, Tangoon Kyo and Kwankong cults, but first before doing that would like to speak of one or two others.

### I. MOHAMMEDANISM

One does not usually think of Mohammedanism in relation to the Pacific Ocean side of Asia, but there are multitudes of believers of that religion in China, variously estimated from six to twelve millions. They are largely in North China, the territory contiguous to Korea. They were strong enough in the eighteenth century to start a rebellion and seriously embarrass the Chinese when they tried to suppress it. One of the five stripes on the Chinese flag stands for these people. The Chinese eat a great deal of pork which, of course, these people will not touch. Possibly as a result of this, the Mohammedans of North China largely have in hand the business of butchering and marketing beef and mutton. When visiting a mosque on a Friday in Manchuria, in 1913, I saw, in the back yard, the carcase of a cow which evidently the people had not finished cutting up before their worship day, and they had left it there in the churchyard till a more convenient time, for their business.

There are mosques in every county seat throughout Manchuria, and there are five flourishing ones in Mukden city. As elsewhere, they use the Arabic language largely in their services. Women seem to have a small part, if any, in the worship. Although the mosques are so close to Korea's border, so far as the records show, there have never been any Mohammedans anywhere in Korea, and certainly they have never had one single mosque, possibly because of the " long wall " which the Koreans are said to have built and guarded through the centuries on the south side of the Yalu and Tumen Rivers from one side of the peninsula to the other.

## II. Taoism

All of the religions and all of the literary productions of Korea are filled with Taoistic ideas. We have noted how Buddhism incorporated in its pictured objects of worship the Kitchen God, and the worship of the North Star Constellation, and even canonized Laotze himself. We shall see, in Shamanism, Ok Wang Sangchei, one of the very highest of the Shamanistic gods who is undoubtedly Yuh Hwang Shangti of the Taoists in China. Many of the books used by the Taoists in their exorcism in China are brought across and used by the Korean Shamans. We have noted, under Shamanism below, several books whose names we have identified with those on a list secured from China. The *Tao Teh Kyung* of Laotze can be bought in the bookstores, though it is probably little read.

Dr. Gale has pointed out in his history how most of the Korean's stories of fairies and dragons come from Taoism,[1] especially the stories of the Suwang Mo, the Western Queen Mother who ruled in that fairy world, the floating gardens of Eden, that hung high in the air above the mountains of Thibet. There the cranes and the phoenixes and the unicorns do her bidding. She gives the magic elixir of life that makes men live forever, etc.

In China, they pride themselves on having the three legs to their religious stool, Confucianism, Buddhism and Taoism, and the Koreans have the same phrase which they use glibly on all occasions, " Yoo Pool Sun Sin, Sam To," but they have always all down through history lacked the third leg to their stool. So far as is known, Taoism as a separate cult with its own temples has never been known in Korea.[2] The Korean histories state that in 642 A. D.,

---

[1] Gale, "History of Korea," in *Korea Mission Field Magazine*, 1924, p. 156.

[2] Underwood, *Religions of Eastern Asia*, p. 108; Jones in *Korea Review*, 1901, p. 41; Gale, *Korea in Transition*, p. 81; Ross, *Corea: Its History, Customs and Manners*, p. 355; *Korean Repository*, 1897, p. 262.

and again in 649, the King of Kogoryu sent to China for Taoist books and teachers, and that because of it certain Buddhist teachers were so incensed that they left his court and went down to Paik-chei, but it was only a flurry and passed away.[8] In 1166, the Koryu King exhorted his people to import Taoism and so get the third leg for their stool, but Buddhism was strong enough to prevent it. In 1882, there was a great effort made to stir up zeal for the cult, and popular editions of the *Tao Teh King* (Korean—*To Tuk Kyung*) and other Taoist books were published, but it all came to nothing.[4] Two of the wards of the city of Seoul, Sam Chun Tong and Sam Kyuk Tong, are said to have Taoist names, and some have thought that possibly there were Taoist temples there at one time, but there is no mention of it in the records. Individuals have been known to practise what they considered to be Sunto[5] (Taoism) with special breathing exercises, all night prayer sessions and the like, but it has never become an organized cult.

In China, all fortune-telling, making of charms, crystal-gazing, spirit exorcism and the like is done by the Taoist priests. Without doubt a part of the Shamanism of Korea either came originally from China and Taoism, or was influenced by it. Still the Shamans are quite emphatic in saying that there has never been any organic connection between their cult and that across the bay.

It is quite curious that Taoism has not made itself more evident as a regular cult since it was at times a missionary faith. Like Mohammedanism, it came clear to the Yalu River boundary. In 1913, I crossed back from Manchuria to Korea six hundred li up from the river's mouth opposite the town of Kosari, and there high up on a mountain pass was a great Taoist temple as fine as almost any Buddhist temple in Korea. Just across the Bay of Pechili in Chefoo, China, a great Taoist temple dominates the whole city and the harbour. The Chinese have practically always had a free right of entry into the country of Korea. Buddhism and Confucianism

---

[8] *Poolkyo Yaksa.*
[4] *Korean Repository,* 1897, p. 262.
[5] Gale, *Korea in Transition,* p. 81.

were welcomed.  Why was the third leg of the stool kept out so meticulously?

### III. Japanese Shinto

Since the Japanese entered the country, in some scores, possibly hundreds of country places, where Japanese officials are located, they have set up on the nearby hilltops Shinto shrines like those in their homeland.  In the city of Seoul, in 1928, high up on the South Mountain overlooking the city, they made a national shrine in memory of the Meiji Emperor of Japan, and there is talk of erecting another in memory of Prince Ito, who was the first Resident General in the country.  More or less voluntary gifts were sought for erecting that Meiji Shrine, which cost in the neighbourhood of a million dollars gold.  As it is a strange sight, and since there is a wonderful view from the terrace there, hundreds of Koreans visit the shrine weekly, but it is doubtful if very many of them really voluntarily worship at any of the Shinto shrines.  So far as is known, not one shrine has ever been erected by the Koreans themselves of their own free will.

The Shinto cult has been compared to the spirit worship of Korea which we shall discuss in another lecture a little later, but, as one examines them a little closely one finds scarcely a point of contact between them.  The pantheons are almost mutually exclusive to begin with, as is the organization and practically every activity of the two religions.  If the Japanese and Korean peoples both came originally from the same ancestral home near the Amur, as some folks have of late years been trying to prove, it would be interesting to hear just how they explain this wide divergence of two cults each of which was undoubtedly primitive and indigenous.  The cult of the Ainus seems to have clear points of contact with the Shamanism of Siberia, but Shinto seems to be of a totally different nature.  Shinto has been vastly " improved " and touched up since the time of its restoration by Motoori about 1800, so that possibly we would have similarities if we could get back to real Shinto, but we cannot be sure of that.

Just on general principles it is interesting to note that not one of the cults from Japan has ever made any headway in Korea.

Korea gave both Buddhism and Confucianism to the Japanese, and
Japan changed in many ways both of these after they received
them, but none of their emendations, so far as is known, ever
came back to Korea, and, so far as I have been able to find out,
none of their commentaries have ever come into any wide use in
this land, either. Perhaps her geographical situation has had a
little to do with this. Naturally Korea has her face towards the
Land of the Dragon and her back turned towards Japan. All of
her good harbours but two are on her western coast, and most
of her contacts with the outside world were there until 1876.
Still, with a people so alert and active as the Japanese are, one
would have expected something different.

### IV. The Pochun Kyo

How old this cult is no one seems to know. It apparently appeared first under the name Yungam Ooto Hoi, and its exercises
seem to have been something like those of some of the Taoists in
China, i. e., there were certain breathing exercises intended to put
one en rapport with the spirits. There were wild dances in which
the whole congregations took part, and sword dances in which a
few skilled members shared. A little later it seems to have been
known as the Heumji Kyo, and at that time blossemed out as a
full-blown Spiritualistic sect, promising to put applicants into
communication with their beloved dead, and to heal sickness, and
do various other sorts of miracles. It created quite a sensation in
some parts of the country, but was looked upon with disfavour by
most of the people because of its open commerce with the spirit
world. Its meetings, like those of Spiritualists everywhere, were
held in the dark, and there were rumours of immoralities which did
not commend it to the average person.

When the Japanese first took charge of affairs, they suppressed
the cult, largely on the ground of its disease-healing claims, saying
that they were deceiving the people and pretending to practise the
art of medicine without having proper qualifications. Latterly
they seem to have dropped, or mitigated that phase of their
activities.

Some twenty years ago it took the present name, " Pochun Kyo," and since then has been recognized as a regular religion. It claims to have some seven thousand believers.

There was an ancient Korean prophecy which stated that, when the Yi Dynasty passed away, a new dynasty of the Chung family would arise and set up its capital on the Keiyong Mountain in South Choong Chung Province. Some twenty years ago, the Pochun Kyo took up that old prophecy and began to make preparations for Chung Si's time. They made a throne and royal robes, so it is said, and kept them in their headquarters in Seoul ready for the great day. Great numbers of families bearing the name of Chung began 'to flock towards the Keiyong Mountains, so as to be on hand for honours when some one of their name should begin to rule. Possibly the Japanese fulfilled in part that old prophecy, for, when they took over the country in 1910, their dynasty name for the period was, in Korean, " Great Chung," " Taichung." At any rate, there was no new capital on Keiyongsan.

The cult has meeting-places all over the country.

### V. Kwankong, the Cult of the God of War [6]

This is the same cult that is found under the same name in China. There it is an integral part of Taoism, although it has its own separate temples. There is a similar cult of a god of war called Hachiman in Japan, but it has no connection with Kwankong.

Kwan Oo, or Kwan Te, or Kwan Ik, as he is impartially called, was originally a curd merchant living in China during the Han Dynasty Period towards the end of the second century A. D. He became a soldier, and rose to a high position in the Empire. He was called the " Tiger General." His sword was known as the " Blue Dragon," and his horse as the " Red Rabbit." Poisoned arrows had no effect upon him. [7] He was finally trapped by members of the Yu and Ma clans and killed. At the time of his death, he was a Baron. After his death, a belief grew up that his spirit

---

[6] *Royal Asiatic Society Records,* 1900, p. 18; Allen in *Korean Repository,* 1895, p. 185.
[7] Gale, " History of Korea," in *Korea Mission Field Magazine,* 1925, p. 50.

was still on duty helping the Chinese in their battles, coming out particularly at critical times and turning the tide for them. During the Mohammedan Rebellion in 1828 and the Taiping Rebellion in 1855, he was said to have been very active.

After his death, his reputation steadily grew, until, in the twelfth century, he was canonized by the Chinese Government under the title " Patriotic and Clever Duke." Later he became a Prince. In 1828, he became a god, and since then has been regularly worshipped, particularly by military men and merchants, but also widely by the common people.

While Kwanoo lived, he had two close friends with whom he made a brother covenant, sealing it by mingling their blood from cuts made on each of their hands.[8] The first friend was Yu Hyun Tuk and the other Changpi. Both were originally, like Kwanoo, men of low degree. There is a saying current among the illiterate as well as the educated Koreans which translated runs as follows: " The spirit of Yu Hyun Tuk became King Sunjong of the Ming Dynasty in China, and the spirit of Changpi became King Sunjo of Korea," and they say that that is why Kwanoo helped the Koreans in 1592 in the year called " Imjin," when the Japanese sent by Hideyoshi ravaged the country all up to Pyengyang. The story goes that the Koreans first asked help of the Ming Emperor at that time and he refused to send it, but, in a dream, Kwanoon came to him and said, " The spirit of my dead brother is in Your Majesty, and that of my younger brother lives in the King of Korea. Will you not help him? "

During the war, the form of Kwanoo and his spirit soldiers appeared suddenly in midair outside the South Gate of Seoul, moved across the city and disappeared in the ground outside the East Gate.[9] At the places where he appeared and disappeared, temples were later erected to him by the Government, and official worship was offered to him to show the people's gratitude. In Pyengyang also he is said to have appeared, and there is a large temple there now which was erected, however, much later than those in Seoul. The two Seoul temples are among the most interesting sights in

[8] Douglass, *Confucianism and Taouism.*
[9] Gale, " History of Korea," in *Korea Mission Field Magazine,* 1926, p. 238.

the city. It is said that to this day no member of the Yu or Ma clans, who have descendants among the Koreans, dares to enter either of the temples or even pass in front of them lest Kwanoo arise and smite them for their treachery to him so many centuries ago.

The temples of Kwanoo are all built upon much the same plan, so a description of one will serve for all. The plan is Chinese. Out in front of the temple is an incinerator of brick perhaps an eight-foot cube with a small window in the side where waste paper may be inserted for burning. In China, any literature, even rough scratches of writing upon pieces of brown paper, is sacred, and to throw such papers into a dirty place such as a ditch, or to leave them lying there after seeing them is considered a sacrilege, or used to be. In 1906, in Chefoo, I saw men going about through the Chinese city with baskets suspended from their shoulders gathering these precious wisps of paper and taking them to the incinerators to be burned. The custom does not exist now in Korea if it ever did, but the incinerators are retained.

The buildings of the South Gate Temple of Kwanoo are immense, great tiled roofs, thick posts like those in the King's palace, and foundations and supporting stones all of smoothly cut white stone. One enters through a lofty, tile-covered gate where the great iron-studded, heavy leaves of the door are five inches thick and nearly ten feet high, and creak dismally in their stone hinge sockets. On the right and the left, under the gate roof, in little rooms guarded by fences, are statues life-size of Kwanoo's horses with statues of men attending. Beyond this is a court, and then another gate, equally formidable. Passing that, we are in another courtyard surrounded on three sides by galleries on the walls of which are paintings showing Kwanoo's various battles and the conspicuous part that he played in them, flashing here and there in the thickest of the fray.

Across this court is a walk made of flat slabs of granite.

On the far side of the court is the Main Temple itself, facing south, as all Chinese buildings must do. This building is perhaps thirty by sixty feet and its roof peak thirty feet from the ground. It is composed of three sections. In front, as one enters the building, is an anteroom for worshippers extending clear across the sixty feet. Three-fourths of the rest of the building is taken by Kwanoo and off in the corner to the left is a small shrine to Pochung, a Buddhist priest who is said to have saved Kwanoo's life at one time. For this act, ancestral worship is offered to him regularly by the worshippers of Kwanoo.

In the main shrine, one sees a large wooden statue of Kwanoo, a little more than life-size, showing just from the waist up in the dimness. His face is a dark red colour, and his heavy beard is black. He is dressed in armour and carries his mighty " Blue Dragon " sword. His face is fierce and menacing.

At his right and left, slightly in front of him and facing one another are two members of his staff, and, still further from him, another pair, so that one looks down a sort of lane between them to Kwanoo. These statues are slightly smaller than the main image, but are no less warlike looking. On the left, Chu Chang has a black face, and Kwan Pyung a white one. On the right, Wang O has a reddish face and Cho Ryoo a cream-coloured one.

In front of them all is a table for incense and for the food offerings. Above, the ceiling is decorated with flowers and birds somewhat as the Buddhist temples are decorated, though there are, of course, no Buddha pictures. Among the birds is the " hak," " the bird that kills dragons," possibly the same as the Garuda, that mythical bird of Vishnu, half eagle, half man which destroys serpents in their character of representatives of evil.[10] It may be the " roc " of *Arabian Nights* fame. In the anteroom are large drums, gongs, bells, and particularly many spears used in the worship and in the processions that used to be held.

The whole institution is in charge of men called " Soopok," low class men, servants. When the members of the royal family in olden days wanted to worship Kwanoo, they did not come in person, as this cult was felt to be of low grade and nothing like the worship in the Confucian temple. A palace-serving woman or eunuch was sent. No man of the nobility would go. Private citizens, when they offered worship, came in person, and, after the

---

[10] Monier-Williams, *Brahmanism and Hinduism*, p. 321.

Soopok had been paid for spreading the food before the images, he retired and the worshipper prostrated himself alone, and prayed for what he wanted. The word used for the Confucian worship was " cheisa." That offered to Kwanoo was not called " cheisa," lest the two become identified in the minds of the people.

Although up until recently the shrines were Government property, and worship was often offered by order of the members of the royal family, it was always counted a private matter of the individual, more commonly of the women folks, and was not considered a national cult. The same raw fruits, grains and meats that were used in the Confucian temples were offered here.

There used to be many old books used in connection with the cult, particularly books telling of the great deeds of Kwanoo, and Books of Forms telling how to offer the sacrifices. The book called *Kyung Sin Nok* in five volumes is said to be about the only one used now.

Special offerings were made on the evening of the fourteenth day of the first lunar month, the day which corresponds with the Jewish Passover and formerly, as in the Buddhist temples, worship was offered regularly on the first and fifteenth of each of the lunar months. We will speak further of that fourteenth day later on.

It is said that of late years they do not often offer sacrifice at the shrine of Pochung, but the shrine itself is retained as a memorial. Candles of wax were formerly used at both shrines. Now paraffine candles are more common. I was astonished in visiting the temple recently to see that they had installed electric bulbs even in the innermost shrines—shades of Edison hobnobbing with the Orient's ancients!

Besides the South Gate and East Gate Temples which have been there for centuries, during the reign of the last real King of Korea, Queen Min, his wife, who was much given to such superstitions, had several other temples built, one outside the west gate, one just inside the northeast gate and a tiny one near the big bell in the very centre of the city.[11] Of these, the first is now utilized by the

---

[11] *Royal Asiatic Society Records,* Vol. II, Part II, p. 23.

Government as a school for the blind, the second was for a time the Buddhist College, but is now the Chunto Kyo Higher School, and the third has been torn down, so that only the two ancient ones remain.

Some years ago, the new Japanese Government, having no use for these ancient temples, since they were nominally Government property, planned to sell off the South Gate building, but the people living near the South Gate, particularly the great merchants, Korean and Chinese, raised a popular subscription, bought it in, and it still stands as it always has. Compared with the old days, it has few worshippers now, but Chinese merchants particularly visit it regularly and, on special days, great numbers of people go.

Outside of Seoul, there are temples to Kwanoo standing in seven places, it is said—Songdo, Pyengyang, Miryang, Sungju, Namwon, and on the island of Kokeum To off the Chulla coast. The temple in Pyengyang was erected privately by the family of Pak Chai Sook, and his descendants still act as custodians of it, but it is considered to be public property. The present incumbent recently told me that, if it were not for the Chinese merchants of the city who come to worship, his temple would be almost deserted.

Far more important than the worship carried on in these nine buildings, however, is the worship of Kwanoo carried on everywhere throughout the country in private homes. There it seems to be more or less connected with Shamanism, as in China it is connected with the degraded Taoism. Under the direction of the sorceresses, images of Kwanoo are made, sometimes just pictures, sometimes great fluffy wall images of paper something like a large valentine, standing out in bas relief from the wall. The ignorant people of the villages believe profoundly in the efficacy of prayer to Kwanoo, and they worship him in their homes most abjectly. The temples seem destined to fall into decay and pass away before many generations. This home worship of Kwanoo bids fair to last long after the other is gone. The whole cult is one of the most curious manifestations of the vagaries of the human mind that has ever existed. It arose of course from the background which made ancestral worship in general possible, but its vitality all down the

KOOKSADANG, NATIONAL SPIRIT SHRINE, SEOUL

centuries has been astonishing. Today, " The crowds that used to frequent the temple have fallen away. Wind-bells tinkle disconsolately over the grass-grown courtyard. Kwan Oo is dead." [12]

## VI. Cult of Choi Il: Tai Chang

Near Songdo, in the county of Poongduk, on the Tukmool Mountains, is a temple [13] similar in meaning to that of Kwanoo, dedicated, however, to a Korea hero, a military man named Choi Il who was very prominent late in the Koryu Period. He was beheaded by the first king of the Yi Dynasty. In his life, he was very powerful, and, because of the violent death that he suffered, the sorceresses of all that region down past Seoul believe in him and invoke him in their seances. His picture is one of the most prominent in the National Shrine on the top of the South Mountain near Seoul, and in the other semi-national shrine just over the Peking Pass near the city.

It is curious how most of the spirits invoked by the Shamans are those of people who have, like Choi Il, died violent deaths, those drowned, eaten by tigers, mothers who have died in giving birth to children, the spirits of dead Shamans, men and women, the spirit of smallpox, General Hojo, etc.

In Choi Il's temple on the Tukmool Mountains, [14] there is an image of him, and worship is offered there very much like that offered to Kwanoo. One well-informed Korean told me that Choi Il, not Kwanoo, ought properly to be called the " god of war " of Korea, but I doubt if that would be the general opinion.

## VII. The Tangoon Kyo [15]

As we have noted several times in these lectures, Tangoon was the mythical founder of Korea who lived in 2332 B. C. (the years being always given exactly), at about the same time that the first legendary rulers of China were living. Dr. Gale says, " Quite

---

[12] " Korea's Receding Pantheon," *Korea Magazine*, 1917, p. 543.
[13] *Korea Review*, 1903, p. 302.
[14] *Korea Review*, 1903, p. 302.
[15] *Royal Asiatic Society Records*, 1900, p. 25; Hulbert, *History of Korea*, I, p. 1.

apart from Confucius, Buddha and Laotze, he has been the guiding spirit of Korean inspiration through all the ages." [16]  In the ancient Korean cosmogony (or rather in one of them, for they seem to have many), the first great Being was a Divine One called "Whanin" or "Cheiso," the Creator.  His son, "Whanung," asked and obtained permission from his father to found a kingdom on the earth in the north of Korea.  Accompanied by three thousand other spirits, he descended upon Taipaik Mountain, now known as "Myohyang" Mountain, near Pyengyang.  This was in the twenty-fifth year of the Emperor Yao of the Chinese, i. e., 2332 B. C.  Whanung gathered his spirit friends or subjects beneath the shade of an ancient "paktal" tree, and there proclaimed himself "King of the Universe." [17]  He governed through three vice-gerents, the "Wind General," "Rain Governor" and the "Cloud Teacher," but, as he had not yet taken human shape, he found it very difficult to take direct charge of a purely human kingdom.  Searching after incarnation, he found it in the following manner:

"At early dawn, a tiger and a bear [18] met on the mountain-side and held a colloquy.  'Would that we might become men!' they said.  Whanung overheard them, and a voice came out of the void to them, saying, 'Here are twenty garlics, and a piece of artemisia for each of you.  Eat and retire from the light of the sun for thrice seven days, and you will become men.'  They ate and retired to a cave, but the tiger, by reason of the fierceness of his nature, could not endure the restraint, and came forth before the allotted time.  The bear, with greater faith and patience, waited the full twenty-one days and stepped forth a perfect woman.

"The first wish of the woman's heart was maternity, and she cried, 'Give me a son!'  Whanung, the Spirit King, passing on the wind, beheld her sitting there beside the stream.  He circled around her, breathed upon her, and her cry was answered.  She cradled her babe in the moss beneath the paktal tree, and it was there that the wild people of the country in after years found him

---

[16] Gale, "History of Korea," in *Korea Mission Field Magazine*, 1924, p. 1.
[17] *Korea Magazine*, 1917, p. 404.
[18] *Korean Repository*, 1895, p. 220.

sitting, and they made him their king. This was Tangoon, whose name translated means the ' Lord of the Paktal Tree.' "

One wonders if this legend of Tangoon's origin from a bear has any connection with the. Ainu bear legends, or with the original source from which those Ainu legends came, especially in view of the possible connections that we shall see later between the Shamanism of the two countries.

" When Tangoon became king, he found nine wild tribes in his dominion. He taught them the relation of king and subject, the rite of marriage, the art of cookery, and the science of house-building. He taught them to bind the hair by tying a cloth around the head, and how to cut down trees and till the soil. He made his capital at Pyengyang, and tradition says that he reigned there for a thousand years until the coming of Keuija in 1122 B. C. When Keuija came, so the story goes, Tangoon retired to Moonhwa in Whanghai Province, resumed his spirit shape and disappeared. There are two or three large, ancient graves in Moonhwa and elsewhere, however, which with sublime confidence and inconsistency are pointed out as Tangoon's graves." [19]

If there be any truth at all in the legend, it may be that there was a line of chieftains of the Tangoon clan that ruled through these thousand years, but the Koreans do not try to spoil their pretty story by rationalizations like that.

" In 2265 B. C., according to tradition, Tangoon first offered sacrifice to ' Hananim,' the God of the Heavens, at Hyulgu on the island of Kanghwa in the mouth of the Han River, twenty-five miles below the modern Seoul. Later he erected on that island on the Marisan Mountain a great altar of stone and earth seventeen feet high and six feet six inches square at the top,[20] and that altar is standing today." [21]

About thirty or so years ago, a number of patriotic Literati in Seoul got to thinking over the condition of their country and mourning over it. Politically, their country was already practically

[19] Hulbert, *History of Korea,* I, Ch. I; *Korea Magazine,* 1917, p. 404.
[20] *Korea Magazine,* 1917, p. 411.
[21] *Royal Asiatic Society Records,* 1900, p. 22; *Korea Magazine,* 1919, p. 411; *Korea Review,* 1904, p. 258.

a dependency of Japan, as it became in fact in 1910. Financially, it was very poor. Educationally, they were just beginning to organize modern schools, and those were largely founded by the missionaries or the Christians. The thing that ground them most was that in all things religious and moral, they were almost entirely dependent upon foreign lands, Buddhism from India, Confucianism from China, etc.

Confucianism as a formal organization seemed about to die, since the old Examinations were gone. Buddhism was entirely foreign, Shamanism was beneath the notice of an educated man (notwithstanding the fact that they ungrudgingly paid the bills when their women folks consulted the sorceresses). Somehow they felt, as patriotic Koreans, that Korea should have at least one religion of its own. Out of this situation, as usual, there came a leader, Kim Yum Paik, who pointed out that the worship which Tangoon once offered to Hananim, the God of Heaven, was purely Korean and worthy of development. The idea was taken up eagerly, and a Tangoon Kyo church was organized.

It should be noted right here that there are really two cults that go by that name in Korea. One is associated with the ancient shrine of Tangoon in the city of Pyengyang, the existing building said to have been erected over five hundred years ago on the exact site of the ancient paktal tree. This building is suffering neglect very much as the Confucian Haingkyo temples are, but worship after the manner of ancestral worship is carried on before Tangoon's tablet there several times a year. The buildings are considered to be Government property, but there are custodians in charge. It is said that at times even some of the Japanese officials have come to share in this worship. The worshippers of the other Tangoon Kyo do not take part in the worship at this shrine.

Kim Yum Paik wrote a doctrinal book called *Sungkyung Palli*, which is accepted as the Bible of the cult. He sent out a call to the Literati everywhere, and there was an enthusiastic meeting for organization. The new religion was launched as an exclusive affair of the Literati. None of the Hoi Polloi were allowed to apply. Every applicant's credentials and genealogical tables were carefully studied. Women were at first not admitted. A church building was provided in Seoul and more or less regular meetings held, periodical worship days being the traditional first and fifteenth of each lunar month.

Word also was sent out to the provinces and the Literati there organized Chapters. The movement took particularly well, it is said, up in the north near Paik Too San, the "Ever White Mountain," on the border, where it was believed that Hananim particularly lived, just as the Jews perhaps once believed that Jehovah lived at Sinai where Moses had first met Him. For a few years, the movement was a great success, but it seems to have lost its initial impetus, and the "Wheels of the chariots seem to be dragging heavily." Women are now admitted. The leader in Pyengyang city said in 1928 that they had about three thousand believers in all the country. A recent newspaper report credits them with seven thousand. Kim Yum Paik was arrested by mistake as a Tonghak and suffered martyrdom during the persecution of that sect. That has helped to give his cult validity.

They have not had time to create a large literature, but they have several books, notably a biography of Kim Yum Paik, whom they reverence as their founder and to whom they offer ancestral worship. The "Bible" of Tangoon Kyo seems to be patterned somewhat after that ancient chart of Chinese Ethics called the *Great Learning* or *Taihak*.[20] Briefly its contents are as follows:

It speaks first of our duty of reverence towards Hananim (God), towards all teachers, and parents; then of love to brethren, husband or wife, and to friends; then of charity due to children, to all men and to animals, and states that, to accomplish these things, there must be study, self-control and practice.

Next, under the heading of "Faith," it goes on to speak of care of the body, which is influenced by poise, alertness and right knowledge; then of care of the Doctrine, which is furthered by meditation, realization of one's influence upon others, and by self-restraint; thirdly of the care for duty, which is exhibited in charity, love of righteousness and breadth of mind or tolerance.

Under the heading of "Faithfulness," it goes on to say that one

---

[20] Martin, *Lore of Cathay*, p. 207.

is to seek the joy which comes from self-denial, soberness of mind and good memories; also blessings which arise out of humility, forgiveness and truthfulness; and lastly it says that there will be eternal good fortune arising from three things, the observance of right customs, from diligence and from the helping of others.

The influence of Confucius can easily be seen in every line of this, and all of it, as far as it goes, is admirable.

The second half of the book is filled with By-laws:

1. Purpose of the society—to worship Tangoon at all times, and particularly on the first and fifteenth of every month and at memorial days. (It is interesting to note that it is Tangoon, not Hananim, who is to be worshipped, even though the cult grew out of discussions of Tangoon's worship to Hananim on Kanghwa. We will discuss the concept of Hananim under Shamanism, later. The Koreans always say that He is the first and greatest of all the gods, but seldom actually worship Him.)

2. Method of propaganda—lectures and sermons to the members.

3. Duties of the members—to do acts of kindness to children, to the childless and to other helpless ones.

4. Rewards to be expected—one puts off this world and becomes spiritual.

5. Humility—to be shown in absolute forgetfulness of self.

6. Desirable things—industriousness, which is the source of long life, peace for parents and brethren, and entrance into the heavenly world.

7. Requisite activity—the cultivation of virtue.

Finally, there are certain penalties provided for those who do not attend the meetings, and honourable mention for those who do, also rules of etiquette for saluting one another (or perhaps passwords) are arranged and provision made for the granting of cards of membership, small cards about two and one-half inches square.

We have said that this cult is only about thirty years old. That is true of its modern form, but there seems to have been more or less ancestral worship offered to Tangoon all down through history. It is such a pity that the people should have concentrated their attention upon Tangoon and not upon Tangoon's God. All over the country on the hilltops, are small altars,[23] many of which tradition connects with the Tangoon altars on Kanghwa. Possibly there was a time when the cult was widespread throughout the land. Jones thought that Tangoon was the first Shaman in the country,[24] but the atmosphere and spirit found wherever he is mentioned in Korean literature is not the miasmic breath of Shamanism. The impression always given is more like that of the earliest kings of China or like that of Abraham, back in the dim dawn of the world, simple-hearted worshippers bowing to a monotheistic God.

There are dolmens in every part of Korea, often long rows of them running off across the country. Whether they were tombs or altars no one knows, though most authorities lean to the former. If they were altars, possibly here is an addition even to the worship of the high altars on the hills.

If Tangoon Kyo in the beginning had taken or even now were to take into consideration the worship of Tangoon's God, we would have a religion without any definite plan of atonement, except that naturally involved in a religion of sacrifice, but it would have been a religion of light as compared with Shamanism and far better even than Korean Buddhism. Its scheme of ethics, albeit, somewhat theoretical, is admirable as far as it goes. The two hints given in the abstract translation above as regards a future world imply a knowledge of one far in excess of those two short clauses.

Tangoon Kyo stopped short of what its founders must have known was the best, and so, like the other miscellaneous cults, it will soon pass away. It is an interesting thing to note, however, as it appears all down through history, and particularly as it appears in this latest development of the soul's outreaching for supreme satisfactions. Many of the Christians in Korea first had their interest in the Christian Gospel aroused through their knowledge of Tangoon and his God, and they have recognized that He is one and the same as the God of their Bible. May the day come when all Korea may be led to do likewise!

---

[23] Underwood, *Religions of Eastern Asia*, p. 100.
[24] *Royal Asiatic Society Records*, 1900, p. 48.

# V

## THE CHUNTOKYO CULT

WE discussed in the last lecture seven of the miscellaneous cults of Korea, and I had thought at first of including this last cult with those, but it is so much larger and more virile than any of them that it did not seem right to submerge it as simply one of seven or eight.

The Chuntokyo cult claims to be the largest religious body in Korea. It is difficult to estimate just how many adherents it has, for its members claim as many as three or four millions. A recent Government report in the *Seoul Press* newspaper credits them with two millions. Possibly at some one time when the cult was at its height, it may have enrolled a million, or three times the whole Christian community of the country. We doubt if it has as many as three hundred thousand actual followers of all types today, but, if it has, that is a company equal to the Christian Church and all of its adherents. Whatever the actual number may be, it is very large we know, and no survey of the religions of Korea would be complete without a study of this cult, too.

The name of the organization means the "Doctrine of the Heavenly Way." There is a religious body in Japan started there by a woman and called Tenrikkyo,[1] and that name translated would be the same as Chuntokyo, but the two cults are not the same in any particular and have never had any contact whatever.

Let us take up the study as we did of the other religions, first as to its history, then as to its ceremonies and its doctrines, and lastly as to its present status and contribution to Korean life and culture.

### I. Its History

The founder of Chuntokyo was Choi Chei Oo (private name,

---

[1] Peery, *The Gist of Japan*, p. 137.

Choi Pok Sool),[2] who lived just before and after 1860 A. D., in the town of Yongdam (Dragon Pool) near Kyungju in southeast Korea.[3] He is said by his cult believers to have been a descendant of one of the last kings of Silla. His mother died when he was six years old, and his father when he was sixteen.[4] His father had been a well known Confucian scholar and the boy was well trained in the characters when a child. After his father's death, he travelled widely, " seeking some doctrine for the salvation of his people."

The Buddhists have a story, told to me by my college president friend, that, at Yoochumsa monastery in the Diamond Mountains, there was a priest who prayed at one time the conventional, continuous forty-nine-day prayer, and, coming out at the end, he found in front of the pagoda of his temple a book containing a mysterious twenty-one character formula. This formula, they say, was the basis of the famous charm formulæ of the Chuntokyo. The priest could not understand the meaning of the writing, so he wandered everywhere trying to get someone to interpret it for him. In his travels, he met Choi Chei Oo, who asked him to leave the book with him, and promised to solve the riddle. The priest did so and, returning three days later, Choi had the interpretation ready for him. The priest heard the explanation, and suddenly vanished out of sight, possibly having by the hearing attained that Enlightenment for which the " Sun " priests were always striving.

Choi Chei Oo's own story is given in the Bible of the cult which he wrote for his people. It is called the *Tongkyung Taichun*. The full translation of the book is given in the Appendix. The part treating of his call is as follows: "About 1860, news came of the arrival in our land of the foreigners (Ed.—these were the French priests) ; that they had not come to take away the wealth of our land or our country itself, but that they were erecting churches and preaching their Doctrine. When I heard this, I pondered over it a great deal, and wondered if their doctrine could be true. Suddenly, in the fourth month of the year 1860, I was

---

[2] *Korea Review*, 1906, p. 419.
[3] *Korean Repository*, 1898, p. 245.
[4] *Chuntokyo Chaykei Yoram*, p. 1.

taken with a mysterious disease, my heart acted strangely and I was shaken with chills. No doctor could understand my symptoms, nor could I describe my feelings clearly.

" One day, as I lay ill, a Spirit spoke to me and said, ' Do not be afraid. I am He whom the people call Sangchei (God). Do you know me?' I said, ' What do you wish, Lord?' He answered, 'At the present time, I have no standing among men. I want to send you into the world to teach my Doctrine to the people. Do you doubt? Do not doubt.' ' Shall I teach them according to the Doctrine of Suhak, " Western Learning " (Ed.—nickname for the Roman Catholic faith)?' I asked. ' No!' he said, ' I have a certain charm (Ryongpoo) which is called " Sunyak " (spirit medicine). It is shaped like the Taikeuk [5] (symbol in the centre of the Korean flag, two commas revolving around one another), or like the Koongkoong (a curved, bow-like figure). Receive it and heal the diseases of the people. Use it as a prayer, and teach it to the people in my name. If you do this, you will have long life, and your fame will go out to all the world.'

" Strength was given me, and I took the paper and swallowed it. Instantly I was cured of my disease, and I knew that it was supernatural medicine. I at once began to use the medicine upon other sick folks. I found that some were helped and some were not. At first, I could not understand the reason for this. I watched carefully, however, and discovered that those who gave their full respect and attention to Hananim (God) received benefit, and that others did not. Again and again I tried it. It was evident that results depended upon the faith of the patient.

" I realized then the reason why our country was in the state in which it was, full of disease and knowing no peace from one year's end to another. On the other hand, I thought of the foreign nations. This did not seem to apply to them, for they were always fighting and seemed always to be victorious (even though their acts were evil). It looked as though the whole world would be gobbled up by them, and we also unless we waked up. I wondered what I could do to protect our people and help our fellow-men. I

---

[5] *Korean Repository*, 1895, p. 135.

determined to write a few words in order to instruct the people and reveal to them the truth!"

The Chuntokyo people today have many stories of the miraculous events attending Choi Chei Oo's visions, of his riding on the clouds enveloped in lightning, of repeated angel visitations, and the like,[6] legends which they were no doubt led to make up so that he might seem as great as Confucius and. Buddha, about whom similar stories were told, but Choi's own account is as here given.

Apparently he began at once to teach in Yongdam, and many disciples gathered around him. He was a scholar, although further along in his book, he tells of the long line of scholars from which he sprang and then says, self-deprecatingly, that he knew so little in comparison with them that he had never even tried to secure public office. These words were likely from excessive modesty.

Tradition says that his wife was a Xanthippe, and that his home life was very unhappy up until he received his revelations. This was because, although desperately poor, he spent his time dreaming over religious and philosophical matters instead of earning a living. When he received his visions, his wife and children, hearing him speaking apparently to the empty air, thought that he was crazy, but he took the Twenty-One Character Formula, which the Spirit had given him, wrote it on a piece of paper, burned it and dropped the ashes into water, and then had his family drink the mixture. Instantly they were all converted and all of his home troubles vanished.

For about four years, he taught quietly, his following gradually growing, although he says in his book that he tried to keep any large numbers of people from coming to his house lest it attract the unfavourable attention of the Government. Careful though he was, he did attract attention, for it was the time of one of the great persecutions of the Roman Catholics when hundreds of them were hunted down and slaughtered like mad dogs, and most of the French priests were either killed or barely escaped with their lives.

Informers reported him to the Government as a Catholic, and he

---

[6] *Korea Magazine,* 1918, pp. 161, 162.

was arrested and taken to Seoul. When he was tried, he stoutly denied any connection with the Catholics, saying that their Doctrine was " Suhak," " Western Learning," while his was " Tonghak," " Eastern Learning." Some have said that the word " Tonghak," like the word " Christian " first used at Antioch, was in the beginning a term of reproach, but evidently this cannot be true, for Choi uses the word in his own " Bible." He also calls the Doctrine " Chuntokyo " in his Bible, so that that name too was used from the beginning, although up until 1900, the more commonly used name was Tonghak.

After keeping him some months in gaol, the Government became convinced that his Doctrine was not essentially different from Catholicism, and so ordered his death. According to the usual custom, he was taken back to the capital of his own province, Taiku, and beheaded there. This was in 1866, and marks what the Chuntokyo call the " time of the Great Tribulation."

Among Choi's most earnest disciples was his nephew, somewhat far removed, Choi Si Hyung, more commonly known as Choi Hai Wul. The Master had tried out the younger man first by giving him the superintendence of the cult in the northern provinces.[7] When the supreme penalty had been paid, the nephew took up the Master's fallen mantle, and secretly carried on for nearly thirty years, the organization growing normally and not interfering with any one. Its meetings were all held in private homes and were worship services, only.

Towards the end of this period, in the nineties, the central Government became more and more corrupt and venal. Magistrates were changed every year instead of every three years as formerly, and all offices were sold to the highest bidder, who had to recoup himself by squeezing the people. To get their money back and a profit, they had to seek out every means of revenue, so, beginning about 1888, they systematically levied blackmail upon the inoffensive Tonghaks, who were technically a proscribed sect, and did not dare to call attention to themselves by protesting.

Gradually indignation began to arise throughout the nation, and,

---

[7] *Chuntokyo Chakei Yoram.*

as the Tonghaks were being abused more than any one else, and
that organization was one of the few in existence among the common people, great numbers of people began to join them in order
to get relief from oppression. A great indignation meeting of the
society was called to meet at the Changansa Monastery in Poeun
County in Choongchung Province. Threats of revolution were
made, and excitement ran high. A noted scholar named O Yoon
Chung was sent from Seoul to reason with the men, and the
excitement was allayed for a time.[8]

Oppression continued, and no relief was given, so more and yet
more people joined the organization for political reasons. Choi
Hai Wul, the head of the society, did not want to enter upon political activity. The "Great Tribulation" and the fate of their
founder were too recent in his mind to make him want that. Some
of the men, however, demanded immediate and drastic action.
Among these a certain man named Chun Pong Choon was most
active.

In 1893, a party of fifty Tonghaks went to Seoul and presented
a petition to the king demanding that the ban be taken off their
organization, and threatening, if it was not done, that they would
rise up and kill off all of the foreigners in the country, as the
Suhaks and not the Tonghaks were the cause of all of the troubles
in the land. The Government temporized with promises of later
action, but, after the delegation departed, nothing was done.

Chun Pong Chun, who was nicknamed "Noktoo," a word that
might be translated "Little Beans,"[9] then seized the leadership of
the Tonghaks away from Choi Hai Wul. A great crusade was
organized which was to start from Kyungsang Province in the
southeast, swing around through Chulla Province on the southwest
and then on up to Seoul to wipe out the foreigners.[10] It started,
gathering momentum and size as it went, all of the pent-up feelings
of the people having for the first time an outlet. The nobility
along the route were handled much as they were in France during
the Revolution, though few were actually killed. Soldiers sent

---

[8] *Korea Review,* 1906, p. 421; *Korean Repository,* 1898, p. 235.
[9] *Korea Magazine,* 1918, p. 163; *Korean Repository,* 1895, p. 30.
[10] Hulbert, *History of Korea,* II, p. 249.

against the crusaders joined them in a body. The greatest alarm was felt at the Court in Seoul, and they appealed to China to send troops to help them.

Some years before this the Chinese had made a contract with the Japanese that they would not send troops to Korea without notifying Japan, but, disregarding this treaty, they now sent an army to overcome the Tonghaks. The Japanese, possibly glad of an excuse, immediately sent an army also.[11] The Japanese troops met the crusaders coming up from the south and scattered them to the four minds, and then engaged the Chinese troops and the great Japan-China War was on. Possibly this war was inevitable, but the Tonghaks were responsible for making the right situation for it.

As soon as the crusade, which in many ways resembled the Boxer Movement in China, was scattered, the Korean Government began to hunt down separately all of those who had taken any part in it. Chun Pong Choon kept actively opposing them, even to the extent of gathering a company and engaging the Government troops. He set up as the head of his organization a young boy of twelve years whom he called " Yidong " or " Wonderful Youth." Chun himself was at length arrested and the boy was killed in battle, although all of his men had been assured that the magic Formula of the cult made them invincible against bullets or any other sort of weapon. Great numbers of the members migrated from Choongchung Province to Kyung-Sang to escape the terrors of the inquisition.[12]

Choi Hai Wul and his first lieutenant, Son Pyung Heui, according to one story, fled to China for asylum; according to another account, they hid in a quiet village in Korea. Many stories are told of the miracles which they wrought while escaping from the soldiers. Choi was said to have had the power of " chukchip," i. e., the ability to wrinkle up the earth, step across, and then smooth it out with himself miles from where he had stood, a sort of modernized seven-league boots. At a wish, he could make houses move out of his path or could leap over them.

[11] *Korea Review*, 1895, p. 60.
[12] *Korea Review*, 1906, p. 419.

He could make himself invisible,[13] etc.   His miracles were not
sufficient, however, or else he slipped up somewhere, for he was
arrested at Wonju, taken to Seoul and executed by strangulation
outside the west gate of the city.

Among the surviving leaders of the movement were Son Pyung
Heui, Yi Yong Koo, Kim Yung Kook and others.   Son Pyung
Heui, whose honourary name was " Wiam," became the head of
the organization.   He is said to have formerly been an ajun, or
magistracy runner, down in Choongchung Province.   Some have
claimed that his real name was Yi Sang Eun, or at least that he
lived in Japan under that name, claiming to be a relative of the
royal Yi family.[14]   This is denied by members of the organization,
who say that his aged father is still living in Seoul and bears the
name of Son Whi Jo.

Yi Yong Koo was much younger than Son, and devoted to him.
Son, having been selected to succeed Choi Hai Wul, appointed Yi
Yong Koo his executive representative, and himself retired to
Japan.   Yi began the preaching of the Doctrine again, confining
himself rigidly to the original religious aspects of the movement.
He also began to erect a halo of sanctity around the absent Son
Pyung Heui, telling how he was gathering multitudes of believers
in other lands [15] and picturing him as a Being who, from far-off
Japan, could know the inmost thoughts of his followers in Korea,
could miraculously heal their diseases from a distance, had the
miraculous gift of tongues, etc.   The devoted Yi Yong Koo gathered the contributions of the faithful, and sent them across to
Son for his living expenses.   Many of the refugees, political and
otherwise, from Korea gathered around Son over there.

About 1905, the Japanese began to press hard upon the country,
demanding many concessions and threatening the sovereignty of
the King.   Many organizations for and against the Japanese were
formed, among them the " Ilchinhoi," or Progressive Society.   It
was started in Seoul about 1905.   Many of the original members were Christians and the chairman of the first public meet-

[13] *Korean Repository*, 1895, p. 58.
[14] *Korea Review*, 1906, p. 424.
[15] *Chuntokyo Chaykei Yoram.*

ing was Saw Sang Yoon, the first Korean Protestant Christian in Korea.

Yi Yong Koo took an active part in the founding of this society, which was at first purely a patriotic one, aiming at correcting the abuses and corruption that had crept into the country. Very early some of the nobility of the country, such as Yoo Kil Choon, Yi Wan Yong, Minister Song of Yangji County, and others interested themselves in it. Because of Yi Yong Koo's interest, great numbers of the Chuntokyo people joined it. They about swamped it, and its original ideals became so submerged that most of the Christians withdrew from it in disgust.

The Court and the Japanese were in a great struggle over the demands. The Ilchinhoi threw in its strength apparently on the side of the Japanese, or at least they were credited with doing so. Yi Yong Koo is said to have formed an alliance with Yi Wan Yong and Song of Yangji, each of whom later became Ministers of State in the Cabinet which turned over the country to the Japanese. Rumour said that, as their reward for their helping in this matter, the Chuntokyo was given a valuable lumber concession on the Yalu River and that that helped to build their cathedral in Seoul.[16] This may be true or not, but it was generally believed by the people. Prince Ito gave 200 yen to this building fund when he was Resident General in Korea.[17]

Son Pyung Heui came back from Japan to find the character of his "church" radically changed from a religious to a political organization, and his former position on a pedestal as a god-like, invisible Being, changed to that of a mere appendage of a political movement. He did not like this. Perhaps he remembered what had happened to his two predecessors when they had meddled or seemed to be meddling in politics. At any rate, he is said to have protested so vigorously that Yi Yong Koo became angry and told him that he did not need him, that it was he himself who had created the Son Pyung Heui myth and kept him supplied with funds over in Japan, and that he could get along without Son entirely.

---

[16] *Korea Review*, 1906, p. 419.
[17] *Korea Magazine*, 1918, p. 165.

Son is said to have suspended Yi and several of his followers. They retorted by causing a schism in the church in 1906, setting up a new denomination, which they called the " Sichun Kyo," this name being taken from the tenth and eleventh letters of their magic prayer Formula, and meaning the " Heaven Honouring Doctrine." They seized the cathedral in Seoul, and, for a time, Son was forced to find another plant for himself in the north part of the city.

Yi sent word to his friends notifying them of the change, telling them that the doctrines of the new church were the same as the old, but only the name and ecclesiastical headship were different. The greater part of the people swung over, and Son was left desolate. Yi had done his work too well, however, when he was creating the Son Pyung Heui myth. He had no substitute for this in his schismatic group. At first, the fact that he was said to control many government positions and other positions helped to hold the people, but they began to drift back to Son. Yi died and was canonized, and his tablet placed in the great cabinet behind the pulpit in the cathedral in Seoul, along with the tablets of the two former founders of the cult. The two cults largely came together then under Son's leadership. Just at first Song Pyung Choon and Kim Yung Kook succeeded Yi, but these two also quarrelled, and Kim Yung Kook made another schism and set up another denomination called the " Kwi Am Kyo."

In the 1919 Independence Movement, Son Pyung Heui and a dozen of the other leaders of the movement signed the Declaration of Independence, and went to gaol. Before being arrested, Son turned over the responsibility of the organization to Kim In Ho. Son died of disease in the prison.

With both Son and Yi gone and other leaders not united, there was no one person able to become leader of the cult, so the form of government was changed from one man leadership (Taitochoo) to committee rule (Chongnichei). In 1924, this again was changed to Choongwichei, i. e., autonomous rule in each of the provinces. In 1926, a National Council was set up, composed of elected delegates from the provinces, and this is now the head of the cult. In each separate group or " church " they have two sets of officers similar to Presbyterian Church elders and deacons, one to have charge of spiritual matters and one for secular matters. They have a Y. M. C. A. Association of *Chuntokyo,* Young Men, and a similar Y. W. C. A. There is a Women's Society, and one for children. The organization has established schools of all grades, and even aspires to found a college. It publishes eight magazines or newspapers, one of which is *Chuntykyo Chaykei Yoram* for children and one for farmers. The members of the original Chuntokyo keep the old-fashioned Chinese lunar calendar. The Sichun Kyo people use the solar calendar.

About 1912, the influence of Protestant Christianity upon the cult became very strong. Chuntokyo churches or halls began to be built everywhere in the villages. Sunday was kept in many places as a day of rest if not as a holy day. The Christians called it Chooil, but the Chuntokyos named it Sungil and the Sichun folks Siil. A hymnbook called the *Palpyunsa* or *Psalter* was formed, largely from the Chinese poems of the founder, Choi Chei Oo, and others of the first leaders. These hymns were mostly sung to Christian tunes, for Korean tunes are most of them not well adapted to congregation singing. The old tune, " Bringing in the Sheaves," seemed to be the most popular with them, as it is also with the Christians. They called their singing Chuntukchung, instead of Chansong, the word used by the Christians.

In the earlier time, women had little place in the cult, and the organization in several places tried to stir up scandals against the Christians because both men and women attended their services. Later, the women began to take an increasing part in the organization, as shown above. A church flag was adopted and run up on a flagpole each Sunday in imitation of the Christian groups who used to indicate Sunday by their flag. Regular organizers began to travel the country.

The Sichun Kyo people particularly began to call their founder " Choi Seichoo," or Choi, the Saviour of the World,[18] and they said that he died for Korea just as Christ died for the foreigners.

The method of financing the organization worked out at an

---

[18] *Korea Magazine,* 1918, p. 165.

early day is unique, but most effective. Each household is required when preparing each meal to set aside in a box from whatever grain the family has to eat, one spoonful for each member of the household. This grain is gathered up twice a year and sent to Seoul.[19] The total gatherings are immense.

Although they use the solar or lunar calendars for the days of the month, and for the months, for the years they have a calendar of their own which dates from the visions of Choi Chei Oo. They call that first year, the year of " Poduk " or Virtue. Nineteen hundred and thirty, therefore, in their calendar becomes the year 69 A. C. " of the Cycle of Choi." In the Orient, time moves in cycles of sixty years, and when a person passes his sixtieth birthday, it is counted a great event, and he begins a new cycle the next day. Ten years ago, in March, 1921, the Chuntokyo organization had a great celebration of their sixtieth year since Choi's visions in Yongdam, and then the Doctrine started on a new cycle of life, vigorous and impelling.

## II. Ceremonies

All of the ceremonies, public and private, of the cult and most of its doctrines centre around that twenty-one character magic Formula which Choi Chei Oo received and made the basis of it all. It reads:

" Chi Keui Keum Chi Wun Wi Tai Kang
Si Chun Chu Cho Hwa Chung
Yung Sei Pool Mang Man Sa Ji."

This has been variously translated by Mr. Junkin[20] and by others,[21] all apparently translating simply the Chinese characters as they stand and not as they are understood by the Chuntokyo men themselves. As nearly as I can judge, they feel it to mean:

" Infinite Energy being now within me, I yearn that it may pour into all living beings and created things.

[19] *Korea Magazine*, 1918, p. 165.
[20] *Ibid.*, p. 161.
[21] *Korean Repository*, 1895, p. 57.

Since this Infinite Energy abides in me, I am identified with
God, and of one nature with all existence.
Should I ever forget these things, all existing things will know
of it."

### 1. Private, Individual Worship

This may be carried on by any member of the cult at any time,
but is particularly enjoined for nine P. M. daily.[22]  No special
paraphernalia is essential, but, if the believer wishes, he may take
cement, clay and stones and erect in the private courtyard of his
home a small altar.[23]  When he worships, he places upon the altar
a bowl of clean water, and then, stepping to the south side of the
altar, bows on his face in the direction across it towards the North
Star, meanwhile repeating the magic Formula.  If he desires, he
may add free petitions to the words of the Formula, but the philosophically initiated do not, for they say, " In Nai Chun," " Man is
God," and so there is no need of petitions.  The Formula puts one
*en rapport* with the Universe, and no more is necessary.

The bowing to the North Star is one element which likely came
from Taoism in China.  One believer told me that the water was
used as a mirror in which the Heavens appeared, and that the
worshipper, as he bowed, looked upon the surface of the water,
and saw " Chun," " The Heavens."  After the worship is completed, the worshipper drinks the water in the bowl, calling it the
" cup of Divine favour."[24]

### 2. Public Worship

In the public worship, the procedure is much the same, the bowl
of water being placed upon the wooden pulpit in the meeting room.
The interior of their churches resembles very much the Christian
churches, with rostrum and pulpit.  Behind the pulpit in the Seoul
cathedral is a great high cabinet containing the tablets of the
Founders.  Most of the buildings are simple halls dedicated to
their purpose.

Whenever the members assemble for a worship-service, as they

---

[22] *Chuntokyo Chaykei Yoram.*
[23] *Korean Repository,* 1895, p. 58.
[24] *Ibid.,* p. 58; *Korea Magazine,* 1918, p. 164.

enter the building, each individual bows first and goes through a ceremony which they call " Yum Chun Yum Sa," " Think Heaven, Think of Matter." They have oral preaching in the services, but never have oral prayer. This silent bowing takes the place of it. It is an adoration of something, but of what it is difficult to say. There is chanting of a hymn or two from the *Palpyunsa,* the leaders often lining it out a line at a time, as they used to do in the Pilgrim Fathers' time, the audience repeating the line as sung. The sermon consists of a ten or fifteen minute address upon some moral subject or an exposition of some of their sacred book. Over and over during the service, they pause and Yum Chun Yum Sa. At the close of the meeting, a number of selected members of the congregation go forward and, dipping up some of the water in the bowl with spoons that are laid beside it, they drink it. The actual worship service is characterized by quite a degree of solemnity.

We have here described the very choicest of their services. As a matter of fact, the customs have had so little time to crystallize and set themselves that one may find a very different service from this in the first church that he visits after reading this. In some places, there is a great deal of confusion and passing in and out and whispering. Sometimes there is no preaching or reading of the sacred books at all. Sometimes there will be a debate rather than a sermon. There are no set rules at all. Usually there is at least relative quiet and reverence during the Yum Chun Yum Sa part of the services.

### 3. Ordination Ceremony

There is no settled priesthood of the cult any more than there used to be in the Confucianism from which Chuntokyo has taken so much of its materials, so there is no special ceremony of ordination for its leaders. At the present time, they are simply elected by the congregation or district which they serve, and drop out when their term of service is over.

### 4. Initiation Ceremony

There is no ceremony corresponding to baptism in the Christian churches. Applicants simply give in their names and are passed upon by the local group. When accepted, they attend a service and perhaps at the end go forward and drink the " cup of Divine favour." Mr. Junkin tells of their being required to bring a feast of fish, bread and wine to the meeting-place, and there repeat in concert the sacred Formula twenty-four times.[25] I have found no record of such a custom, but, as we have said above, there are no fixed rules. After the ceremony, sometimes the new members give a feast to the assembly.

### 5. Special Days

There are three special memorial days when special services are held, the fifth day of the fourth lunar month in memory of Choi Chei Oo and his receiving of the Doctrine. It is called " Chunil," or " Heaven Day." The second is the fourteenth of the eighth month in memory of Choi Hai Wul. This is called " Chiil," or " Earth Day." The third is the twenty-fourth of the twelfth lunar month, and is called " Man Day." The Korean New Year's Day is also a special occasion.

### 6. Rosary

It is interesting to note that the Chuntokyo believers carry a rosary much like that of the Buddhists for the registering of the number of times that they recite the sacred Formula. It has, however, only 105 beads, while the Buddhists have 108.

### III. DOCTRINES OF THE CULT

It is extremely difficult to disengage and isolate the doctrines of the religion. In the first place, the Korean language at the present time is in a state of chaos due to the sudden opening of the country, the control of education by the Japanese, and the sudden influx of new ideas for which there never were any words in old Korea. The great reservoir of Chinese characters is right at hand, and a word can be made instantly for any concept in the mind of man, but the difficulty is that no one may understand the new word and

---

[25] *Korean Repository*, 1895, p. 58.

what it represents except the man who put together that particular combination of Chinese characters. Westerners sometimes find the same difficulty when words are newly made from esoteric Greek or Latin roots.

Secondly, those who write on these matters are not philosophically trained, and hence are unable to express clearly what they do believe. Thirdly, there is no authoritative book or decision of any council that can say the final word for all of the cult. There is the little booklet called the *Chuntokyo Chaykei Yoram*, which purports to give an official statement of their beliefs, and we will quote from that:

"Five Things Required of All Believers.

" *1. Chookmoon, i. e., Repetition of the Sacred Formula*

If this is repeated at all times, the thoughts will be kept clean, and bad thoughts expelled, a realization of the Doctrine will be increased and the mind strengthened. Mind and body will also be brought into harmony. If any one wishes to know the meaning of this Formula, let them read the explanation given by Choi, the ' Water Cloud Teacher.' " (Note—this is one of the honourary names of Choi Chei Oo, and the " Explanation " referred to is that in the Tong Chun Tai Chun, which is translated in full in the Appendix of this book.)

" *2. Chungsoo—Clean Water*

" When the Great Teacher was beheaded at Taiku, he personally gave the clean water as a symbol of his shed blood. Every believer at nine P. M. daily must set out a bowl of clean water. This is the order of the Great Teacher. This clean water is also a symbol of the original elements of Heaven and Earth, so one should use it whenever giving themselves to meditation.

" *3. Sül—Keeping Sunday*

"According to the command of the Great Teacher, all believers should assemble themselves each Sunday in the places of meeting to study the Doctrine, and to learn the mind and purpose of the Great Teacher.

## " 4. Sungmi—Rice Offering

" Every believer must daily set aside his spoonful of rice. This is the fund for the making firm of Heaven and Earth. It is the means of financing the organization and is a sacrifice to Heaven and to Earth.

## " 5. Chisung, or ' Reverencing,' or Prayer, Yum Chun Yum Sa

" It shall be offered daily, and on Sundays formally, and there shall also be particular prayer seasons every year.

## " IV. BASAL DOCTRINAL IDEAS OF CHUNTOKYO

### " 1. In Nai Chun—Man is God. Identity of Man and God

" This may be thought of in two ways, philosophically and practically. As to the first, the words ' In Nai Chun ' express the unity of man and the Universe, i. e., man and the Universe both unitedly reveal the grandeur of God. Secondly, it expresses the greatness of mankind, since man is the summit of evolution in the Universe. It means that one should not make any idols above man, or alongside of man. As man's nature reveals perfectly the nature of the Universe, this shows that man is the ruler and best expression of that Universe.

" Practically, ' In Nai Chun ' reveals the relation between man and man, between man and Matter, and between man and the whole world. As to the first, it shows that, among men, there should be no higher and no lower. As to the second, it shows that there should be no physical objects used as idols by men. One should be interested only in better ethics for men. The principles of In Nai Chun oppose all setting of men in graded classes, and they promote the principles of human liberty.

### " 2. Sungsin Sangchun

" This first word refers to possible psychic changes in man (e. g., reformations) ; the second refers to social movements. If these things are perfect, all is perfect. As man identifies himself with Heaven (In Nai Chun), this perfection is brought about. At present, there are many imperfections both in nature and in society, but all of these may be corrected by a realization of In Nai Chun, that man is one with God.

### " 3. Chi Sang Chun Kook

" We should strive to make this earth a heaven. This is the highest objective of In Nai Chun. To bring this about, three things are required:

" (1) Men's thoughts must be changed. This involves a casting out of evil, a reorienting of minds and changes in social situations. Those entering the Chuntokyo must begin to think in a way different from ordinary men. They must put away evil thoughts and old habits, and go back to their original nature, begin to study and think straight. It is difficult to mention all of the things included in bad habits. They include, of course, in the realm of religion, all superstitions and idol worship; in the realm of ethics, all foolish and selfish thoughts. Our Great Teacher, when he first began to preach, wrote out the motto, ' Yung Poo Sung,' ' Keep the Spirit Always Holy,' and, through the contemplation of that, he changed his whole nature.

" (2) Civil changes must be brought about. Before one can look for these, there must be changes in the human spirit. There must be a widening of interests and a sympathy for all the peoples of the world.

" (3) Social changes must be brought about. These grow out of the previous two. Social changes of the right sort bring about everlasting peace for society and goodwill to everyone outside. Our Great Teacher spoke of these social changes as the last step in the establishing of paradise on earth.

### "V. CHUNTOKYO TEACHING

#### " 1. Relation of the Chuntokyo to Religion in General

" Some say that Chuntokyo is a religion, and some that it is only an imitation of one; some say that it is simply a method of thinking. There is no clear decision on the matter. The Chuntokyo does not concern itself with a future world, but only with this world. Externally, its activities have been more with matters of government of the country than with morals, so that some people say that it is not a spiritual religion. Others say that it is one. Today religions in general do not seem to concern themselves with all of life. They confine themselves simply to man's hidden emotional life, and so religion has become largely divorced from morals, civilization, government and economics. Civilization is a visible thing, but religion is hidden. If one thinks of religion as an affair of the inner life only, Chuntokyo is not a religion. In that case, one might call Chuntokyo simply the ' Modern Thought of Korea.' However, a judgment like this is unfair, for it judges Chuntokyo by the modern instances of religion as to whether it is simply an inner, hidden thing, and does not judge by the original meaning of the word ' religion.' In the beginning, religion did not concern itself with just a few matters, as it now does, but it included all life. The religion of today is a matter of the last two thousand years only. Before that time, government, civilization, etc., were not separate things. Religion included them all. In that age, all civilization was a part of religion.

" Jesus, Confucius, Mohammed, Buddha and like persons may be thought of not only as founders of religions but as founders of civilizations. All of our religious teaching came about originally, not for the sake of religion but for the sake of civilization. During the last two thousand years, as science has spread knowledge abroad, gradually religion has become divorced from life and it has become a separate thing. Therefore today we speak of one thing, and say that that is religion. Of another thing we say, that is not religion. Chuntokyo should be judged by the definitions of religion which were current two thousand years ago. It arose to incorporate in itself all of the good movements of the day. If it does not represent those matters fairly, it has no value whatever in the world. In olden times, religion arose to make changes in men. It was for the same purpose that Chuntokyo was founded. For that reason, one may fittingly call it not ' New Thought ' merely, but ' New Religion.' Religion and civilization now seem to stand apart from one another. Chuntokyo is not that sort of a religion. Whenever religion includes all of civilization, it may be called a real religion. Chuntokyo does that, so there is no special value in debating whether it should be given the name of a religion or not.

## " 2. Relation of the Chuntokyo to Thinking

" The word ' thought ' includes so much that it is difficult to say anything about it. The thoughts of the Chuntokyo are the thoughts of Choi Soo Oon, the Master. What were his thoughts? As he pondered over the sad situation of the people, the thought that came to him was a patriotic one, how he might help his people. He asked himself, ' How may I find a means to make the nation safe and the people peaceful? ' and ' You poor dying people, how may you be kept in safety? ' As to the time after he received his revelations, his thoughts were busy not only with his own people, but with the peoples of all the world. This is the thing of which we spoke a moment ago—changes of the spirit of men and changes in society. The Master asked himself, ' Can the whole world thus be changed? If it can, we may have Paradise right here upon the earth.'

" The Master said, ' When the Spring comes, we shall see these things drawing nigh (therefore the Chuntokyo looks forward to each Springtime hoping that the time will be then). The Teacher said, 'At that time, men will be made good, not by law, but by virtue. At that time, even my Doctrine will be unnecessary. It will be practised as a matter of course.' Briefly, then, the message of the Master is that subjectively there must be a change in men, and then that objectively there will come a change in society, and in all the world. Through virtue, all the world will be changed.

## " 3. All Things Come from One Source

" Many people ask, ' Did the Great Teacher say that spirit is supreme or Matter supreme? ' It is a very difficult question to answer. He does not use either expression. He simply says that all things come from one source, and this source is described in the Formula—Chi Keui, ' Infinite or Cosmic Energy.' ' Chi ' means Infinite, ' Keui ' means Emptiness, or All Power. One may say that Chi Keui seems to imply something like matter, but that is not clear. He really seems to mean both spirit and matter with the one word. ' Keui ' seems to imply something material, but it also implies the idea of ' Emptiness,' which is something like spirit. Therefore the phrase ' Chi Keui ' represents both spirit and matter as a matter of fact. They are not two, but one. There is nothing that exists apart from them. Everything goes back to one source. At first we had neither matter nor spirit, but something behind both, the original source of all. This original source we can only know by instinct or by intuition."

So much for their own statement of their faith. Some of the sentences are not very lucid, but they are fully as lucid as the original.

In the *Bookman Magazine* for June, 1924, Mr. W. C. Kerr has given a translation of an article in the Chuntokyo magazine *Kai-pyuck,* an article written by a Chuntokyo believer as a statement of their beliefs. It runs as follows:

" 1. In Nai Chun—pantheistic monotheism.

" 2. Heaven here on earth, not in a future world.

" 3. Punishments and rewards according to a man's actions.

" 4. The Universe a product of evolution.

" 5. There can be no distinction of good and bad in man, for man is himself Chun, or Heaven.

" 6. This world is a theocracy in which the man-god creates his own perfect happiness.

" 7. Self-achievement through self-effacement.

" 8. Progress is through alternate stress and relaxation.

" 9. The future should consist in a gradual making of this world a better place to live in.

" 10. Resurrection is spiritual and in this world.

" 11. There should be a love which serves men as it serves God."

The above two statements are probably as accurate and authoritative as any that could be found anywhere else. Added to the Bible of the cult given in the Appendix of this book, they give at least a general idea of what they teach.

Mr. Kerr has characterized " In Nai Chun " as implying pantheistic monotheism. That seems about to express it. They talk freely at all times of Chun Chu and of Hananim and seem to imply a personal God in almost the same way that the Christians do. The actual words " Chun Chu " come in the second line of the magic Formula. They say that Chun Chu sends the harvest, that He rules all things, etc., but, if one asks them if this Chun Chu is a personal God as the Christians conceive Him to be, they immediately draw back and deny it, saying that Chun Chu has no personality, and that they are one with Chun Chu, that Chun Chu is just one element in a continuous entity, the Universe.

The first two words in the magic Formula seem to be the most important of all. If we knew clearly what " Chi Keui " means, the rest might perhaps be easier. It seems to mean " Infinite Force " or " Cosmic Energy." One wonders if that old philosopher of Yongdam did evolve a conception as broad as that all through his own mentality, a conception so similar to those that have been busying Western philosophers during the recent decades. Nowadays one always suspects that ideas of this sort have been brought back from abroad by returning students, but Korea had no touch with the outside world in 1860, and " Chi Keui " is quite fully explained in the Tong Chun Tai Chun Bible. However they may have gotten it, it seems to be the " Cosmic Urge," the " Spirit of Life in the Universe," the " Elan Vital " of Bergson, or something of that general class, something that seems to satisfy the hearts of their believers as they Yum Chun Yum Sa in their services, something that makes the devout ones among them each night at nine o'clock set out the bowl of water and bow in secret devotion.

The translation of the magic Formula given above would seem to indicate almost ordinary pantheism, but the Chuntokyo people always deny that. Infinite or Cosmic Energy does flow through everything, and yet Chun Chu is a real living entity in it, as man is. One cannot help but feel that Chun Chu's actual place in it all is a lot more important than even the Chuntokyo leaders realize. The philosophically initiated may concentrate upon Chi Keui, Infinite Emptiness or Cosmic Energy, when they Yum Chun Yum Sa, but one wonders if the ordinary believer's thoughts go farther than semi-personal Chun Chu or Hananim whom their fathers have known since Tangoon's time. Probably pantheistic monotheism is the best characterization that we can get for it.

As to their other doctrines, they have been fairly clearly indicated in the quotations given.

They state that they have no distinction of good and bad in

man, that is, no doctrine of sin, because man is identified with God, and so there is no transcendent Being to set standards and apply them objectively. The good in man is God, but so is the evil in man, God. God cannot be at odds with Himself. The theory of this cannot be attacked, but in the first quotation above we can see that practically they do recognize the distinction of good and evil, and, even in the second quotation, they speak of rewards and punishments awarded according to men's actions.

They repudiate a belief in any future world, or at least they have no doctrine of punishments there. They call death, " Hwan-wun," or a " falling back " of the spirit of man. They deny the idea of the transmigration of souls, but are not very clear as to exactly what they do believe as to the state of the dead. As they explain it, it sounds a bit like the idea promulgated by Nagarjuna the Buddhist at about the time of Christ, the so-called " Madhy-amika " explanation of how the soul exists. He taught that the soul after death might be said to exist, or not to exist, according to the manner in which one looked at it. The soul of an individ-ual is like a wave on the surface of the sea. It has apparent exis-tence for a moment, and then disappears in the body of the ocean once more.[26]

They have no doctrine of the atonement, although, to counteract the teaching of the Christians, they speak of Choi Chei Oo as the " Saviour," " Choi Sei Choo," and, in the " Five Things Required " above, they speak of the water as the " symbol of his blood." Those things are probably both imitations of Christian teaching, and not parts of Chuntokyo. Simply turning over a new leaf and starting a new, clean line of living is all that they feel to be neces-sary. The past will care for its own mistakes. Future good be-haviour is more important than sorrow for past sin.

They repudiate all images with the exception of the ancestral tablets of their parents and the Founders of the cult, and even as to those, they claim that they do not offer " Cheisa " as do the Confucianists. They say that they simply " Chisung," i. e., " rev-erence " the tablets. They repudiate all of the superstitious prac-

---

[26] Lloyd, *Creed of Half Japan*, p. 109.

tices of the Shamanistic worship, and refuse to take any part in the village worship on the hills.

We have spoken of the Koreans' cosmological idea of Whanin, Whanung and Tangoon, as the first founders and creators of the world. They also all know the ancient Taoist idea of China of the great giant, Panku, who was supposed to have carved out this world and started it going.[27] He is supposed to have laboured for some 18,000 years. After him came three mythical dynasties which also reigned each for 18,000 years. In the first of these, the Chun Wang, or Heavenly Kings, were twelve " brothers " who seem to have reigned consecutively; in the second the Chi Wang, or Earth Kings, eleven brothers, ruled; and in the third, the In-wang with nine brothers sat on the throne. The ancient Tong Kook Tong Kam book has this story.

The Chuntokyo early laid hands upon this legend, and, in order to get hold of " sanctions " for their cult, they taught that, at the very end of the above 54,000 years of the three royal periods as above, Choi Chei Oo had his visions in Yongdam, and that at that time he ushered in another period also of 54,000 years. Following the analogy of that cosmology, therefore, Choi Chei Oo was always called by them " Chun Wang," or Ruler of the Universe; Choi Si Hyung, his successor, was called " Chi Wang," or Ruler of all the Earth; while Son Pyung Heui was given the name of " In Wang," or Ruler of all Humanity. In addition to these names, others were given which at least point toward Divine honours being given them. Choi Chei Oo, The Dragon Pool Teacher, was called sometimes " Soo Oon," or " Water Cloud." This name was given to one of Whanung's ministers in the Tangoon story.[28] Choi Si Hyung was almost always called " Hai Wul," or the " Ocean Moon " Teacher, while Son Pyung Heui was " Wiam," the " Righteous House," " Sungchoo," " Holy Master," or " Tai To Choo," the " Great Doctrine Teacher." No doubt the use of these semi-Divine names and the cosmological setting given to the cult were very helpful in giving it standing. One wonders what will happen now when those things are gone. Possibly the psycho-

---

[27] Hawks-Potts, *A Sketch of Chinese History*, p. 7.
[28] Hulbert, *History of Korea*, I, p. 1.

logical " fallacy of the absent " may work out, however, and the cult be stronger in the absence of the living teachers than it was when they were present, but could not always be standing on their pedestals.

It is interesting to note that the modern Buddhists in their college in Seoul are also teaching the doctrine of In Nai Chun, and a group of them whom I met at the Haiinsa Monastery wanted to debate with me the truth of the teaching. They used to have a similar phrase of their own, " Sim Cheuk Pool," " Mind is Buddha," but they seem more interested now to prove In Nai Chun.

It is quite easy to see that what Choi Chei Oo has achieved is more or less of a synthetic cult. A Chuntokyo friend said to me, " Our religion is a combination of Yoo Pool Sun Sin (i. e., of Confucianism, Buddhism and Taoism). Choi Chei Oo received his great vision when visiting the Yoochumsa temple, and came to realize that the three religions were one." Another friend said, " The essence of Choi Chei Oo's great vision was that he sat down a long time in meditation as Buddha did under the Bodhi tree, and suddenly he came to enlightenment when in a flash he grasped the truth of In Nai Chun."

There are twenty-one beads in one of the Buddhist rosaries and twenty-one characters in the magic Formula which tradition says was first found by the Buddhist priest. Note the repetitions of the number twenty-one in the Rosary Classic in Appendix III. That may have been coincidence, but the very fact that the Chuntokyo believers use a rosary at all shows some borrowing from Buddhism. Both Taiseiji and Kwanseieum of the Buddha images carry vases of the " Dew of Divine Favour," and they may quite possibly have suggested the name for the " cup of Divine favour " of Chuntokyo. The Taoists all make much of the North Star Constellation and the Buddhists borrowed the idea, and Chuntokyo seems to have followed it. The name " Chun Chu " for God they perhaps borrowed from the Roman Catholics, and possibly also their idea of a monotheistic God as far as they have such an idea. Even Shamanism and the degraded Buddhism seem to have contributed to Chuntokyo their doctrine of charms and talismans. There is little doubt, however, that their greatest debt is to Confucianism

as interpreted by Chuja and his school.    Probably this is the only
element which they would willingly acknowledge as borrowed.    As
a matter of fact, they probably would not even acknowledge that,
for a part of their stock in trade has been their boast that theirs is
a purely native religion, purely Korean, and not at all borrowed
from anywhere.    It is said that even their pet phrase, In Nai Chun,
was first used by Chuja to justify his materialistic interpretation
of the Universe.

### IV. Estimate of the Cult

One cannot help but admire the organization a little as the
product of Korean genius, albeit made largely of borrowed materials.    In its short career of only seventy years, it has had a
most varied history, not unlike that of the Christian Church down
the ages.    It has endured persecutions even unto death, and has
helped to cause some persecution in places where it was in a position to hector Christians or other cults.    It has had its martyrdoms
of every type.    It has built up a library of sacred books, and a
voluminous other literature filled with a most interesting philosophical view of the constitution of the Universe.    Probably it
may have had at one time even a million of the two million adherents with which the recent newspaper article credits it.    There
must be something in a movement that can win the interest and
hold the financial and moral support of a million people of any
class.    There is little doubt that they have even today a couple of
hundred thousand nominal adherents.

Whether the cult will continue to live and grow, of course, remains a question.    The element of divinity and mystery which
surrounded the first three Masters has been taken away.    Patriotic movements are not looked upon with favour by the existing
government.    Political offices on a very limited scale are open to
Koreans.    It would look as though there were relatively few
physical benefits which one could hope for as a member of the
cult, and it frankly states that it is not primarily interested in
" hidden religion."    Will the religious aspects alone of the cult
hold its people when all of the other benefits pass away?

The emphasis upon Chun Chu and Hananim in the cult cannot

help but prepare the believers for passing over into the Christian Church if the cult ever should pass away, for those are the words used by the Christians to describe their personal God. The words are the same, but, into his words, the Christian has brought all of the warm, rich, comforting content of the Christian's Father God idea while the Chuntokyo brother at best deals with elusive concepts and abstractions. One wonders if the richer concept will not conquer and drive out the abstract one. Already in the last two decades hundreds of Chuntokyo people have crossed over to the churches. I have never yet heard of any one crossing the other way.

An interesting incident in this connection happened at the time of the Independence Movement of 1919, while I was living in Seoul and was pastor there of the Central Presbyterian Church.

Most of the leaders of the Chuntokyo were then in gaol, including Son Pyung Heui himself and some thousands of his people and of other leaders of the nation. Rumours were rife that the whole Chuntokyo organization was going to be suppressed by the Government because of its political activities.

One Sunday morning a young Korean Christian, graduate of a famous American university, came to see me and said that he had been asked by certain leading members of the Chuntokyo to sound out some of the missionaries on the possibility of combining the Chuntokyo organization and the Christian Church. He asked what I thought of it, and I told him that I thought that it would be a wonderful thing for them and for us, if they adjusted themselves to the requirements of our Church and came in. He said that that was just the point, that they were all good members in good standing in their own organization, that they were willing to consider joining in a body with us, but that they were unwilling to enter as raw new believers, and pass one by one through probation, and have to make a public confession of sin, professions of faith, etc. He asked if it would not be possible for us to waive our rigid entrance requirements in view of the unprecedented opportunity, and take them all in as a group. I called his attention to the fact that certain of their leaders were said to have plural wives, and that our Church could not endorse that; that many of them were drinking men, and none of them had repented of any sins or changed their lives, that they had no knowledge whatsoever of Christian doctrine, and that the very mass of them coming over would determine the future character of the Church and ruin every single thing for which the Christian Church stood.

The young man was unconvinced, and urged me to talk with some of the leaders of the General Assembly of the Church, which was then in session. I have no doubt also that he talked with many leading Koreans also, but I heard nothing further of the matter, so judge that he met an *impasse* everywhere and gave the matter up. Whether in the first place those who had approached him had any right to speak for the Chuntokyo or not I do not know, but at least the incident was a diverting one.

Many have crossed over as individuals into the Christian Church, but there are a number of factors which will no doubt operate for a long time to prevent any wholesale crossing. The leaders of the organization are able men and will hold their people as long as they can. First of all, as has been noted, the movement is pressed as a purely native, Korean one, whereas every other religion in the country except the degraded Shamanism, they say, is imported. They tell their people that as patriots they must be true to Chuntokyo.

The organization prides itself upon its participation in "social movements," as it says in the Chaykei Yoram, and then mentions dates which indicate that it means "political" ones. In the peculiar situation in Korea today this appeal is not without cogency. The Christians are patriotic also, but the Church, as an organization, has held strongly aloof from political movements and takes no part in any of them.

Koreans, with their Shamanistic ancestry, have always clung to such things as charms and talismans, and they have delighted to find magical methods for circumventing the spirits which cause sickness. The sacred Formulæ of Chuntokyo appeal to Korean psychology.

Not the least reason for their holding aloof are the strict rules for entrance into the Christian Church, far more rigid than those required for Western churches. The Chuntokyo is not so hard upon human frailty. If a man drinks, or has a secondary wife, they do not particularly praise him for it, but they live and let live, and say nothing about it, where men of that type cannot even be catechumens in the Christian Church without complete repentance.

Chuntokyo is just another brave but pathetic effort of the human spirit by its own outreach of reason trying to find its God. As compared with the Shamanism or even the Buddhism of Korea, it has gone a long distance on its way. It has found Omnipotence and Omniscience and Omnipresence, and a sort of a will-o'-the-wisp phantom shadow of God. One would be ungracious if he withheld a tribute of admiration for what they have attained. How much help Choi Chei Oo received from philosophical books of China we cannot know. In any event, he seems to have been a man of whom any nation could be proud. One only regrets that when that spirit " Sangchei " spoke to him, he did not fully accept the Being in the Christian conception of God and give his full allegiance to Him. Chun Chu and Hananim and Sangchei are all one and the same Person, God, and his followers would no doubt have accepted the personal Chun Chu as quickly as they did this attenuated one. What the future of Chuntokyo will be, no one knows. Possibly it depends upon the future of the Christian Church. The magic Formula will perhaps lose its power in this scientific age, especially now that the Masters are gone. If the Christian Church can put content into those words, " Chun Chu," in that Formula by making its own concept of God so vivid throughout the land that any one thinking those syllables must inevitably think of the personal God, Chuntokyo's inadequacy will become evident even to passersby and it will be sloughed off and forgotten. That is the hope of the coming generation.

# VI

## SHAMANISM

THE *Encyclopædia of Religion and Ethics* defines Shamanism as follows: "It is a primitive religion of polytheism or polydemonism with strong roots in nature worship, and generally with a supreme god over all. While the Shaman exercises certain priestly functions, his main powers are connected with healing and divination. These he exercises by virtue of his intimate relation with the supernatural world. Certain spirits aid him, possess him, are at his command. He has direct intercourse with spirits, and actual (bodily or spiritual) access to the spirit world. With the aid of these, he obtains knowledge superior to that of the ordinary man, and can drive out hostile spirits or powers and generally during the exercise of his powers, the altered mental state of the Shaman is in evidence.

"Through auto-hypnotism caused by different methods, a state of trance or alternate personality is produced. He becomes a mediator between gods and spirits on the one hand and men on the other. He knows the secrets of the gods and spirits, often malevolent, and the wellbeing of all depends upon his power to cajole or overcome them by various actions, rites or sacrifices. By these he can enlist the services of spirits. Among the Yakuts, a Shaman has a guardian spirit, or the spirit of some dead Shaman, who aids and advises him. In other cases, he may have many spirits under his control, and the more he has the more powerful he is."[1]

The author of that article was writing from the standpoint of Siberian Shamanism, and knew absolutely nothing of Korean Shamanism, but, with just a few tiny exceptions, this is an exact picture of what is found in Korea today.

---

[1] Article " Shamanism."

Banzaroff says, " Careful study of the subject shows that the Shamanistic religion did not arise out of Buddhism or any other religion, but originated among the Mongolic nations, and consists not only in superstitions and Shamanistic ceremonies, but in a certain primitive way of observing the outer world, Nature, and the inner world, the soul."[2]

The *Encyclopædia of Religion and Ethics* further says, " The word Shaman appears to be derived from a native Tungus name for priest, ' saman,' used also among the Buriats and Yakuts. Saman has been thought to be an adaptation of the Pali word Samana (Sanscrit—Shramana), a Buddhist monk, or mendicant, through the Chinese, but evidence is lacking. Still less likely is it a derivative from the Persian word Shamen, an idol or temple. The Tungus word, saman, means ' one who is excited, moved, raised.' "[3]  Klemutz, in the *Encyclopædia* article on " Buriat," says that the word is not now used by any one in Siberia, but he quotes Banzaroff as authority for its having been used in the seventh century. The word has never been used in Korea, although the thing is here. The Koreans call the whole cult of Shamanism simply Sinkyo, Spirit worship.

Shamanism is found in essence in other parts of the world, as, for example, in the case of the voodoo doctors in Africa and in the witch doctors of Ceylon, but it is more particularly the form of religion or religio-magic practised by the aborigines of northern Asia, in a strip of territory extending from the Baltic straight across to and including Alaska, and extending from the Arctic regions down into Manchuria and Mongolia and to the Ainus in Japan.[4] Along these southern fringes, of course, there have been profound modifications caused by contact with the more developed religions such as Buddhism, Confucianism and Taoism, and the influence has been to some extent reciprocal, for it is said that in Mongolia the Buddhist priests have been compelled to learn to Shamanize, and we have already seen the same in the case of the Buddhism of Korea.

---

[2] *Black Faith*, pp. 4, 5.
[3] Article " Shamanism;" Underwood, *Religions of Eastern Asia*, p. 93.
[4] Czaplicka, *Aboriginal Siberia*, p. 166.

The Shamanism of Korea is without doubt a product of those contacts. Its original basis far antedates the coming into Korea of any of the great religions which we have discussed. It has been enriched and modified by the spirit worship of Taoism and many things taken from Buddhism. In 1901, Hulbert said, " The native demonology of Korea united with Buddhism and formed a composite religion that can hardly be called one or the other, but running through it all, we can see the underlying Buddhistic fabric, with its four fundamentals—mysticism, fatalism, pessimism and quietism." [5] I think that he has much too strongly emphasized the effect of Buddhism, but endorse his general idea of the combination that has taken place.

The original home of the Koreans is said to have been up in the Amur Valley in Siberia.[6] Their language clearly belongs to the Turanian group.[7] They came very early under the influence of China, and, since 1122 b. c., probably have had more contacts westward with China than directly northward to their ancestral home. Still this great underlying belief in spirits, once acquired, seems to cling in the very blood of a people and persist through all changes of civilization and exterior religion. The Confucianists, even after Chuja, with all their contempt of the spiritual world, could never abolish the belief in Kwei and Shen, and their own selves believed in, and at times offered sacrifices to, the Dragon spirit. Burmah claims to be all Buddhist through and through, yet the belief in the Nats persists and has almost more power than Buddhism itself. The inner urge to Shamanize did not die when the higher religions came into the country, and we shall see, as we go along, the many points of similarity, at least, between the Shamanism of Korea and that of their northern ancestral home.

## I. History of the Cult in Korea

We have taken it for granted above that there is a history of the direct connection of Korean Shamanism with that of Siberia, but there is little in the way of written records to prove it.

[5] Royal Asiatic Society Records, 1901, p. 39.
[6] Griffis, The Hermit Nation, p. 19.
[7] Annual Report Administration of Chosen, 1926-7, p. 6.

Jones believed that Tangoon, the founder of Korea, in 2332 B. C., was simply a great Shaman,[8] and that his worship on the great altar on Kanghwa was simply a Shamanistic performance. I do not believe it, for the whole atmosphere of every account given of it, and of every reference made to it in Korean literature breathes a vastly different spirit. He rightly says that Korea had its own demon worship long before its first contacts with China and did not need to go there to get it. He notes that the Chinese ideograph for " spirit " or " ghost " in Korea is fully as old as the ideographs for " heaven " or for " God."

The oldest Korean histories state that Ye Kook, one of the primitive peoples in the province of Kangwon directly east of Seoul, near the Japan Sea, " worshipped the heavens in the tenth month of each year " and also that they " worshipped the tiger spirit." [9] Of the Okju, another primitive people, it says, " The dead were buried and left until their bones only remained, after which they were dug up and the bones were placed in a hollow tree. Beside the tree, an image of the person was set up," presumably to be worshipped. This custom has some resemblances to the Buriat ceremony and others in Siberia.[10] Of the Fuyu people, just across the border in Manchuria, possibly one of the races from which the Korean people came, it is said, " They sacrificed to Heaven, to the spirits of the land, to the morning star, and to the celestial and invisible powers." [11]

In our discussion of Confucianism, we noticed in the story of Keuija's coming to Korea in 1122 B. C., that he " brought sorcery and incantation." This was probably the first injection of Chinese influence into the aboriginal Shamanism. Down through history, the cult continued to develop under the influence of those two strains. The history states that in 773 B. C., there was one king who " forbade sorcery and incantation." [12]

Edkins says, " The Han, or genuine Koreans of the third cen-

[8] *Royal Asiatic Society Records*, 1900, pp. 35-41.
[9] Hulbert, *History of Korea*, I, pp. 21, 23; *Korean Repository*, 1892, p. 200.
[10] Czaplicka, *Aboriginal Siberia*, p. 157; Ross, *Corea: Its History, Customs and Manners*, p. 19.
[11] Griffis, *The Hermit Nation*, p. 24.
[12] Hulbert, *History of Korea*, I, p. 11.

tury after Christ, are described (in Chinese literature) as worshipping the spirits in the fifth and tenth months when the sowing and reaping of the year were concluded. On such occasions, they sang, danced, and drank wine. Several tens of them took part in the dance, and their hands and feet kept time carefully. One particular person was set apart to sacrifice to the spirit of heaven, and he was called the ' Heavenly Ruler.' " [13]  " Magic and divination of the Koreans is said to have followed the teachings of Wun Chang Kang, an ancient Chinese sorcerer." [14]  Of course, this could refer only to that strain which came from the West, not that which came from their original home in Siberia.

The histories state that in 618 A. D., the Emperor of the Tang Dynasty in China sent " Shinto " books to Korea. [15]  These, of course, were not books like those of Japanese Shinto. The Koreans never had that. In 1409 A. D., in the authentic histories of that date, we read that at one time all sorcerers and sorceresses and geomancers were required to send in their books to be burned. [16] In 1472, such persons were all driven out of the capital city. [17]  This ebullition of virtue was, of course, due to the re-adoption of Confucianism at about that time as the state cult of the Yi Dynasty. No doubt the Shamans crept back little by little again, as they always have done.

The wife of the last real king of the Yi Dynasty, Queen Min, probably raised the cult to the highest place of glory which it ever enjoyed, for she was supremely devoted to it, and brought Shamans right into the palace itself. She tried to organize the cult of the whole nation under one centralized control. She elevated her favourite sorceress, Yi Chi Yong, to the rank of Princess, and tried to force grave old Confucian statesmen to do her reverence. [18] When the Queen was murdered by the Japanese in 1895, all of this came to an abrupt end. The whole cult was cleared out of the

---

[13] *Korean Repository*, 1892, p. 200.
[14] *Royal Asiatic Society Records*, 1900, p. 18.
[15] Hulbert, *History of Korea*, I, p. 92.
[16] Hulbert, *History of Korea*, I, p. 302.
[17] *Ibid.*, p. 319.
[18] *Ibid.*, Vol. II, p. 248; Bishop, *Korea and Her Neighbours*, p. 402.

palace, and has gone back to its old status as an individual, more or less secret, anti-social affair.

## II. Importance of the Cult

Hulbert said in 1900, " The religion of the vast majority of the Korean people consists of a perfunctory acceptance of Confucianism and its teachings, and a vital clinging to the immemorial fetichism, the latter being modified by the Indian Buddhist philosophy." [19]

W. M. Clark, in 1925, wrote, " Today it may be safely said that this Shamanism is the strongest power, from a religious point of view, in Korea." [20]

Similar testimony could be brought from numerous writers who have lived between these dates. Confucianism was the religion of state and, as such, a charge upon the national revenues. Buddhism throughout Korea's history was a state cult or a semi-state cult. Shamanism has been often condemned publicly, as noted above, and has always been despised by the literati, and more or less shamefacedly practised by everyone, yet it has had more vitality than them all.

Jones says, " Shamanism has absorbed from the other two cults (Confucianism and Buddhism) nearly everything of a supernatural character which they possessed." [21] Confucianism has its belief in spirit dragons, in Kwei and Shen spirits, in the spirits of the winds, the hills and the rivers. Korean Shamanism, by affinity, took them over, so that it was always difficult to decide whether those paying attention to these entities and ideas were acting as Confucianists, or believers of the Shamanistic cult. Shamanism took away from Buddhism most of that accretion of magic, of charm-making, crystal-gazing, dream interpretation and the like which it had taken over from the degraded Taoism of China. Shamanism even adopted many of the magical dharani prayer sentences invented by the Buddhist community in Thibet, and it uses them freely in its incantations, although the Shamans never

---

[19] Royal Asiatic Society Records, 1900, p. 41.
[20] Korea Mission Field Magazine, 1925, p. 79.
[21] Royal Asiatic Society Records, 1901, p. 39.

visit or have anything to do with the worship in the regular Buddhist temples.

The cult was despised and considered only fit for the most ignorant of the people and for women, but it was always a power among the common people, and it is still a power today. In 1900, Gifford said, " It is estimated that demon worship costs the people of Korea two million five hundred thousand dollars a year." [28]

### III. BUILDINGS

Of the buildings, Moose says,[29] " Spirit worship builds no temples. It is contented with its fetiches and shrines, which are to be found everywhere throughout the country." This is true. There are no great temples like those of the Buddhists, and nothing like the Haingkyo temples of Confucius. On the outskirts of every village, or on a nearby hilltop, there will be a tiny shrine, varying from a two-foot cube to a building sometimes eight feet square. The "koot" ceremonies are held outside the shrines, not in them. In Seoul, the deserted "Kooksa Dang," "National Spirit Shrine," on the South Mountain, is a building that might take in fifty people, and the shrine just over the Peking Pass, the one inside the Cha Moon, and the one that used to stand outside the South Gate along the side of the wall would each accommodate thirty or so. No such congregations ever gathered there, however. Most of the Koot ceremonies were private affairs, just for an individual or a household or, at most, a half-dozen households in a single village. Not only so, these ceremonies were in the great majority of cases held in the homes of the believers, and not at these small shrines. The Shamans and Shamanesses used the public shrines more as practice places, or for Koots which, for any reason, could not be held in the private homes.

There were communal services of worship to the gods of the mountains, etc., and sometimes hundreds of people gathered for those, but they were always on the mountain-top in the open air. There were no stated meetings of any sort anywhere, and so no assembly buildings were needed.

[28] *Every Day Life in Korea*, p. 107.
[29] *Village Life in Korea*, p. 191.

Inside of the smaller shrines, there was never anything more than a hideous, grotesque daub of a picture in bright yellow and red colours, representing the spirit, or else just a wooden tablet bearing his name. In the Kooksa Dang, National Shrine, in Seoul, there is a row of somewhat better pictures extending the full length of the wall, conspicuous among them being one of Choi Il Taichang, the " God of War " mentioned above, and one of the Old Man Spirit of the Mountain, seated, as usual, upon a tiger. In the other Seoul shrines, in some cases, there are single images of some one of the Buddhas. There is one on the South Mountain in a building just below the National Shrine. In the other places, practically all have wall charts with decorative panels hanging all around the wall bearing such names as Suk Wang, *i. e.,* Sakra of India; of Hojo, the spirit of smallpox; of the spirits of women who have died in childbirth, of men who have been devoured by tigers, of deceased blind sorcerers and sorceresses, etc. Back in the past ages, there was one king of Korea who conceived the idea that his son, the Crown Prince, was plotting against him, so he ordered a coffin made, and placed it before his throne. Then he called his son, and ordered him to lie down in it. The son obeyed. The King ordered the coffin lid nailed down Everyone thought that he was simply trying to frighten the son, but he was in earnest. The son suffocated in the coffin and then was taken out and buried. His spirit, called " Tooji Tai Wang," the Coffin King, is supplicated near Seoul more than almost any other.

The above are the spirits mentioned in shrines near Seoul. In other parts of the country, others are mentioned, as, for example; down near Kyungju, they call upon the name of one of their earlier kings who is said to have been powerful enough to turn the course of the river in front of that city and send it down another valley to the sea.

When Koots are held in private homes, usually a large tent or awning is set up over the courtyard of the patient's home, forming a temporary temple just for the occasion.

Beside the hilltip and mountain-pass shrines, there are sacred pillars of wood or stone, and usually an old gnarled tree and a pile of pebbles. These are a part of the physical properties of the cult, but we will speak of them later in another connection.

We have already spoken of the dolmens which may have had something to do with Shamanism. Whether they were altars or graves, no one knows. We do know that, in connection with geomancy, they are sometimes deliberately set up in order to control the Fungsui of places, to shunt off evil influences which might run down certain mountain backbone ridges into villages where people live.[24] We have mentioned below how the monk, Tosun, earned the eternal gratitude of the people of Choongchung Province by placing such a dolmen. We have also mentioned above the great stone face Miryucks on the mountain sides and suggested that, although today the Buddhists have laid hold of them to represent Miryuck, the Coming Messiah Buddha, quite probably they originally belonged to the animistic or Shamanistic cult.[25]

### IV. TYPES OF SHAMANS

In Siberia, there are various classifications of Shamans,[26] e. g., the Family Shamans who serve only on accasion either in their own households, or in the communal rites of the villages, and the Professional ones, who do nothing else; then the Black Shamans, who do their work with the help of the evil spirits, and the White, who cultivate the good; then the Great, the Middling and the Little Shamans; the male and the female Shamans, etc.

In Korea, there seem to be family Shamans, although of less permanence of function than those in Siberia, and there are also large numbers of the Professional ones. There are no classes definitely called Black and White, although there are individuals who seek to prevail over the spirits by cultivating the evil ones and those who prefer to cultivate the good. The blind men seem to do the latter.

There are three unquestioned classes of Shamans in Korea, the Mootangs, the Paksoos (who are men but do the identically same work as the Mootangs) and the Pansoos, or blind Diviners. Then

---

[24] Underwood, *Religions of Eastern Asia*, p. 102.
[25] Hulbert, *Passing of Korea*, p. 296.
[26] Czaplicka, *Aboriginal Siberia*, p. 191 f.

there are the non-professional village temporary Shamans, also
the Chikwan, or Geomancers, and the Ilkwan, or selectors of favourable days. This last class is doubtful. There is a class of
blind women fortune-tellers also, called Yubok. They do not hold
Koots like the Mootangs.[27]

A. Of these various classes, the evidence indicates that the
Mootangs and Paksoos are directly due to the Siberian tradition,
and the other classes seem to be more the result of the inheritance
and influences from China. We will discuss, therefore, the first
two classes first.

Troshchanski believes that the original Shamans of Siberia were
women, and that the men only took up the vocation much later.[28]
He thinks that these men were originally the smiths who made the
magical iron ornaments which hang upon the sorceress's robe. In
Siberia, there are far more women Shamans than men. As proof
that the original Shamans were women, the following is adduced:

1. On the Yakut Shaman's robe are sewn two iron circles,
representing breasts.

2. The man Shaman dresses his hair like a woman on two sides
of his head, and braids it; during a performance he lets his hair
down.

3. Both women and Shamans (male or female) are forbidden
to lie on the right side of a horse-skin in the yurta tent.

4. The man-Shaman wears the Shaman's costume only upon
very important occasions.

5. During the first three days of any believer woman's confinement, access to her house is forbidden to all men, but not to the
men-Shamans.

It is known that only certain smiths who had great psychic
powers were able to make the magic iron ornaments. " In modern
times, there are no longer any ' magical smiths ' and *new Shamanistic garments cannot now be made.*"[29] It certainly looks as though
possibly the smiths, feeling that they had within themselves powers
such as the women Shamans were using, and desiring to share in

[27] *Korea Review*, 1903, p. 305.
[28] *Evolution of the Black Faith*, p. 123.
[29] Czaplicka, *Aboriginal Siberia*, p. 199.

YAKUT SHAMAN OF SIBERIA

the large emoluments of the latter, deserted their trades and took to Shamanizing, which up till then had been a woman's monopoly.

In Korea, too, by far the greater number of Shamans are women, called Mootangs. There is a class of men, called Paksoos, who Shamanize exactly as do the women, but there are probably not one of these to a hundred Mootangs. On the dress of the women, small round disks of iron are hung, flat shield-like pieces two to five inches in diameter.[80] The people speak of these pieces of iron with awe and say that great power resides in them, and, *per contra,* in the one who wears the robe. When they Shamanize, the women also carry in their hands rude iron swords or three-tined forks which are supposed to enhance their mystic powers. When the Paksoos Shamanize, they put on the outer garments of a woman.

2. This last sentence contains an interesting item that again, connects Korea with Siberia. While the Paksoo wears the outer dress of a woman while Shamanizing, the Mootang, on the other hand, always wears the outer dress of a man. This sort of thing is called by some writers in Siberia " change of sex," [81] by others merely a " change of dress," [82] but it is of some mystic significance and far more than simply a change of garments. The Koreans do not now know where the custom came from, nor any good reason for it, but they follow it meticulously. It is no doubt a legacy from their ancestral home.

3. A third thing that connects Korea and Siberia is seen in the names given for the Shamans. This also is a proof given as to women having been the first Shamans there. In every different tribe across Siberia, the name used for a man Shaman differs, but, for women Shamans, it is practically the same among the Mongols, the Buriats, Yakut, Altaians, Torgout, Kidan and Kirgis, particularly; where the names read respectively—utagan, udagan, udaghan, ubakhan, utygan, utiugun and iduan.[83] The name " Mootang " in Korean is quite evidently the same word, slightly changed to fit the exigencies of writing it with two Chinese characters

[80] Tyler, *Primitive Culture,* I, p. 140.
[81] Jochelson, *The Koryak,* I, p. 53.
[82] Czaplicka, *Aboriginal Siberia,* p. 248.
[83] *Ibid.,* p. 198.

which would represent the sound and, at the same time, somewhat explain the thing itself. " Moo " is the Chinese character meaning " deceiving," and " tang " might be translated " company." [34] Sometimes " Moonyu " was used, which means " Deceiving Woman." Any one of the above Siberian pronunciations could have been written in the Korean alphabet script, but the Chinese scholar always tried, in translating a foreign word, to find an existing character or set of characters which would sound like the foreign word, and which would intrinsically give the meaning of the concept to be represented. This is fully as close as they ordinarily hit things and has served very well to express it.

4. The séances of the Siberian Shamans were nearly always held at night. [35] So also for the Korean Shamans. They were always connected with dancing and the beating of the drums. No Mootang séance would be complete without both of these.

5. The Mootangs, like the Black Shamans, cultivate the friendship of the evil spirits in order that they may cajole them and coax them to do their will. The Mootangs claim to be able to cure all sicknesses, since they are all caused by evil spirits, and will leave when the given spirit has been propitiated. They claim to quiet the ghosts of those who have been drowned, and who would otherwise have no peace until they had drawn some other unfortunate into the water, and had drowned him. They claim to purify wells after people have drowned themselves therein. After death, it is believed that the spirits of the dead linger around the home and may become dangerous to the household. The Mootang, for a consideration, contracts to send the spirit on to its permanent abode, and so remove all anxiety. The Mootang makes the little wooden charms called " choryung," which are tied on children's belts to protect them from the wandering " Deunsin," tramp spirits. She places the " Sungjoo," or House Lord, envelop on the ridgepole of every new house that is built, and readjusts it later if a series of misfortunes following the family indicate that some of the spirits, or the House Lord himself, is peeved about something. She will find lost articles and predict the future, will propitiate

[34] *Korea Review*, 1903, p. 145; Bishop, *Korea and Her Neighbours*, p. 409.
[35] Czaplicka, *Aboriginal Siberia*, p. 228 f.

the dragon spirit who controls the rain, and will guarantee to travellers a safe journey if they start only on the days which she indicates.

Several of her séances are described below. It will be noticed in them that she always accompanies her séances with blood offerings, a chicken, or pig, or some such animal. Years ago it is said that on occasion, they offered human sacrifices, notably at certain places to the spirits of the sea, the victims, usually young girls, being cast into the water and drowned to appease the spirits. A wise magistrate, happening to be assigned to that place, broke up the custom, by stating that he thought the spirits would be better pleased to have one of their servants, the Mootangs, cast in to them than any other sort of sacrifice. When he ordered one of them cast in instead, the whole group of Mootangs agreed to use some other sort of sacrifice.[86]

The Mootangs and most of the Paksoos are of the lowest class in society, and usually densely ignorant. They use no books in their séances, and read none unless it be the *Chunsoo Kyung,* compilation of Buddhist dharani charm sentences. Their incantations and methods of controlling the spirits are not in any way standardized. They are handed down from generation to generation, each individual making such variations as suit her. Common rumour credits these women with being of questionable moral character. They usually marry men as base as themselves, and these husbands accompany them on their séances and beat the drum and blow on the pipes for them.

6. In divination, the Siberia Shamans use the thighbone of a sheep. The Mootang takes ashes from the fireplace, spreads them smoothly out in a winnowing pan, repeats her incantation, and then interprets the spidery lines which show themselves on the smooth surface of the wood ashes.

B. The Pansoo divides with the Mootang the field of Shamanizing. He also does many things similar to those done in Siberia, as, for example, uses the drum continuously throughout his séances, holds the meetings at night, etc. On the other hand, his

---

[86] *Korea Review,* 1903, p. 303; *Korean Repository,* 1896, p. 165.

technique rests upon certain printed books of incantations, more like some of the things in Confucianism, and in general he seems to derive his technique as much or more from Chinese as from Siberian sources.

1. All of the Pansoos are blind, or pretend to be. The name is taken from two Chinese characters, " Pan," to decide, and " Soo," destiny.[37] The Pansoos are held in much higher esteem than the Mootangs. Having been deprived of their physical eyes, people believe that they have somehow acquired an inner vision.

The Mootangs cultivate the evil spirits with a view to winning their favour and cajoling them. The Pansoos, like the White Shamans, cultivate the favour and seek the assistance of one or more powerful Sinchangs, good spirits, and then thereafter, by the use of certain spells and incantations, and with the help of the good Sinchangs, they force the evil spirits to do their will. Often their Sinchangs are the spirits of deceased Shamans, just as among the Yakuts of Siberia. Below we will describe one of their séances which will show their technique in such matters.

Perhaps the best known work of the Pansoo is that of healing, or that of driving obnoxious spirits away, but, as his name indicates, he also gives a large part of his time to telling fortunes, and giving advice on all sorts of business and other matters, advice which his familiarity with the Sinchangs makes valuable. There are three general sorts of things which the Pansoo uses most in his divination—little bars of metal with notches on them which he casts, jack-straw fashion out of little dice boxes; secondly, coins; and thirdly, Chinese characters. By means of these things, he can decide almost any question that is of interest to any man. Hulbert mentions thirty-four types of questions which they agree to answer.[38] They include almost every possible contingency of the future; financial, marital, domestic, private or public. The mastery of these forms of divination is a terrific task and usually takes years, as they are extremely complicated. Usually any one individual tries to master but one of the types. It is distinctly understood by the believers, however, that the success of the Pansoo in

[37] Underwood, *Religions of Eastern Asia*, p. 123.
[38] *Korea Review*, 1903, p. 344.

making his prophecies is not due to his skill in manipulation of these articles. It is his fellowship with the spirit world which gives him authority. Shamanistic worshippers have a belief that after death the soul sometimes enters into animals, the fox, or crow, or the dog, etc.[89] They say that this is not the Buddhist idea of transmigration, but it is probably based upon that. The Mootang in the tracks in her winnowing pan will find footprints that will tell the individual what he may expect. The Pansoo will be told the same by his Sinchangs.

## 2. Books of the Pansoo

The Pansoos have many books which they use, books of spells and powerful incantations. It is said to take at least five years to master enough of them to become full-fledged Shamans, and it involves hard study to keep informed thereafter. Of course they all have to be committed to memory so as to be recited at the proper time freely and appropriately for the controlling of the evil spirits.

The most common of these books is the *Okju Kyung*, or the *Jade Book*. This book tells of a supreme Being called Chunchon, the "Shaker of the Nine Heavens," and of the myriads of his satellites. The book makes for itself the most extravagant claims. For example, it says that "When one has infectious fevers of the heavenly or earthly sort, any one of the twenty-five types; or when he has stomach worms of any one of the twenty-four kinds, or any of the other thirty-six sorts of bodily weakness, reading this book will immediately drive them all away. In the time of pestilence, when whole villages are dying, one reading of this book will make one perfectly immune.

On journeys, when threatened by robbers, or leopards or wolves, on land; or, on water, when threatened by sharks or sea-serpents; or, on rivers, when in danger because of the rapids, one reading of this book will make all of troubles pass away. In drought, it will bring rain. When there is too much rain, it will cause it to moderate. It will put out fires and stop tidal waves.

---

[89] Tyler. *Primitive Culture*, II, p. 7

The book states that Chunchon has the power of enforcing his decrees, consigning those who displease him to an Avernus presided over by Whangkwun Yuksa.

These various claims sound a good deal like those which some patent medicines used to make, guaranteeing to cure everything from tuberculosis and cancer to stubbed toes and milkmaid's knee. A full translation is given in the Appendix. So far as there is any Bible of Shamanism, this is it, so that it is worthy of study.

There are many other books that are sometimes used, as, for example, the *Eumpoo Kyung* (or *Hades Book*), the *Paiktoo Kyung* (*White Head*) the *Chookki Kyung*, the *Palaing Kyung*. The *Pupsin Kyung* tells particularly of the kitchen god, snake gods, mountain gods, etc. The *Chilsung Yunmyung Kyung* tells of the Great Bear Constellation. For crystal-gazing, which is not much followed in Korea, there is the *Yoji Kyung*. There are also certain books on phrenology. Most of these books seem to be bought in China. At least three of the above I have identified from a list of Taoist books received from a friend in China.

### C. The Chikwan or Geomancer

Ross, quoting from an ancient Korean book, says, " Geomancy originated with Hu and Ho, ministers of Yao (the famous King of China about 2000 B. c.). Any man who takes up with it *becomes a devoted servant of the Kwisin, spirits.*" [40] Martin calls geomancy the " debased offshoot of a degenerate Taoism." [41] Dr. Gale writes, " In 1022 A. D., Han Cho brought from China the literature of geomancy, the book called *Chiga Su.*" [42]

Possibly some might question whether these men were Shamans. They seem to deal more with noxious influences, rather than with spiritual personalities such as engaged the Mootangs and Pansoos. However, the above quotation from Ross would indicate that the people consider these men to be busied with spirits. These men seem to get their cult entirely from China, for there seems to be nothing like it in Siberia.

---

[40] Ross, *Corea: Her History, Customs and Manners,* p. 358.
[41] *Lore of Cathay,* p. 252.
[42] *Royal Asiatic Society Records,* 1900, p. 10.

The " science " [a] which these men follow is that known in China as Fungsui and in Korea as Poongsoo, the Science of Wind and Water, the work of selecting propitious sites for residences and other buildings, but particularly of selecting sites for graves. In old Korea, the people were far more worried about getting proper grave sites, dominated by proper spirit surroundings, for their parents than they were about getting proper homes and sanitary surroundings for themselves and for their children. Usually villages were built down in the unhygienic lowlands close to the malaria-filled rice-fields, but the grave sites were up on the airy uplands or hilltops, and their spiritual hygiene was well attended to. Woe to the family if it was not, for the spirit of the ancestor would come back to his former home, and bring dire disaster upon all of his descendants.

The selecting of those sites was a most complicated business, and it was necessary that the Chikwans be most highly educated. In addition to the book already mentioned, in more modern times, the source of knowledge has been a book called the *Chun Keui Tayo*. The Chikwan went out over the hills with his compass and spyglass and stakes and lines for measurements. Influences which might be malign started from the Everywhite Mountains on the northern border and flowed down the diminishing ridges and backbones of mountains to the southward. A grave must be so placed that only good influences could come to play upon it, and so that all the evil ones were shunted away. A " Blue Dragon " spur must stand in just the right relation to an opposing " Yellow Tiger " arm of the mountain. Observations must be carefully taken to prove that no " Spying Peak " of another mountain could show itself near or far over the top of the near mountains. When all was rightly laid out and certified, the family could rest in comfort. If the lack of skill on the Chikwan's part caused misgivings, peace of mind could not be hoped for.

All sites had their guardian spirits, the earth gods, and gods of the mountains, and the Chikwan in Korea needed to cultivate them in order to be successful in his business. When the earth was

---

[a] *Korean Repository*, 1892, p. 169; *Ibid.*, 1896, p. 387; *Korea Review*, 1903, p. 109.

broken in the digging of the grave, he must be capable of so
directing matters that the spirits of the soil would not be outraged
too much and themselves bring about disaster. The actual exorcising away of any spirits in the soil just before the body was laid
to rest was usually the work of the Mootangs, or done under their
direction, but preparations for it were made by the Chikwan in so
arranging things that the interment would go off smoothly.

Many of these Chikwans acquired national reputations and were
called upon to locate royal graves and buildings. They also located the places for those geomantic masts " which are still found
in many places in Korea, holding the ship of state steady in its
course. In the carefully selected location, two great slabs of stone,
four to ten feet high, two feet wide and six inches thick were set
up in the ground facing one another, and then a lofty wooden pillar
was clamped between them pointing skyward. Just what effect
was expected from them we do not know, but they evidently had
some power as regards the keeping away of influences or spirits
malign. The wooden posts have all rotted away in most places
today, but the stone supports are there to show the industry of
the Earth Doctors."

Since the Japanese have taken over the country, they have forced
the people to use public cemeteries with just small plots of ground
for each household, so the profession of Chikwan is now confined
to the selection of building sites, and even that is rapidly
disappearing.

### D. The Ilkwan, or Chooser of Lucky Days

This, too, was once quite a profession in old Korea, for so many
important things depended upon the matters of days and of hours.
Every person born into the world came under the influence of one
of the five Elements, fire, water, wood, iron or earth. If a fire
boy married a water girl, they were sure to have a most terribly
fizzy time, and if the iron boy married a wood girl, cutting things
might be expected. The Ilkwan set the lucky times for marriages

---

" *Korea Magazine,* 1918, p. 4.
" *Korea Mission Field Magazine,* 1925, p. 233; Starr, *Korean Buddhism,*
p. 6.

and indicated who might safely take the leap, and with whom. There were many books used in the Ilkwan's professions, but the *Yookkap* was the commonest. As in the case of the Pansoo, the Ilkwan's decisions were accepted as final, not because of the intellectual skill which he had received in working out the puzzles of birthdays and hours and minutes, but because it was believed that he had inside knowledge of the spiritual realities behind these evident things, and because of that had authority.

### E. The Family Shaman

In connection with Confucianism, we have spoken of the Chunchei ceremonies for bringing rain, ordered by the king in times of drought and carried out in the villages. The professional Mootangs almost never [46] took part in those ceremonies.[47] From among the village headmen or other men known for their clean lives, Masters of the ceremonies were chosen to do much the sort of acts which the Mootangs and Pansoos did in their Koots, although they did not dance or beat the drum. Again, each year in the Fall after the harvest, nearly every village laid an assessment upon each household, and a cow was bought and sacrificed to the god of the mountain in a " Sanchei " ceremony, and there, too, the village leader conducted the service.[48] In Whanghai Province, in one place near the sea, each year they used to kill a dog and take off the skin and then stuff the skin with straw so as to make it look as though alive. The village assembled and the Mootang held a special village Koot, and besought blessings for the people, and at the end the dog effigy was cast over a nearby cliff into the sea, a scapegoat taking away the evils due to come upon the town. This was almost like the Sanchei ceremony, yet in that Sanchei ceremony only the Family Shamans temporarily served. The Family Shamans in Korea were not so permanent as in Siberia, but they seem to have existed. A ceremony conducted by one of them will be described a little later.

[46] Underwood, *Religions of Eastern Asia*, p. 119.
[47] *Ibid.*, p. 40.
[48] " Village Guild Laws," in *Royal Asiatic Society Records*, 1913, Vol. IV, Part 2, p. 21.

There may be some question as to whether these last three types mentioned should really be considered as Shamans. Mrs. Bishop says, " The term Shaman may be applied to all persons, male or female, whose profession it is to have direct dealings with demons, and to possess the power of securing their good will and averting malignant influences by various magical rites, charms and incantations." [49] If that is a proper definition, the classification is true, for that is what the Master of Ceremonies tried to do.

## V. The Call and Preparation of the Shamans

Of this it is difficult to get much information, since the cult is so relatively moribund now, and the Shamans do not like to discuss such questions with outsiders.

1. As to the Mootangs, it may be said that almost the identical situation exists as in Siberia. The women are usually neurotics, wherever they are sincere. New Mootangs are recruited from among the children of Mootangs, or from among the nearby women relatives. The Koreans all firmly believe that when a Mootang dies, her spirit lays hold upon some one and that that person has no volition in the matter. The spirits force her to serve them. Quite often, when the Mootang has no children of her own, she buys or adopts a little orphan girl, taking her first as a servant and then gradually training her in the vocation. It is usually in these long years of apprenticeship that the Mootang gradually gets her power. There being every inducement for her to " cultivate the demon's presence and power," she does it, and if she is nervously properly constituted, sooner or later she begins by auto-suggestion to receive the visions and auditions which she seeks. Sometimes they say that a special demon, as, for example, the falcon spirit has come into them. Most Koreans are terribly afraid of that particular spirit. [50]

2. As to the Pansoos, the case seems somewhat different. No doubt there are neurotics among them also, but they usually seem far better balanced and masters of themselves. It is likely that in

---

[49] Bishop, *Korea and Her Neighbours*, p. 422.
[50] Bishop, *Korea and Her Neighbours*, p. 422; Czaplicka, *Aboriginal Siberia*, p. 78.

the olden days, the thing that first called most of them to the calling was the very fact that they were blind and that very few vocations of any sort outside of that of beggar were open to a blind man. I have asked many of them how they happened to take up their work, and they nearly always make that reply.

Having once decided to enter the cult, however, those who excel have made it their business not only to master the books of the cult but to " practise the presence of the demon " in order to win their Sinchangs and secure the needed power. In the olden days, they tell of many of these blind Shamans who went away into mountain caves for a hundred days at a time to seek for power alone. This custom likely came from Taoism.[51]

Whether there was much mental or physical agony involved in securing the psychic power by either Mootang or Pansoo is difficult to find out today, but in a number of cases where women who used to be Mootangs have decided to throw it off and become Christians, there have been some acute periods of stress when they believed that the spirits were fighting against losing them. In recent decades, there has been no formal ordination ceremony for Shamans.

## VI. ORGANIZATION OF THE CULT

Of this, there has never been much except sporadically. We have noted the effort of Queen Min to organize it nationally. This was probably the most ambitious effort in history. As there were no temples, so there was no widespread organization. The Shamans of a given small district might unite to erect or maintain one single shrine which all might on occasion separately use. Usually two or three of the women or the men seem to band themselves together as a family for mutual comfort and encouragement.

Since the Japanese occupation of the country, the cult has met with special difficulties. At first, apparently, the officials intended to suppress it entirely, but there was such vigorous opposition that they felt it necessary to recognize it. To insure a real recognition,

---

[51] *Korea Magazine*, 1917, p. 544.

the Shamans themselves were compelled to form a closer corporation. In and around the city of Pyengyang, the Shamans have a society called the "Sinsung" Society, and in that one town of 100,000 inhabitants, they claim to have three hundred practising Shamans.

## VII. The Kinds of Spirits Worshipped

The reader will have already noticed that we have used the term Shamanism to cover quite a bit more than legitimately comes under that category. In these documentless, indefinite religions, animism, fetichism, animatism, and all of the rest shade off into one another and it is almost impossible to put one's hand on a single item and say that that is purely this or purely that. This situation will appear still more as we name these things that are regularly worshipped, but possibly, if we give all of the data, the reader may later separate it out to suit himself.

Koreans say that there are eight million Buddhas of various kinds. Hinduism claims thirty-three million gods,[52] and Japanese Shinto eight hundred thousand,[53] or some say eight million.[54] Korean Shamanism is generous in just the same way. The name of its pantheon is legion, for its gods are so many. It is a land of demons. It simply swarms with them, spirits of the earth, and spirits of the air, spirits of the waters and spirits of the hills, spirits of the living and spirits of the dead, spirits in rocks and spirits in trees, spirits which act in a rational manner, and frolicsome, capricious sprites like the "Tokkeibi" goblins, who spend all of their time playing pranks upon these stupid unresisting mortals.

A few, a very few, of the spirits are benevolent. Almost all are definitely malignant. Shamanism is a religion of fear. One of the distinctive things in it is the variety of Chiksung or Soosal Yungsan, i. e., articles used as preventative measures to shunt off prospective evils, or to prevent the entrance of wandering spirits.

---

[52] Monier-Williams, *Brahmanism and Hinduism*, p. 44.
[53] Aston, *Shinto*, p. 66.
[54] Jones in *Royal Asiatic Society Records*, 1901, p. 46; Clodd, *Animism*, p. 91.

One never enters a house by going straight in from the gate to the door. Inside the gate is a screen with a picture of a tiger or dragon to frighten out the spirits. One goes around the screen and sometimes around two or three of them before he arrives before the house door, walls within walls.

As one turned off from a main road towards a village in the old days, there was nearly always a wooden goose on a pole set up to shunt off any passing spirits that might have a mind to take the smaller road. Even ten years ago when the " flu " was raging, archways of brambles were made over such roads between villages and sacrificial blood of a bull or dog poured out on the stones near it to block the " flu " demon's passage to the other village.

It is impossible to name all of the multitudinous spirits, but possibly we may get some idea of them if we think of them under six classes.—

### 1. The Spirits of the Heavens, or of the Air

(a) Hananim. At the head of all the spirit host stands this one. His name has been variously translated. " Hanal " is the ordinary word for " blue sky," and " Nim " is honorific, so that the ordinary idea has been that the name meant " Honourable Heavens," or something of that sort. Hulbert translates the honorific slightly differently and makes the word mean " Sky Master." [55] Dr. Gale, taking a suggestion made several hundred years ago by one of the ancient poets, says that the word comes, not from " hanal," " Heaven," but from " Hana," meaning " One," [56] so that it would mean, the one " Great One."

In the definition at the beginning of this whole discussion, it was stated that in Shamanism " generally there is a supreme god over all." Griffis, who had studied the Shinto of Japan, says, " In the Creed of Shamanism, there may or may not be a conception of a single all-powerful Creator above all." [57] We have already mentioned Chunchon as one apparently supreme god, and have spoken

[55] Hulbert, *Passing of Korea*, p. 404.
[56] Gale, *Korea in Transition*, p. 78.
[57] *Religions of Japan*, p. 15.

of the fact that the supreme Yuh Hwang Shangti [58] of the China Taoists, under the name of Ok Wang Sangchei,[59] is also thought of as a supreme god.  Both of these are at times said to be the same as Hananim, but it is interesting to note that they seldom reverse that statement and say that Hananim is the same as the others.

Hananim is unique.  There is scarcely a question that he goes far back into the dim ages of Korean history long before any of the foreign religions came into the country.  In the earliest history of Shamanism, we noted how the Ye Kook people worshipped Hananim.  It was Hananim whom Tangoon worshipped on his high altar on Kanghwa.  Dr. Underwood speaks of meeting a Buddhist priest in a temple who said,[60] " Hananim is of course supreme.  Buddha is one of the lesser gods," and he says that " the supremacy of Hananim is apparently acknowledged alike by Confucianists, Buddhists and Shamanists."  Hulbert says, " The Koreans consider this Being to be the supreme Ruler of the Universe." [61]  The Protestant Christians of the country have seized upon this word and have defined it and defined it until, for the Christians, it holds all of the content in the English word for God. The Roman Catholics use the Chinese word " Chunchu."

Koreans universally say that Hananim sends the harvest, that he sends the rain, that by his grace we live and breathe.  The Rain Bringing Ceremonies of Confucianism are addressed to Hananim, not to Sangchei, or any other of the Chinese names.  In times of mortal danger, almost the first cry of the Korean is to Hananim. Hananim seems to dominate their lives, since his name is continually on their lips, but curious to note, they seem never to really worship him, unless we except the Rain Ceremonies.  They say that he sends the harvest, yet in the Fall they offer their sacrifices not to him, but to the gods of the hills, or to the house gods, or to the ancestral tablets.  He seems to be everything to them, and then again he seems to be nothing, judging from the way in which they disregard him when all goes well.

---

[58] Nevius, *Demon Possession in China*, p. 22.
[59] Gale, *Korea in Transition*, p. 69.
[60] *Religions of Eastern Asia*, p. 110.
[61] Hulbert, *Passing of Korea*, p. 404.

How much of personality attaches to the word it is difficult to discover. If one pins a Korean down and demands a statement on the matter, the non-Christian will take refuge in the defence reaction, saying that Hananim is simply the blue sky as over against the earth, and that the two are, as Chuja taught, the Father and Mother of man. Actually, however, they do seem to attach far more of personality to Hananim than that. Still they do not worship him, to any great extent.

Hulbert says, " Hananim is entirely separated from and outside of the circle of the various spirits and demons that infest all nature." [62] Gifford seems to place him within that circle.[63] I think that Hulbert is undoubtedly correct. That atmosphere about Hananim is different from that about the other spirits. In the Koreans' attitude towards him, along with what we have already said about Tangoon's altar, there is much evidence for a primitive monotheism which has degenerated, leaving Hananim as a name with little of its former content of meaning and authority. At least there is as much reason to believe in a primitive monotheism as there is in China.[64]

Hananim is at the head of the Korean's Shamanistic pantheon, or rather he is up above the head of it so far that the connection between is not very clear. Underwood says, " There seems to be no system in Korea's Shintoism. There is no chief deity clearly recognized as being over a whole hierarchy of gods. Buddhism early broke up its tendency to form a system." [65] Hulbert says, " If the Koreans had been left to themselves, they would have developed a pantheon like the Greeks, but the rival cults from across the Yellow Sea came in and stopped the tendency." [66]

(b) The O Pang Chang Koon, or Five-Point Generals. Here we come down to the unquestioned gods of Shamanism. These are some of the spirits whom the Pansoos, particularly, cultivate

[62] *Passing of Korea*, p. 404.
[63] *Every Day Life in Korea*, p. 88.
[64] Hulbert, *Passing of Korea*, p. 404.
[65] *Korea Review*, 1906, p. 89.
[66] *Royal Asiatic Society Records*, 1902, Vol. II, Part II, p. 62.

industriously, and who are said to rule the five great wards of the heavens.[67] They are separately named:

(1) Chung Chei Chang Koon, the Green General of the Eastern Sky.
(2) Chuk Chei Chang Koon, the Red General of the Southern Sky.
(3) Paik Chei Chang Koon, the White General of the Western Sky.
(4) Heuk Chei Chang Koon, the Black General of the Northern Sky.
(5) Hwang Chei Chang Koon, the Yellow General of the Zenith.

Each of these in his own ward is supreme and each controls a mighty spirit host which does his bidding. The Pansoo, in his séances, first locates the offending demons in the proper ward, and then proceeds to bring pressure upon him through the Changkoon and others to force him to cease his wickedness.

Rudely carved posts representing these Generals are often set up at the entrance of villages to protect against the coming in of free lance spirits or goblins that might work harm to the people. In the Fall, often the whole village gathers and offers sacrifices of rice bread and fruits to these symbolic posts. Each year a new one is set up, and all of the old ones left standing. Sometimes one sees a dozen of them standing in a row, the last all new and shiny, and the first one all crumbling down to dust. On one occasion, while looking at such a row, a long snake came meandering out from under the oldest one, reminding one startlingly of the Eden story and the body which the evil one wore there.

Sometimes twin posts are set up in this way, one marked " General of the Upper Heavens," and the other " Mrs. General of Hell," [68] not very complimentary to the fair sex. Probably these are not the Five Generals, but they belong in the clan or family.

It is interesting to note that, by the roadside entering many Buddhist temples, one will find these same protecting posts. Evidently the priests are not willing to trust entirely to the Buddhas to protect them.

(c) The Sinchangs. These are officers under the great Generals in the five wards, and are the familiar spirits invoked by the

[67] Underwood, *Religions of Eastern Asia*, p. 112; *Korean Repository*, 1895, p. 71.
[68] Gale, *Korea in Transition*, p. 87.

Mootangs and particularly by the Pansoos. Some Pansoos say that there are eighty thousand of them. Some say that there are more. Each Sinchang has under his direction great numbers of inferior spirits, so that there is never any dearth of helpers in spirit affairs. Each Pansoo tries in some way to secure the goodwill and assistance of one or more of the Sinchangs, after which his power is secure.

### 2. *The Second Great Class Comprises the Spirits of the Soil*

Of these there are four general types that might be mentioned:

(a) Site gods. Under Confucianism, we mentioned the worship of the site god of all the land up beneath Paiktoosan, the Ever White Mountain on the northern border; also the Pookoontang, or guardian spirit of smaller areas, a country or so, and also of the actual grounds of the Confucian temples. Whether these are Confucian or Shamanistic gods may be a matter of opinion. The Oriental does get his religions most dreadfully mixed at times.

The next unit is the separate dwelling, and, for this, in old Korea, nearly every house had its " Tujoo," site god. Around behind the house one would find them, small jars perhaps with a few pennies in them, covered by peaked tent-like roofs of thatch. Once or twice a year or oftener, cooked rice or rice bread and fruits were spread out before them and the household bowed and did them reverence. This spirit is almost forgotten now, but not more than ten years ago, one of my workers got into a bit of hot water by taking me, in the man's absence, to see his " Tujoo." His mother was a Christian and invited me, but the son was very angry about it.

(b) The Sansin, or mountain gods. These are the Baals of Korea and almost exactly like the gods of the mountains in Palestine. Most people read Psalms 121:1 all as one single sentence. It probably should be two. " I will lift up mine eyes to the hills. From whence cometh my help? My help cometh from God who made the heavens and the earth." The psalmist did not look for help from the gods of the hills, but from far higher up. The Koreans used to be largely satisfied with the hill gods. These beings, like the Baalim, were fertility gods, and were worshipped particularly just after the harvest. Usually on the top of the hill was a sacred grove, as in Israel, and also a small shrine containing a picture of the Old Man Spirit seated upon a tiger. The spirit was lord of everything on or within the mountains, its trees, and minerals, its birds and its animals. The medicine dealers, searching for medicinal roots, particularly sacrificed to the Sansin. Hunters and miners did him reverence. It was believed that the crop in the lowlands beneath the mountain depended largely upon his favour. In case of drought, a Koot was held beside his shrine and the blood of a cow, a pig or a dog poured out over the stones. They believed that then the spirit, to cleanse the rocks from defilement, would send the purifying rains. Ross said, " More people believe in the god of the mountain than in Buddhism. The mode of worship of this god differs radically from that in China, but probably the custom came from there, where it has always existed." [69]

(c) The Sunghwang Dang, or Mountain Pass Gods. Wherever a road went over a mountain pass in the old days, there was a little shrine by the roadside, usually with an old gnarled, twisted tree beside it and a pile of pebbles, and quite commonly also with some of the Point General wooden pillars. The Jews used to worship pillar gods, and they called them "Ashera." The Koreans and Japanese used to make much of them, and, in the Japanese language, they are called " Hashira." A picture of an Arab " Wely " shrine shown in Macalister's *Century of Excavation in Palestine,* (p. 272) might well be taken for a photograph from Korea.

Across the front of these little shrines, hanging from a piece of straw rope, or suspended from the limbs of the old tree, one would see many strips of cloth of various colours. Some of these were the collars off the coats of passersby, or of sick children in nearby villages, offered to secure the spirit's protection against threatened death. Some are from the clothing of brides journeying to the homes of their husbands. It was believed that the spirits of her father's house might follow her. A small feast spread at the

---

[69] Monier-Williams, *Brahmanism and Hinduism,* p. 219; Ross, *Corea: Its History, Customs and Manners,* p. 356.

shrine and a wisp of her clothing would delay them until she had gone on, and, after that, of course there was nothing for them but to return where they came from. Robertson Smith says,[70] that these offerings in all lands are supposed to bring one ideally in contact with the god. Tyler suggests that the rags were tied there as the actual receptacles of the disease, transferred there.[71]

Merchants offered bits of silk there, or cotton, or salt. Others offered rice in order to get good crops. Horse-boys offered tiny iron or chinaware images of horses. Petitions of many sorts were written on strips of paper and tied to the tree. Hezekiah, and others of the good kings of Israel, hewed down these Ashera and the groves on the hilltops. When some of the Korean Christians tried it, they landed in the police station.

Beside the shrine is the pile of pebbles and, in the old days, no one dared to pass the shrine without either adding a stone to the pile or spitting upon it. Many explanations are given of this last curious custom. One is that there was a beautiful maiden long years ago who committed adultery, and, to pillory her and her crime, everyone cast a stone on the pile or spat upon it, as representing her. Another story that comes from China tells of Kang Tai Kong, who spent his whole life up to the age of eighty studying the Classics or fishing. His wife got out of patience with him for not earning a better living, and she deserted him. At the mature age of eighty, the Emperor heard of his attainments in the Classics and summoned him and made him Prime Minister. Then the faithless wife returned and tried to attach herself to his ménage, but he spurned her and she fell down on the top of a pass and gave up the ghost. To pillory faithless wives, the passersby cast stones upon her grave. Likely these explanations are later rationalizations to account for a custom of recognizing the existence of the spirit in this way, but there is some slight reason for them, since we know that something similar happened to a man. There was once a Minister of State in Korea called Chang Seung [72] who committed adultery with his own daughter. To express the nation's

[70] *Religion of the Semites.*
[71] *Primitive Culture,* II, p. 150.
[72] *Korean Repository,* 1895, p. 143.

horror at the crime, the King ordered that posts be set up along all of the main roads of the country. Some thrifty official placed the posts just ten li apart, so they were useful to all the nation. They look something like the Five-Point General posts, but are called " Changseungpaki."

(d) The Chunsin. These gods are the tutelary divinities presiding over villages located in a plain. Their function is almost the same as that of the Sansin, but they are perhaps more closely connected with the agriculture. Confucianists tell of Sillongsi, the mythical legendary ruler of China who invented agriculture, and is reverenced as the patron of it. Outside of him, Korea has no god of agriculture, although there is one spirit that approaches it.

The monk, Tosun, was advisor to the founder of the Koryu Dynasty in 935 A. D., and he was a master of the rules of Fungsui. In the two provinces just south of Seoul, for several years they had had repeated crop failures, and they called Tosun to help them. He worked out the cause and set up a dolmen to intercept the malign influences that were playing upon them, and since then they have always had good harvests. In gratitude, they vowed to offer perpetual sacrifices to his mother, Ko Si. Even today, when a mid-morning or noon lunch is carried to the farmers in the fields, before eating, they flip a spoonful of it out on the ground, crying, " Ko Si Nay," " Mrs. Ko, come and partake of this ! " This practice has now spread quite widely through the country, so that Ko Si might be thought of as the Demeter or Ceres of Chosen. This practice of casting out the first spoonful makes another contact with Siberia, for in a recent magazine,[73] a writer speaks of seeing libations of wine thrown out in this way by the Buriats of Lake Baikal.

The Shamans have contact with all of the above soil gods. We have noted their use of the Generals. As to the site god, it is usually the Mootang who comes and enshrines him in the jar, or the " nest," as it is called. In the country territory, nearly all Koots of the Mootang, which are not held in private homes, are

---

[73] Magazine called *Asia*, Jan., 1928, p. 48 f.

held alongside of the Sansin, or Chunsin, or Sungwhangdang shrines.

### 3. Water Spirits

(a) The best known of all the water spirits is the Dragon,[74] who was taken from, or shared with, Confucianism. He is the lord of all oceans, rivers, lakes and wells. He is supposed to reside more particularly in certain bottomless lakes or ponds. He is worshipped by casting food into the waters and offering prayer. There are special shrines to him in many places, usually erected where he has at some time shown himself. Although lord of the waters, he can also soar up into the heavens. There is a shrine at Kwangnarro, forty li east of Seoul. erected to commemorate such an event.

There was a dragon well some years ago a hundred li east of Seoul, not far from the river bank. In a period of drought, sacrifices were offered and no rain came, so the people of the village determined to punish the Dragon by emptying out his well. They bailed and bailed for days, but the water kept fairly constant in the well, as it had underground connections with the river. They finally gave it up as an impossible task, but rain came, and so their faith in the Dragon was justified.

(b) Spirits of people drowned. All of the spirits of people who have suffered violent deaths are dangerous, but those of the drowned are almost the most malignant of them all. They are said to be in torment confined to the water until they can pull some other poor unfortunate in to take their places. Then they can come out on land. They wail around the side of the water and try to entice people near. The boatmen are terribly afraid of them, and arrange periodically for Koots to lay the spirits. The Mootangs come and offer blood sacrifices by the side of the water to calm them.[75]

(c) Guardian spirits of boats. In each of the river boats near Seoul in the old days, there used to be tiny shrine amidships where sacrifices were offered to the spirit of that boat It is thought to

---

[74] Ross, *Corea: Its History, Customs and Manners,* p. 356.

[75] *Korea Review,* 1903, p. 259; *Korea Mission Field Magazine,* 1925, p. 80.

have been a female spirit, for the boatmen, when they had to strip and get out in the river to lift the boats off shoals, always put on part of their clothing when passing from one end to the other of the boat afterwards.

When a boat on the river or the sea started on a journey, they usually engaged in a big hurrah with tomtons and gongs to attract all of the nearby spirits, then dropped food and incense on a bundle of straw floating in the water, set fire to it and sailed away while the spirits were busy at the feast and could not follow. On the river boats, if this former ceremony was too cumbersome, they at least made some of the noise and then cast a gourd full of water around the bow and the stern of the boat to cut off any clinging spirits. The Koreans used to say that Hapaik was the king of the water spirits, but they did not know any details about him. Possibly that is just another name for the Dragon.

#### 4. House-Gods

These are the various Lares and Penates that belong more particularly to the residences. We have already spoken of one who might be counted among these, i. e., the site god. There are others.

(a) The Sungjoo, or Holy Lord, the main spirit of the house. When a new house is built, the sorceress comes, and holds a Koot and calls up the spirit of the house. She makes a rude sort of paper envelope, puts some rice and money in it, soaks it in wine, and, after appropriate ceremonies, pastes it to the side of the ridge-pole, where it hangs all puffy with the enclosed air. Dry rice is thrown at it, and, if much of it sticks, it is considered a favourable sign. On all important occasions thereafter, particularly at harvest times, food is spread before this spirit and prayer is offered.

Sometimes, after a while, things begin to go wrong in the household, thereby conclusively proving that the Sungjoo is angry or has deserted the home. The Mootang comes again, coaxes back the spirit, makes a new envelope and again enshrines him. When a man in those early days bought a house, it was about as necessary to inquire minutely about how to keep the Sungjoo happy as it was to get the house title investigated. Stepping on the threshold of the house was a thing carefully avoided, as that was the neck of the god. This custom also may have come from Siberia.[76]

Sometimes, after one had bought a house, things would suddenly begin to go radically wrong, and the new owner would sometimes have to journey a long way to find the old owner and ask more particularly about the spirits. The Samaritans did that once in Israel.[77]

(b) The Keullip. This spirit lived in a great bunch of strings, the selvage edges taken from cloth, and hung up against the wall. Merchants in shops often had this particular spirit " nest," so it is thought by some to have been a god of wealth, there being no other one of that distinctive name in the pantheon.

(c) The Luck Gods. Behind the house, alongside of the site god's " nest," was another made almost like it for the so-called luck gods. The snake luck (Kurumi Up), the weasel luck[78] (Chokchebi Up) and the child luck (In Up). People actually believed in the live animals as luck bringers and were pleased if the snakes or weasels would come and live in the woodpile or tent-like home that they had made, but it was not necessarily the animals that they worshipped. It was the spirits of those animals that brought luck, too. One of my evangelistic helpers told me that for years before becoming a Christian he had a snake in his back yard whom he worshipped and to whom he offered food periodically to make it stay at his home.

(d) The Sonkaksi. Of all the malignant spirits, that of a young girl who died just before her marriage was the one most feared. They were often buried in the middle of travelled roads in graves eight feet deep, with roof tiles fastened around their heads to keep the spirit in the grave, and keep it from wandering about to plague the living. Baskets of silken wedding clothes were made and placed up on a shelf, and sacrifice was regularly offered to appease the restless spirit.[79] Few families would allow any of their young people to marry into a family that had a Sonkaksi spirit, for the

---

[76] *Korea Review Magazine,* 1895, p. 20; Tyler, *Primitive Culture,* I, p. 70.
[77] *Korea Mission Field Magazine,* 1925, p. 81.
[78] II Kings 17:28; *Korea Magazine,* 1917, p. 546.
[79] *Korea Review,* 1901, p. 69.

spirit might thereby pass over into those other homes and drive them to distraction.

(e) The Cheisuk Jar.  We have noted under Buddhism and in our survey of the Shaman shrines that Sakra of India was revered by the Koreans.  This Cheisuk Jar is dedicated to Sakra's spirit.  In olden days, it was an earthenware jar full of dry rice set up on a shelf.  Periodical worship was offered to it.  If the rice swelled and overflowed the jar, it meant good fortune.  If it soured, there was trouble ahead.  This particular worship of Sakra had nothing to do with Buddhism.[80]

(f) The "Samsin" or Three Spirits.  This is the Trinity formerly worshipped by women who longed for children.[81]  The Koreans say that these gods "look over the shoulders of little children" until they are ten years of age, i. e., they are a sort of guardian spirits or angels.  Usually they live in a paper bag or gourd containing rice and some strips of paper with writing on, placed there by the Mootangs.  They are hung in the warmest, most honourable part of the living-rooms, and periodically women spread out food before them and worship them.

Who these Three Spirits may be, no one seems to know.  Underwood suggests that they are the Trinity of Chinese Taoism. There are many Buddhist Trinities, and one man suggested that they might be the Vairochana Trinity, the Puppohwasin.  My Buddhist college friend said that they were probably Whanin, Whanung and Tangoon.

(g) The Kitchen God.  The Kitchen God was taken from Taoism and adopted by both Buddhism and Shamanism.  Images of him were seldom made.  Sometimes there were pictures, and sometimes just a bundle of cloths hung up on the ridge-pole served as his " nest."

(h) The Hongpi Kwisin, or Red Diploma Spirit.  In the ancient Confucian Examinations, the diplomas won at so great a cost in labour were genuine sheepskins nearly three feet square and coloured a dark red.  Because of the difficulty in securing them, many ignorant people believed that they contained some " Mana " or

---

[80] *Korea Mission Field Magazine*, 1925, p. 81.
[81] Underwood, *Religions of Eastern Asia*, p. 11.

other sort of potency, so households that had one among their ancestral possessions often set them up on the wall behind a curtain and worshipped the Kwisin or spirit that was supposed to dwell in them.

Most of these household gods were actually fabricated by the Mootangs, or at least at times the Mootang had to come in as priestess mediator to see that they were all behaving well.

### 5. Spirits in Trees

There are no particular species of trees in Korea that are worshipped more than others.[82] Any tree will do if it is in the right place and properly formed. Many of them are worshipped in various ways. We have already spoken of the pillar gods, and the groves on the hilltops and beside the Sunghwangdangs.

In addition to these, often a village will adopt all of the trees of a nearby grove, each house taking one as its own, and worship will be offered separately to each tree by its proper household. Left-woven straw rope is often taken and tied around the tree to indicate that it is set apart for this purpose. Sometimes a bit of thatch two feet wide and two long is hung on the rope, making it look like a woman's apron, and then again like a person kneeling at the foot of the tree embracing it. On the sacred fourteenth night of the first lunar month, red earth was spread around the tree and food laid out at its foot and prayers offered.[83] The Yakuts of Siberia have ceremonies very much like this.[84]

When any one was killed and devoured in whole or part by a tiger, the family often selected a tree to be the abode of the man's spirit, and the Mootang was called to enshrine him there.[85]

Usually the tree was thought of simply as the abode of the spirit. Sometimes the people conceived of the tree itself as alive. In one of my villages, we bought a piece of ground and built a church. Just next to the site was an old demon tree, which the village people had formerly worshipped, but which they had apparently

[82] Gale in Korean Repository, 1892, p. 21.
[83] Korea Mission Field Magazine, 1925, p. 80.
[84] Tyler, Primitive Culture, II, p. 224.
[85] Griffis, Religions of Japan, p. 30.

totally forgotten. The Christians decided to cut it down, as it was in the way. One man in the village came and pleaded against it. "Cut off my head, if you must," he said, "but do not cut down my god."

### 6. *Free-Lance Spirits*

(a) The first of these perhaps would be the Tokeibis or goblins, who are said to take such delight in gratuitously tormenting people. They cause the iron kettle covers which are larger than the kettles to fall down inside. They misplace articles so that they must be hunted for, and make general nuisances of themselves.[86] They can be propitiated by offerings set out under the trees and by prayer. Often the offerings take the form of clothing placed in an earthen jar. The offerings are usually outdoors, not in houses.

(b) The Deunsin, or Floating Spirits, Tramps. These are un-attached unclean spirits of various sorts, people who have died violent deaths, etc. The spirits of boys and young men who have died are often among them. Like the Sonkaksi, they are much feared. They are called respectively Namshakui and Duosuni. There is a dead magistrate spirit called Koonoong that is often mentioned. Spirits of the various diseases also wander abroad. The sixteenth night of the Korean first lunar month is a sort of Hallowe'en or Walpurgis Night called Talki Kwisin Night, when all of the spirits turn loose and no sensible man is out on the streets. For that particular night, the best protection is to hang a sieve in the front doorway, for the spirit will get busy counting the holes in the sieve and not come further into the house.

In a great deal of their traffic with spirits, the Shamans act as though the spirits were not ordinarily intelligent, as in the case just mentioned. All roads in the Orient are crooked, they say, because spirits travel in straight lines only, and this kept them from moving freely from one town to another. When sickness entered a house, sometimes they used to block up the front door and open another gate elsewhere. Then the spirit coming again could not get in, and all would be well. Sometimes, to prevent the

---

[86] *Korea Mission Field Magazine,* 1925, p. 100.

spirit there getting angry and causing a fire, they offer sacrifice outside the newly blocked door. Sometimes, again, when there was sickness, a little straw man was made and cast out into the road before the door. Often they have on them the name of the sick person. I picked up one one day at the crossroads, and the placard on it read, "I am little Kim Won Suni. I've had the scarlet fever, and I'm dead." What sensible spirit would enter that house to do any more damage there? I have even seen a small bier made of poles and straw matting placed outside of the house with the straw man on it, so that the spirit could see that the sick person's body was already sent out for burial, and so needed no more of its attentions.

### VIII. Apotropæic Rites and Devices

We have already spoken of the Five-Point General posts, and the wooden ducks at the road forks, and the thorny archway sprinkled with blood to keep spirits shunted off. There are the much-screened doors of all of the gentry's houses, guarded by tiger pictures, where one has to edge his way through the maze to get in; and the blocked doors just mentioned. When the family anticipates a possible return of some deceased member to trouble them, a knife thrust into the ridge-pole at the ceiling of the room will make him hesitate about entering.[87] Often in roadside inns, where the building extends clear out to the street line, little wooden spears a foot long will be seen extending out above the outer door. Food is pierced upon the spears and left there for the refreshment of passing spirits, who may eat and pass on, and not come in. The whole lintel and sides of the doors are often covered with bundles of thorns, also, as the spirits will not then pass through. On the ridge thatch of a house outside, on the fifteenth day of the first lunar month, little silver disks to represent the moon and golden or yellow disks to represent the sun were set up on little sticks to ward off evil for the coming year. All of these things come from the Shamans' lore, and many of them are even set in place by the Shamans. Children are given names which include the character

---

[87] *Korean Repository,* 1892, p. 54.

for "dragon" in order that lesser spirits may bring no harm to them. There actually used to be a ceremony of "selling" children to the Mootang nominally since, once recognized as belonging to her, her familiar spirits must protect them.

The reverse of apotropæic rites is seen in the rites for harming an enemy at a distance, writing an enemy's name on the belly of a rat, and placing it under his bed or in some room which he regularly occupied; writing his name on a piece of paper, and piercing it with needles while calling down curses upon him, etc.

## IX. Ceremonies and Seances of the Shamans

The séances of the various Shamans are concerned with the dispersing of spirits, the curing of sickness, and the searching for concrete blessings. Possibly a brief description of four ceremonies may explain the cult most clearly.

### 1. Funerals and Burial

I have not spoken of these items before because, while they have in them much of Confucian and Buddhist customs, they seem more to belong to the Shamans.

When it was seen that any sick person was about to die, in the old days, he was, if in any way possible, carried out into the open air that he might die there, possibly in order that there might be less danger of his spirit later clinging to the home and making his descendants uncomfortable. He was always placed with his head to the west, that the spirit might pass directly in that direction. Just as the spirit passed away, some one was supposed to take some of the deceased's inner garments and throw them up on the roof, announcing in a loud voice to the spirit world the event that had just come about. These things partake of Shamanism.

A squash is brought and broken, and three pairs of new shoes and some rice are laid out on a platter in front of the house for the three Sajas,[88] or spirit messengers sent to escort the spirit of the deceased into the presence of King Yumna of the Buddhist under world.

---

[88] Gifford, *Every Day Life in Korea*, p. 91.

If it was a Confucian household, the next step was to prepare
the temporary and then the permanent ancestral tablet, according
to the customs of that cult, but the body was bound upon a plank
four inches thick, where, under the head, seven holes had been
bored half through the wood in the positions occupied by the North
Star Constellation. Was that Taoism, or did it come from
Buddha? Coffins were not used ordinarily in the olden days. The
body was tightly bound upon the plank with whole bolts of cloth
till it resembles a mummy case. The Shamanistic Chikwan then
came in and scientifically located the proper grave site with the
exact orientation and depth decided. Then, on the day of the
funeral, Shamanism again took charge to send before the body on
the way to the grave men wearing hideous four- or six-eyed masks
to frighten all Deunsin that might want to tag along, and, at the
grave side, the Mootang or the Pansoo saw to it that all interfering spirits were kept at a distance, so that only the body went
into the grave alone. Confucianism dressed the mourners in sack-
cloth before they left the house, robes with unsewed hems and
with long pendulous sleeves to the ground and round-topped miters
tied on by pieces of straw rope. Shamanism escorted the third
soul back to the tablet in the home, and Confucianism offered
sacrifice and wailed before it. Shamanism, in an extended Koot,
separated the last clinging vestiges of the spirit's presence from
the clothing and other effects in the household, and Confucianism
took over thereafter the continuous worship of the tablets. The
particular technique of the several Koots carried out in this connection will be seen in the next two ceremonies. It is interesting
to note how all three religions collaborated in bringing rest to
the dead.

## 2. The Mootang's Koot for Healing Disease

Of all of the activities of the Shamans, probably this is more
like the cult of Siberia than anything else in Chosen. We have
mentioned already the fact that the Mootang in her official ceremonies wears the outer dress of a man, as the Paksoo, her male
imitator, wears the outer dress of a woman. We have mentioned
the iron disks that she wears on her robe, and the iron swords or

tridents that she carries in her hand. She also has a sort of rattle called Pangool, made of bits of iron and wire, and quite often has upon her head a round helmet of bronze. There are many Mootangs who do not have these iron-spangled properties, but wear simply a round felt horsehair hat with a two-inch rim, and the blue or red, split-half-way-up-the-back over-garments such as used to be worn by petty officials around the Korean Court. These women also Shamanize, but they do not have the prestige of those who are fully equipped in the ancient way.

The drums of Siberia are said to be all round or oval. Those of Korea are usually shaped like an hour-glass and are about three feet long, and possibly fourteen inches in diameter. Some are the size and shape of snare drums. They are beaten with the hands alone, one hand on each drumhead, or with a baton in certain definite ways which take a long time to learn. Along with the drum, they always use also a small trumpet-like horn which makes a wailing, mournful sound not very pleasant to uninitiated ears. Two assistants, one of them usually the woman's husband, preside over the drum and the pipes, leaving the Mootang free.

First, sacrificial blood is shed, of a chicken, or pig, or dog, and a generous meal of rice and other things with this meat is prepared. An awning is spread overhead covering the courtyard of the house, and thick grain-drying mats are spread over the ground. When the meal is ready, it is placed upon a small table and set out in the courtyard on the mats, and then the drums begin to sound, the pipes to wail and the Mootang to dance. She holds in her hands the sword or trident, or sometimes only a fan, and she postures and dances, calling out to the spirits from time to time and inviting them to join the revelry. Faster and faster she goes, whirling like a dervish, leaping high in the air. Her eyes flash wildly. Even the sound of her voice changes. People shrink away from her in fear. Sometimes, to help her, one of her assistants will take a basket and scrape upon it, making a sound like that which the boys make on the rocks along the river bank when they try to entice fresh-water crabs out from under big stones. On and on she goes, calling and calling to the spirits to come and join her, begging them to come, cajoling them with all sorts of

A MOOTANG'S KOOT—SORCERESSES IN A SEANCE

promises, explaining the wonderful feast that has been prepared, reminding them of their friendship to her, teasing, joking, pleading. Sometimes she gets absolutely exhausted and falls down almost in a faint without getting any results. She lies still a while, and then arises and begins again, or a companion takes her place and they serve alternately, calling and calling. Sometimes the spirits are quite obdurate, and the Koot has to go on for days, usually when there is extra money to be had for the extra effort. New food has to be prepared if they go too long. The séances are mostly in the night and often last all night long. Sometimes they stop at morning time, and then go on the following night.

Usually, sooner or later, a change comes, and she announces that the evil spirit has come out of the sick person and is partaking of the feast. Then she must use some device to persuade the spirit to go away after eating, and not to go back into the person who was ill. She does this sometimes by cajolery and perhaps more often with guile. Among her properties will be a small horse sometimes, made of woven straw. She will beg the spirit to mount the horse at the end of the meal, and, when he has done so, she will seize the horse, run out the door and throw it up into a tree or into a stream. The poor, simple-minded evil spirit cannot find his way back to the same house again, so the sick person gets well.

### 3. The Pansoo's Koot for Ejecting Spirits That Trouble.[90]

The technique of the Pansoo, as befits its Chinese origin, runs along with more of decorum, although with no less of intensity. Naturally, the blind man does not dance, so that at once changes everything. He has the drum, however, and beats it entirely himself, sitting on the floor of the porch with his helpers standing around him. First of all, he has the ceiling of the porch marked off into wards like the four wards of the heavens, and puts up in each and at the zenith, the banners of the Five-Point Generals. One assistant sits before him, holding perpendicularly[90] a club of peach wood about a foot long, the same resting at its bottom on a

---

[89] Bishop, *Korea and Her Neighbours,* p. 405.
[90] Gifford, *Every Day Life in Korea,* p. 112.

solid slab of wood. Other assistants stand around with leafy branches from the peach tree, which is particularly feared by the demons.[91]

The Pansoo begins to boom the drum and recite sections of the *Okju Kyung* and other books which he has learned. His first purpose is to get into communication with his own friendly Sinchangso, or single Sinchang, if he has but one. Sometimes this part of the ceremony will take two or three hours or more, sometimes longer. Every little while, the Pansoo stops and asks towards his assistant's club, " Have you come? " If the Sinchang is not there, the club will wag wildly from side to side, no matter how much force the assistant puts in to hold it. The Ouija board, so popular in the Christian Occident, was in use in Korea when England was still populated with savages.

At last, when he asks, the club no longer wags from side to side, but bounces up and down. Then the Pansoo asks until he finds from what ward of the heavens the spirit comes who is troubling the household or institution. Learning that, he begins to call the roll of the various spirits in that ward of the heavens who might be the guilty one, and he keeps on until he finds the culprit. Then he begins to read the books in earnest, putting pressure upon the guilty one, beating him, overwhelming him, benumbing him with his great and powerful formulæ. Presently he asks in what part of the house the spirit is keeping himself, and, finding that, the assistants rush into that place with the peach branches and drive him out, chasing him from place to place until he comes up on the porch where the Pansoo is.

The Pansoo has all prepared and ready an earthenware or stone bottle and a lump of buckwheat dough. The harassed spirit is ordered to enter the bottle, and is unable to resist longer. He goes in, the assistant jams the dough in for a cork, and the bottle is taken out on the hills and buried. Perhaps some Aladdin or Sinbad of future years, digging around on Korea's mountains, will find some of these bottles and some very troublesome genii in them.

---

[91] Underwood, *Religions of Eastern Asia*, p. 60; *Korea Review*, 1902, p. 344; Bishop, p. 406.

## 4. The Family Shamans, the Chunchei or Sanchei

Whether these should be called Shamanistic rites at all or not, I am not entirely persuaded, but they seem to be like those of the Family Shamans in Siberia, and not unlike some of those of the Mootangs and Pansoos, so we will consider them as such.

These ceremonies are usually held in the Fall just after the harvest, but may be held once a quarter regularly and at other times of great calamity. The spirits supplicated are sometimes the gods of the mountains or neighbourhood, sometimes come very near to Hananim alone. In many ways, they are similar to the Peace Offerings of the Jews.

Seven days before the ceremony, the village has a meeting and elects from among the " clean " men of the village one to be a Chief Shaman or Master of Ceremonies, Chei Kwan, one to be Prayer Reader, Chook Kwan, and several to be assistants.[92] A bull without blemish is chosen, all of one solid colour, not spotted. For a week, the animal is carefully kept, immaculately clean and well fed. The men bathe, wear clean clothes, put bits of pine on each side of their front doors and a left-woven straw rope across it and red earth in front of it, to show any possible visitors that they are set aside and cannot do any business until after the sacrifice. They refrain from tobacco and liquor or fellowship with their families. No mourner or person defiled from touching a dead body is allowed to go near them.

The night before the ceremony, a small booth is erected on an elevated point of land on the mountain-side, or, if it is Chunchei, on the plain; the bull is killed by the village butcher and the meat, and particularly the blood, is placed in the booth over night, before the gods.

At cock-crow next morning, all of the men of the town assemble around the booth. The Shaman Master of Ceremonies and the Prayer Reader, clad in robes of ceremony, alone approach the booth, worshipping the spirit there. Then the Reader reads the prayer of the community, section by section, presenting petitions for good crops, for freedom from disease, for many sons, etc.

---

[92] " Village Guild Laws " in *Royal Asiatic Society Records*, 1913, p. 21.

After each section, the men assembled on the lower land around the booth respond with the sound, "A-eum," equivalent to our word "Amen." The Master of Ceremonies bows all during the reading, worshipping continuously. After the ceremony is over, the meat is divided among the villagers according to their several contributions. Part of it is taken down below the hill, cooked and eaten there in a sort of barbecue.

Those chosen to be Masters of Ceremonies and Readers are usually the same over a long period of years. Their Shamanizing, if this is Shamanizing, is only on these special days. Ordinarily they do not show much of the " altered mental state " mentioned in the definition at the beginning of this discussion. If they do reveal such states, they are more appreciated. One would expect that the Mootangs or Pansoos would be called upon to do this work. They are sometimes asked to indicate favourable days for it, but are almost never asked to lead. The ceremony has no possible contact with Buddhism and only a tenuous possible connection as similar to the Sajik Shrine worship. It would seem that it is Shamanistic, and is surely an ancient custom. Possibly these men were the original Shamans, as some writers on Siberia believe that theirs were at first family ones, and later became professionals. Possibly these men are the result of a degeneration or drawing away from professional Shaman control under the influence of Confucianism and the worship of the Sajik Shrine. Each one may decide this for themselves, but these are the facts of what is done.

## IX. Doctrines and Morality of Shamanism

1. We have noted that there is no supreme Deity served by all of the Shamans. Hananim was apparently too high for them. The Five-Point Generals have much power, but are never thought of as having final authority. Ok Wang Sangchei comes near to being God, but he is a foreign importation. Chunchon in the Okjukyung seems to have a high place " in the Nine Heavens," but not in any sense supreme control. It would seem that the definition given at the beginning of this study comes very near to describing what we have been studying, a " primitive religion of

polytheism or polydemonism with strong roots in nature worship, and generally with a supreme god over all." The last clause failed of fulfilment, as Hulbert and Underwood have shown, because the more developed religions from China came in and stopped the right development of a pantheon, throwing everything into confusion. Possibly, in the beginning, there was one supreme God, Hananim, the concept of whom has degenerated down the ages.

2. As to ideas of sin and questions of morality, Shamanism does not seem to have been very much exercised, at least the women Shamans of the Siberia strain do not. It is not that they have taught evil to others. Outside of their example in cultivating the intimate friendship of the evil spirits, and the rumoured suggestions as to their own private lives, they had no message on or interest in the matter. They were busy getting men free from the omnipresent, harassing spirits and the discomfort which they brought. They had no doctrine of a judgment day or anything resembling it. It was outside of their line of vision.

The Pansoos, from their presumed contacts with Confucianism due to their better education, seem to have done a little better in this line. The Okjukyung translation in the Appendix suggests that. Still they, too, considered it more or less a matter outside of their line, possibly because Confucianism was taking care of it, and of nothing much else. Their interest was in spirits and the supernatural world.

It is interesting to note that, even under the most degraded Shamanism, there have never been in Korea any patron spirits of gambling hells and brothels such as are found in her immediate neighbour lands, nor has immorality been practised near any of Korea's temples as a part of, or approved by any of its cults.[98] There has been almost none of the phallic worship which is so common in some other lands. Many of the Koot ceremonies include prayers for progeny. Outside the Chamoon Gate of Seoul is a large boulder pitted with holes half as large as one's fist. Rumour has said that any woman who could place a pebble in one of those holes and make it stick would in due time have a son.

---

[98] Underwood, *Religions of Eastern Asia*, p. 131.

Another similar stone used to stand outside the South Gate and one by the Peking Pass. Still there are no suggestive phallic symbols shown anywhere, and never an obscene picture in any of its temples.

3. As to immortality, all Koreans of all of the cults seem to take for granted continual existence of some possible type, although, for all except the Buddhists, it seems to be the hazy Avernus type, or realm of the shades type, of the ancient Mediterranean world. Buddhism has helped the other cults to give more content and meaning to what beliefs they do have. Believers of all of the cults seem to somewhat accept by common consent the belief that everyone goes ultimately to "Chu Seung," "that place," to King Yumna's judgment seat. Yumna is Buddhist now, but he may have antedated Buddhism and represent a much older tradition, as many things in Buddhism do.

## X. The Future of Shamanism

Let it be noted again that in describing this cult, we have taken the liberty of describing it as it used to be when it was still in its full bloom. It is far from being in full bloom now. It is far too superstitious and baseless a cult to endure the light of a modern scientific world. Today one might enter a hundred houses consecutively and find not a single one of the house gods mentioned above. The shrines still stand on the hilltops, but there are relatively few villages that turn out *en masse* as they used to do for the Sanchei or Chunchei ceremonies. There are thousands of Five-Point General posts standing along the highways, and one occasionally sees a new one all glistening with its new paint and axe-marks. but a new one is the exception, not the rule now, and the old ones are crumbling away. People speak shamefacedly when they have celebrated a Koot ceremony in their homes, and wonder subconsciously if the money would not have been better spent on hospital medicine. There are more than six hundred thousand pupils of all ages in the modern missionary and government schools of the country, and probably fully that many more have been graduated or have had a large part of a course in some of the schools in the last two decades. Gale says, "This form of worship is on the wane in the more enlightened parts of the country, and will disappear with this generation." [94]

Still, the cult dies hard, and is a long way from being dead today. The Shamans have joined into district societies for mutual counsel and encouragement. How many there are still in Korea, probably no one knows, but the Paksoo who is Chairman of the Pyengyang city Sinsung Guild told me that there were three hundred accredited members in that one town of 100,000 souls. There are nearly twenty millions of people in all Korea, so there must be thousands of the Shamans altogether. Even in these much modernized cities, one hears quite often the boom of the Shaman's drum, and, in Seoul, it is not uncommon to hear the piercing call, " Moonsoo " (Manjusri Boddhisattva) which the Pansoo gives as he walks around drumming up trade. Just a few months ago, three of them carrying their drums got on an electric tramcar in which I was riding in the city. I wondered if they felt any lack of harmony between Chunchon and modern charged, high voltage wires. Inevitably the cult must decrease from now on steadily, but, judging from the persistence of the Friday, and number thirteen, and ladder and broken looking-glass superstitions in some other lands, it will take a long time to die. For the good of this awakened Hermit Land, we hope that the time will be as short as possible.

---

[94] Gale in *Korea Magazine*, 1917, p. 546.

# VII

# FIRST CONTACTS WITH CHRISTIANITY IN OLD CHOSEN

IN our discussion of Buddhism, we have spoken of that belief which some scholars have that Buddhism and Christianity touched down in the southwestern corner of China in the first century A. D., and that there Buddhism, following its immemorial custom of combining with other religions, absorbed from Christianity ideas of an eternal Deity, of a Saviour Buddha, of vicarious salvation, of a coming Messiah, of real prayer, and of a future world of bliss, not one of these ideas apparently having been in the Buddhism before that time, and none of them being today held in the Southern Buddhism of Ceylon. We grant freely that theories of borrowing by one religion from another must all be scrutinized very carefully before being allowed. It is undoubtedly often not a question of borrowing, but simply of human psychology which, under certain conditions, in far distant places, without a possibility of borrowing, has produced the same effects. Still, it certainly does put a good deal of strain upon one's credulity to try to believe that those six new doctrines suddenly evolved of themselves, especially when we know that Christians were working in that neighbourhood and that not over five centuries later, the Tang Emperor had to rebuke the Christian maker of the " Nestorian Tablet " of Sianfu because he had done that very thing,[1] openly collaborated with the Buddhist, Prajna, in writing the so-called Christian inscription on that tablet. If those theories of borrowing by Buddhism are true, Korea's first touch with the Christian Gospel was indirect, and came three hundred years before Buddhism itself entered Korea territory.

---

[1] Lloyd, *Creed of Half Japan*, p. 203.

One hesitates to quote Madame Gordon after the many mistakes in her information which we have noted in the pages past, but she points out one interesting fact[2] about Soonto's first coming to Korea in 372 A. D., extremely interesting if it be true, *i. e.,* that one of the two monasteries which King Soosoorim built for Soonto is called " Ibullam," and that is exactly the way in which the word " Ephraim " would be written with Chinese characters, and no one knows what the word " Ibullam " really does mean. Korean tradition says that it was the transliteration of some foreign word. Quite likely it is simply a coincidence, and there is absolutely nothing in it.

Another most interesting thing which we hope to see some day checked up is the full story of the wonderful Cave of Sukoolam near Kyungju, which we have already described in the lecture on Buddhism. Meukhoja, who is reputed to have built that cave or have caused it to be built was, if we may judge from his name, a black man, a foreigner. The cave itself is undoubtedly Buddhist. The central figure is the wonderful eleven-foot high image, which some think was the prototype of the great Japanese Buddha at Kamakura. There are other Buddha statues in niches in the walls up high, and the Wheel is carved on the ceiling, but the thing that makes one wonder is that row of sixteen standing figures on the sidewalls of the cave, a little more than life-size, men and women all with Jewish faces, totally unlike Koreans. The women have boat-shaped haloes on their heads like those in Syrian cave temples. One carries a flabellum like those used around the Mediterranean, and unlike anything in this land. One is presenting a cup to the person next her, very much after the manner of the Communion chalice. We have already noted how Greek culture, through the Greek Bactrian states, came in contact with Indian life long ago in northwest India, so that a possible reasonable explanation for it comes from that, and from the fact that Meukhoja himself, this "black man," may have been a native of northwest India, a missionary who had come across as did many of the others whom we have mentioned before. The explanation is a good one,

---

[2] *Royal Asiatic Society Records,* 1914, p. 14.

but certainly the appearance of those images is startling, and one cannot help be dubious about the explanation.

The cave itself, large as it is, is wholly artificial, and Mrs. Gordon claimed that it was built after the model of Christian cave churches in Syria. It has first a tunnel-like outer cave, and then a small stretch unroofed, and then the circular inner cave with its dome-like ceiling. The Japanese engineers sent to repair it, being ignorant of the fact that the outer cave was an integral part of it all, tore it all away and cast the long, curved roof-stones upon the rubbish heap, erecting a level platform of new shiny stones in front of the inner cave door, more usable and solid than the original, but the whole constituting a bit of philistinism to make one weep.

Madame Gordon quotes [a] Walter Lowrie's *Christian Art and Archeology* as authority for her statement that Syrian temples were built on the same model as this cave. I have not been able to secure that, or any other book upon the subject, so simply quote what she has said. If what she has said can be established, it once more opens the question of those strange bas-relief figures inside, and makes one wonder if here again we may not have a case of Buddhist-Christian syncretism exactly like that which we find in the Nestorian stone. Meukhoja probably lived in the fifth century and the great tablet was made in the seventh.

We have noted that Korean Shamanism was an indigenous cult which came from two sources, probably, from their original home in the Amur Valley, and from the west in the land of the Dragon. In discussing the customs and ceremonies of that cult, we purposely left out those connected with the fourteenth day of the first lunar month of the year. We would like to mention them now.

First of all, let it be noted that that is the night of the Jewish Passover, the fourteenth day of Nisan, with which all of the Old Testament Passover ceremonies are connected. The Jewish first lunar month comes two months later than the Korean first month, but that makes it all the more significant that the Koreans should have on their day nearly all of the customs of the Jewish Passover.

[a] *Royal Asiatic Society Records,* 1914, p. 22.

On the night of the fourteenth, no Korean used to go out of his house, if he could in any way avoid it.  They went in early, and even placed their shoes inside of their sleeping-rooms that night, something that they did on no other night in the year.  That night, the only night in the year, they ate bean pulse and bitter herbs, instead of good rice and red pepper pickle.  Before evening, they prepared little straw men about a foot high and put pennies in the heads of them so that the beggar boys would come and carry them off when they had been thrown out.  At midnight, they took these little men and cast them into the street, preferably somewhere at a cross-road, where Comparative Religion Doctors tell us folks expected all of the roving spirits from four directions to congregate.  They then went into their houses, and came out no more that night.  In the city of Seoul, they used to tie a red cord upon the outside handle of their door.  What is this but the Redeemer idea, the little straw man, on the night of the Passover, taking over, on behalf of the householder, all the evils due to come upon him all that year?

Here is a series of "coincidences" which one would like to have someone rationally explain.  Apparently there are no customs of this sort in Manchuria or North China contiguous to Korea.  In Korea, these customs, with minor variations, used to be followed throughout all the land.  Where did the customs come from?  Is it possible that Jewish missionaries at some time in the past ages came all the way to Korea and introduced the Passover here?

We have noted above how the Mohammedans, starting from the Mediterranean world not less than 621 years after Christ, were strongly established in Manchuria many centuries ago.  A few years ago a colony of Chinese Jews was discovered in Western China, the descendants of immigrants who had come there centuries before.[4]  In the ninth century A. D., Khordadbeh, an Arab writer, spoke of the Korean kingdom of Silla in one of his books, and mentioned ten of its products, showing that Arab sailors did business there.[5]  Possibly the world needs to study a lot more attentively than it has till now the whole question of the spread of

[4] Lloyd, *Creed of Half Japan*, p. 49.
[5] Griffis, *The Hermit Nation*, p. 2.

religious cults.  The little note in the Preface of this book also indicates this.

## II. REAL CHRISTIANITY IN HIDEYOSHA'S TIME

What we have mentioned above are simply hints and suggestions. It is difficult to know anything very clearly about the earliest years of any land.  Still, the things mentioned are significant.  The first unquestioned contact of Christianity with Korea came in 1592 A. D., at the time of the great invasion of the country by the Japanese.  As is well known, the Portuguese Jesuits established themselves in Japan early in the sixteenth century, and the religion early won for itself many thousands of converts.  Many people of high degree were believers, and many of the best soldiers in the land also.  When Hideyoshi became Shogun, he found this movement on his hands, and he did not like it a little bit.  He had already planned an expedition into Korea as a preliminary to an invasion of China.  He seized upon the opportunity of carrying that out, and, at the same time, of ridding himself of the powerful Christians.

Two armies were selected to go to Korea.  One was placed in charge of the Christian general, Konishi,[6] and the other under a bitterly anti-Christian Nichiren Buddhist, General Kato.  In Konishi's army, a score or more of the leaders were Christian men.  Hideyoshi seems to have thought that, if the army got beaten, and the Christians killed, he was well rid of them; while, if they won out, he could assign them the conquered territory to rule, and equally be rid of them.  Possibly his appointment of the hostile Kato was to insure disharmony and make assurance doubly sure.

The two armies landed together at Fusan, and started to march to Seoul, Kato by way of Chun Chu City and Konishi up past Andong.  Luck favoured Konishi, and he reached the capital first. The Court there, upon his approach, deserted the city, and fled away to the north.  The Japanese followed on up to the city of Pyengyang, and stayed there some months, but were finally forced

---

[6] *Royal Asiatic Society Records,* 1913, p. 2.

by cold and hunger to retreat to Fusan, where they set up garrisons, one near the city, and one further up the coast on a hill near Eulsan.

It was during this period of garrison life that Christianity really came to Korea. Konishi, who had been baptized by the Jesuits with the name "Augustin Arimandono," sent to the Jesuits in Japan for a missionary, and one of them named Gregorio de Cespedes came, accompanied by a Japanese priest called "Foucan Eion." These two men laboured for a whole year among the scattered Japanese camps, but Kato, hating all Christians, laid charges against Konishi of disloyalty, and Konishi was forced to return to Japan to defend himself. The priests were recalled and the organized work stopped, and apparently it was never renewed.

It is hardly likely that any of the Koreans of the country were influenced by the priests, or heard their teaching, for the Koreans had no dealings with the invaders. The people voluntarily devastated the whole country for miles around the camps, so as to cut off all support from the soldiers, and they either fought the soldiers when they came out on raids, or took to their heels and ran. Hundreds of Koreans were seized, however, and sent to Japan as slaves, both at this time and at earlier and later times, and, among them, there were many converts to the Christian Catholic faith. Record is made by Dallet, in his wonderful *Histoire de l'Eglise de Corée,* from which most of the following account is taken, of two such men in particular who were captured by Konishi and sent to his daughter, who was the wife of the governor of the island of Tsushima, half way between Korea and Japan, opposite Fusan. These two young men were of noble birth, one of them the son of the secretary of the King of Korea. The lady, herself a Christian, took pity on them, and sent one of them at once to the Jesuit school, purposing to send the other when he was old enough to go. Gregorio had preached in Tsushima on his way to Korea, and many of the people, including four of the Councillors, had been baptized. The boy sent to the Jesuit school graduated, taking the name of "Vincent." He was ordained as a priest, and was sent around to Peking to see if he might not be able to enter Korea from that side, and take the Gospel with him. He was unable to do so after several trials, so was recalled, and some years later died a martyr in the terrible, bloody persecutions which came to all of the Catholics in Japan.

Although no free Koreans within Korea heard the Gospel at this time or adopted it, hundreds in Japan became Christians, according to the reports sent home to Europe in those days by the Jesuit Fathers. Just a few years afterwards, when the bloody persecutions began, and the Catholic Church in Japan was practically annihilated, many Koreans died bravely for their faith. Dallet records the following as known cases among them,—In 1614, a Korean labourer at Nagasaki refused to recant. He was hung up on a cross like a fork, his legs were crushed, the cords of his thighs cut. When dead, his head was cut off, and the body chopped to pieces. The same year, another Korean, finding that his name was left off the list of those proscribed, came and demanded that it be put on. He was arrested and decapitated. In 1619, another was executed at Nagasaki, and, the following year, his wife also was killed. In 1622, of fifty-two martyrs, five were Koreans. In 1624, a man and his wife were executed at " Chambocon." In 1626, a student of the Jesuit school was put in gaol, beaten, exposed naked to the icy wind, given poison, which he vomited up, and was then burned alive. In 1629, sixty-four Christians were submerged alive in a sulphur lake, one being a Korean woman. Dallet gives the names of all of these, but they are taken from the Japanese, through the French, so it is impossible to guess what they would be in the Korean writing.

### III. Seventeenth Century Contacts

No Christians were made in Korea itself during the Japanese invasion, but, during the next one hundred and fifty years, the Korean embassies sent each year to Peking, often met the priests there, and reported the fact upon their return. In 1631, one of the ambassadors reported having seen an European (possibly Father Jean de la Roque [7]), ninety-seven years old, who seemed to be in the full possession of his faculties. He judged that the man

---

[7] Gale in *Korea Magazine*, 1918, p. 390.

must be a Taoist, since the members of that cult claim that through certain exercises one may live forever.

A famous Korean writer, named An Chung Pok, in 1785, wrote a vigorous criticism of Christianity,[3] in which among, other things, he says the following, " Books concerning the Western teaching arrived here during the last years of King Sunjo (1568–1609). Officials and ministers saw them, but they understood them to be like the books of the Taoists and Buddhists, and so set them aside as mere objects of curiosity.

" In the years Kemyo (1603) and Kapchin (1604), Christianity became popular with a certain class of young men, who contended for it, saying that God Himself had come down to earth, and given His commands through angels.  Alas, in a single day, their hearts were changed, and turned away from the writings of the Sages! It was like the boy who graduates in the Classics, and then comes home to call his mother by her first name, a sad state of affairs, indeed!

" There is a book called *Distant Messages,* by a priest, Aleni (arrived in China 1597), which says, ' Judea was a part of ancient Rome.  It is also called Palestine, the land where God visited the earth.'  Matteo Ricci (arrived in China 1592), in his book called *Truths About God,* says, ' In the second year of the Emperor Wunsoo, and, on the third day after the winter solstice, God chose a virgin, and, by means of birth, came and dwelt among men. His name was called " Jesus," which means " Saviour."  He taught for thirty-three years on that western frontier, and then He ascended again to heaven.'

' The foreign missionary claims to worship ' Chun ' (God?), and, in that respect, we are at one, but we do it in a right and proper way, while his is a wicked and deceitful way, and I oppose it.  For the Western missionary to call his teaching the ' Religion of God ' is most foolish, not to say blasphemous.  They think that, if they claim for their teaching the name of the Supreme Ruler of the Universe, no one will dare to oppose them on account of that all-prevailing name.  It is like using the name of the Em-

---

[3] *Korea Magazine,* 1917, p. 262; Gale, " History of Korea," 1927, *Korea Mission Field Magazine,* p. 82.

peror in order to accomplish one's private ends, a very clever trick, indeed!

" The religion of the literati puts the Sage in the place of God, to work for God in the governing of the people; to reward the good, and punish the evil.  Thus it makes God all in all, and shows that the literati act according to His Divine decrees.  How can the mere calling of it the 'Religion of God' make it Truth and Holiness?

" There was once a man called Meukja (Chinese—Mooti) (450 B. C.), a Chinaman, who wrote a book called the *Will of God*, in which he says, ' Those who follow the will of God know only love for all mankind, and, in love, seek other's profit.  Doing so, they will find their reward; running counter to His will, and hating will find punishment!'  The Western missionaries, exhorting us to put away enmity, and love all other people, talk just the same things as Meukja's ' Kyum-ai,' ' loving another as one's self.' When they teach to endure hardship and practice self-denial, that is the same as Meukja's ' Sang-keum,' ' Taking the hard way.' The only difference is that Meukja speaks of this present world and the missionaries of the future world.

" The Sages of China are very high and very great, and yet they never pretend to equal God Himself.  How foolish are these foreign missionaries to speak of their Founder in such extravagant and unreasonable terms!"

In 1720, another ambassador reports meeting and talking with the Catholic priests, and states that their doctrine was like Buddhism in some ways and like Confucianism in others.  Ni Ik[9] compared their doctrine of heaven and earth with that of Buddhism, and mentions the " seven virtues and seven vices " about which the priests taught.  Tradition says that a certain man named Hong Yoo Han, in 1770, studied what Ni Ik had written, and adopted the doctrine as his own.  Not having any Christian calendar, he kept the seventh, fourteenth, twenty-first, and twenty-eighth days of each lunar month, and, not knowing which days were fast days, he observed all days by refraining from pleasing

---

[9] *Korea Magazine*, 1917, p. 347.

foods. There is a record of a single Korean taken to Rome by Carlotte about 1600.[10]

In 1644, the Crown Prince of Korea and his younger brother were carried away as hostages to China, and there met and formed a friendship for Adam Schall, one of the German Jesuits.[11] The younger brother later became King of Korea in 1649. The young prince was not converted, but naturally felt friendly to the religion of his friend. In 1627, a Dutch ship, off its course and short of water, sent three sailors ashore in South Korea, and they were taken prisoner. Two of them later died fighting for their captors in Mnachuria, but the third, John Wettevree, remained in the service of the Korean Court for thirty years. In 1653,[12] another Dutch ship was wrecked on the coast, and thirty-six sailors became captives. Later several of them escaped to Japan and got back home. What contact Korea may have had with Christianity through these two parties, no one knows, but it is likely that Wettervree had some influence.

## IV. REAL INTRODUCTION OF CHRISTIANITY INTO OLD KOREA [13]

The founder of the Catholic Church in Korea was Yi Tuk So, called Yi Pyucki, one of the Yi family of Kyungju in Southeast Korea. Before him, in his family, there had been many military officials. He was large and strong, and his father wanted him to take the Mookwa examinations, but he refused, for he was interested only in literature and philosophy.

In the year 1777, Kwun Chul Sin, a famous scholar from Yangeun, 120 li southeast of Seoul, with Chung Yak Sun and a number of other nobles, went to an isolated Buddhist temple to rest and study together certain philosophical books. Pyucki heard of it, and went to join them. They had the usual Confucian books, and, in addition, several Catholic books that had been brought over from Peking. They read these last, and discussed them at great length together. Pyucki became convinced that the Catholic books

---

[10] *Royal Asiatic Society Records,* 1918, p. 95.
[11] Trollope in *Korea Magazine,* 1918, p. 391.
[12] *Korea Magazine,* 1917, p. 102.
[13] Most of what follows is from Dallet's *Histoire de l'Eglise de Coree.*

contained the truth with regard to all of the philosophical puzzles that had been bothering him, and he began from that time to keep holy one day in seven. As he had no calendar, he followed the plan of Hong Yoo Han mentioned above, and kept the seventh, fourteenth, twenty-first and twenty-eighth days of each lunar month, praying those days night and morning. Apparently he carried on all alone for six or seven years until 1783, when he met Chung Yak Sun and his brother, Chung Yak Yong, on a boat going down the Han River. He discussed these questions with them, and found them already so much interested that his own convictions were strengthened. He was sure in his mind that the doctrine was true, but he had no books beyond a tract or two. He did not know what the Church was like, how it was organized or managed, or anything about it.

At Seoul, when they arrived, he found that one of his friends, Yi Sung Heun, had been appointed the third member of the annual embassy that was to go to Peking that year. Pyucki went after him with all of his power, and, by his enthusiasm, convinced him that the doctrine was a wonderful thing, and that he must get in touch with the priests at Peking, and bring back copies of all of their books, and of all other articles that they used, and all possible information with regard to the religion. Sung Heun went to Peking, met the priests, was himself baptized by the priests with the new name of " Pierre," and brought back, in his baggage, books, crosses, images, and all sorts of other paraphernalia.

Pyucki studied the new books very thoroughly, and was more than ever convinced that he had found a wonderful thing. He began preaching it to his friends, and many nobles accepted the faith. Many opposed it strongly, but he held several notable debates with them, and silenced them all. Pyucki decided that, in order to get the movement better started, he must get a few big names of leaders for it. He selected the Kwuns of Yangeun, and went down to see them. There were five brothers in this family, all of the high nobility and so famous as scholars that students from far-off provinces flocked to their house for study. The oldest brother, and head of the house, was Kwun Chul Sin, the leader of the summer conference group back in 1777. Under Pyucki's exhortations, Chulsini was not at first converted, but his third brother, Ilsin, immediately adopted the faith, and was later baptized with the name of Xavier. Later, Chulsini and the entire household were converted. Yangeum, therefore, became the first strong centre of Christianity in Korea. The writer was most favoured, when he went to Korea in 1902, to have the privilege of starting some of the first Protestant churches in that county, and to minister to them thereafter for some twenty busy years.

At the time when the Kwuns were converted, there was a student living there and studying with them, a young man named Yi Tan Won. He was from far-off Chunan County in the province of Choong Chung. He also was converted, and baptized, and sent back to establish the Church in his home neighbourhood. He was very successful in winning converts, and in establishing there a second strong centre for the Gospel. Yoo Hang Kyum, of Chunju in Chulla Province, heard that the Kwuns had accepted a new doctrine of some sort, and came to find out about it. He, also, was converted, and, going back home, established a third thriving centre of influence. A little later, Chi Chongi, of Chinsoo, another place in Chulla Province, came, was converted, and went to establish the Church in his home town. Chung Yak Sun and his brother, Chung Yak Yong, lived at Matsuri, near the branching of the Han River, eighty li from Seoul. The next centre was opened there. In Seoul, two officials, brothers of Hong Nak Min (he himself was later christened " Luke," and baptized), were received, as were also Chi Chang Hong, one of the Court musicians, and Choi Chang Hyun, one of the Court interpreters. This last individual copied many of the Chinese books of doctrine which had been secured, and made them available for the new centres.

One reason why the doctrine spread so quickly was the existence of the " sarangs," guest-houses of the nobles. The people could not discuss politics freely, as it was dangerous. They spent a large part of their time visiting and gossiping in one another's guest-houses. The doctrine was a new and live topic of conversation, and was considered with the most intense interest.

In 1785, just one year after the doctrine had been taken up seriously, we find the first martyr for the faith, Kim Pum Oo, baptized "Thomas," one of the Court interpreters. He was arrested for having given up his national religion, and was being tortured when "Xavier" Kwun, and a group of the other believing nobles, went to the court, and demanded that the judge have them also arrested, since they believed the same as Thomas did. The judge did not dare order the arrest of men of such high rank. He put them off somehow, and went on with the trial. Thomas was finally exiled to Tanyang County in Choong Chung Province, but his health was so broken by his tortures that he died almost as soon as he got there.

That same year, Chung Sooki, tutor of the King, published a violent circular against the doctrine, but nothing came of it. Two other sad things happened that year when Yi Pyucki and Yi Sung Heuni, the two first believers, both apostatized. Sung Heuni's younger brother was violently opposed to the doctrine, and persecuted him, so that Sung Heuni recanted, and burned the books in his possession. Yi Pyucki's father beat him, and used every possible method to get him to recant. Finally the father took a rope, and threatened to hang himself, if Pyucki did not give up the doctrine, and Pyucki yielded. If he had not, Korean public opinion universally would have condemned him as lower than the beasts. Possibly he hoped to renew his vows later, but, if so, he had no chance, for, a few months later, he was taken sick and died. The next year, Yi Sung Heuni repented of his apostasy, and came back. He was taken in again by Kwun Ilsin, and the two Chung brothers (Yak Sun and Yak Yong), who were the leaders of the work.

That year these men decided that they would establish a hierarchy for the Church like that which Sung Heuni had seen in Peking. Xavier Kwun was elected by them as Bishop; Sung Heuni, Yi Tan Won, Yoon Hang Kyum and Choi Chang Hyun were elected priests. Choi Kwan Chun rented a house in Seoul for a church. For two years, these men exercised their office as priests, administering the Sacraments, and penances. The usual penance was beating on the shins, a typical old-time Korean punishment. One day, in reading one of the books, a doubt was raised as to the right of the hierarchy to serve, so they at once all resigned, and sent a messenger in the next embassy to ask about the matter. Yoon Yoo Il, a former pupil of the Kwuns, who lived in Yujoo, was the messenger. He was baptized in Peking and received the Communion there.

In the letter brought 'back, the Bishop confirmed their doubts about the hierarchy, forbidding it to serve. He praised their zeal, however, and sent many articles to be used in their worship. A second letter was sent the next year, asking many questions. Among the replies that came back was one which came like a bomb to the Christians. The Bishop of Peking forbade the Christians taking any part in ancestral worship in their homes. Immediately there was a great exodus from the Church, Yi Sung Heuni again among them. Only Kwun Il Sin, Yi Tan Won, Yoon Hang Kyum and Choi Kwan Chun of the old leaders were left. At this time, Choi Pil Kong, who later became a strong leader, was converted.

### Persecution of 1791

" Paul " Chi Chongi (also called Chi Yoo Song), of Chinsan in Chulla province, was a well known scholar. When he heard of the Bishop's order regarding ancestral worship, he burned the tablets which he already had. Shortly after that, his mother died, and he did not set up a tablet for her, or carry on the customary worship. Two anti-Christian noblemen in Seoul, Hong Nak An and Yi Kei Kyung, stirred up the Prime Minister to have Paul arrested, and he was seized with his cousin, " Jacques ' Kwun, who, as nephew to the deceased, should have performed the sacrifices if Paul refused. Kwun was also a nobleman whose family originally came from Andong, but he lived at the time in Kongju. The prisoners were submitted to the usual torture. The son claimed at first that it was on account of the pest then raging that he had omitted the sacrifices, but later he came out with a clear acknowledgment, saying that he had read the Catholic books. Both men were condemned to death, but the permission of the King was necessary before the sentence could be carried out, since they were noblemen. The King, who was of a kindly temperament, at first refused to give his permission, but he was bombarded so hard that he gave in. The next day he repented of it, as he feared that this one case might become a precedent, and many others be arrested. A second messenger was sent, but he arrived too late. Both prisoners had been decapitated.

The King's fears were amply justified. Immediately all of the enemies of the Christians felt that they could torture them at will. Word of the execution of the two Christians for burning the tablets and refusing to offer worship was published in every county in the country. Xavier Kwun was arrested, tortured terribly, but refused to recant, and he was exiled to the island of Quelpart. Choi Pil Kong was arrested, and tortured, and the magistrate claimed that he had recanted, so he was released. Many other Christians, including Yi Tan Won, of Chunan, founder of that centre, were arrested, but saved themselves by apostatizing. In later persecutions, most of them redeemed themselves.

There were many arrests near Kongju. The brother of " Laurent " Pak, of whom we shall hear much later, was among those seized there. Laurent himself went and rebuked the Governor for arresting the people, and was himself seized, beaten, had the cangue placed upon his neck, and was kept in gaol a whole month, during which time he refused to recant one single word. The grandfather of Andre Kim, who later became the first ordained Korean priest, was arrested, tortured and released. Pierre Wun Si Chang, of Hongju, was tortured repeatedly, beaten off and on all day long, and then, since he would not die, he was stripped naked, water was poured over him, and he was left out doors in zero weather, and froze to death. In 1794, twelve Christians were arrested and tortured. Eleven apostatized, the last man stood firm. They were all released. These cases, and the ones to follow, are not mere hearsay. They were all minutely investigated by Daveluy on the spot just a few years after the occurrences, and the reports are all from eye-witnesses.

Summary: In 1794, ten years after the baptism of Yi Sung Heuni, in spite of the lack of teachers, and in spite of persecutions and defections, there were four thousand Christians in Korea. At least four well known Christians had met public martyrdom, and likely there were many others. There are records of over fifty other Christians having been arrested and tortured. Likely there were hundreds of them in all.

### ARRIVAL OF THE CHINESE PRIEST

From the beginning in 1784, each year the Koreans had begged that a priest be sent to minister to them. In 1791, an Italian, Jean dos Remedios, was actually appointed, and went to the place opposite Wiju on the border to try to enter in, but, hearing of the great persecution, he delayed for a year. That year he died.

In 1794, a Chinese priest, Jacques Choo, crossed the border, and got safely to Seoul. He immediately began his work, but soon found that he must labour in secret, else he would be arrested and the work stopped. Two years after the priest came, the first traitor appeared among the Christians, Han Yung Ik. Through information filed by him, the two men who had escorted the priest from the border were arrested, tortured and beheaded. The traitor died that Fall far from home and alone.

During most of the time that the Chinese priest was in Korea, he lived in Seoul in the home of a devout widow, named Colombe Kang Wun Sook. She was formerly from Hongju, where she had been arrested once in 1791 and released. Her husband had apparently deserted her, and she came to Seoul with her stepson, and his wife, and her husband's mother. The priest at times stayed temporarily elsewhere, but his main home was here. The priest at least once visited in Yujoo, the home of Paul Yoon Yoo Il, the messenger who was martyred for bringing him into the country. We know also that he visited Chunju, Kongju, Nampo, Onyang, and the Chunan districts. His zeal was very great, and he was most industrious, but was hampered all the time by having to keep under cover. He founded one special men's brotherhood, called "Myungto," for the sake of special study. Colombe taught many of the women. There were four thousand Christians when the priest arrived. Just a few months later there were six thousand.

Persecution again breaking out, Yi Sung Heuni and Chung Yak Yong, two of the earliest Christians, made written statements of their apostacy and were exiled, the former to Yeisan and the latter to Kimseng. Yi Ka Hwan was the head of the " Namin " political party. He was not a Christian, and was one of those who had opposed Pyucki in debate in 1784. He lost his Court rank at this time, and was made a simple magistrate at Yujoo. In 1796, " Thomas " Kim Pong Heui, the minor district headman of Chung-yang in Choong Chung Province, was arrested, and tortured for being a Christian. They heated a cart-axle red-hot, and made him walk the length of it barefooted. They put a drum on his back, whitened his face, as was done for all condemned criminals ready for death, and paraded him around the market-place. A new magistrate arrived, re-tried his case, and freed him, but ordered him to leave the county.

In 1797, the Governor of Choong Chung Province ordered all Christians arrested and the Church annihilated. Many were arrested, but we do not have a record of their names. One, Paul of Chungyang, was tortured, was in gaol over a year, suffered the fever and terrible hunger, and the gaolers jumped on his cangue to make him yield. His bones were broken, and the marrow oozed out. There was no part of his body without wounds. They again jumped on his cangue, crushed his ribs in, and finally got rid of him.

Laurent Pak, who had been arrested before, was taken again in 1797. He was first beaten and had his flesh torn with pincers. He wore the cangue day and night for three months until his friends bribed the gaolers and got them to take it off. At his third trial, he was tortured and threatened with death; at the fourth, he was beaten and sent to Haimi; at the fifth at Haimi, he received five blows from the big club, and then was sent back to gaol; at the sixth trial, he was given twenty blows; at the seventh, he was beaten until his bones were broken; on a later occasion, he was left out all night in the mud to freeze to death. On his eighteenth trial, he was given fifty blows of the big club after water had been poured over him. In all, he received four hundred blows of the club and was eight days without water. They thought that he was dead, so washed off some of the blood and threw him out the door of the gaol. The Christians picked him up, and brought him back to life and fed him. The next day he was seized again and beaten. The judge asked if he was still alive, and, finding that he was, threatened to kill the gaoler if he did not finish him.  The gaoler beat him until he himself was totally exhausted, and Laurent would not die, so the gaoler strangled him.  He had been two years under the tortures, and yet did not deny his faith.

Others martyrized at this same time were—Jacques Wun of Hongju, cousin of Pierre Wun, who was martyrized in 1793.  He was beaten, both legs broken, was sent to Chungju, tortured a whole day there with whips, punching batons, and the big clubs, had his bones pulled out of their sockets, and died under the torture.  Pierre Chung of Tuksan, in Choong Chung, was beheaded in 1798, François Pang, a lower official, died in prison in Hongju, either by clubs or strangulation.  François Pai Kwan Kyum had apostatized in 1791, but repented.  He was beaten many times at Chungju till his flesh hung in shreds, and the bones protruded.  He died under the blows.

In 1800, the King, who had more or less protected the Christians, died, and, since many of the Christian leaders had been members of the " Namin " political party, their enemies of the other parties seized the pretext of religion to wipe them out.  Five months after the death of the King, came an Edict of the Regent against the Christians, and immediately arrests began.

### PERSECUTION OF 1801

Justin Choi Tong Sun, one of the original band at the monastery retreat in 1777, was exiled to Whanghai.  Choi Pil Kong and Pierre Choi were arrested.  Houses everywhere were searched and pillaged.  Many Christians fled.  Some apostatized to save their lives.  The second traitor appeared, Kim Ee Sam, originally a man from Choong Chung.  He gave evidence against crowds, and the gaols were crammed.  All who would apostatize were set free.  One judge tried to release wholesale the ordinary prisoners, but the Regent deposed him and sent him into exile for his clemency.  Yi Ka Hwan, former head of the Namin party, though not a Christian, was counted as one and arrested, and with him the twice-apostate Yi Sung Heun, Chung Yak Yong, also Kwun Chul Sin, eldest of the Yangeun brothers, also Chung Yak Sun, " Luke " Hong Nak Min, and several other famous men.  Kwun died in the prison under torture, as he was old. Nine others were decapitated. Many new believers in Yangeun and Yujoo were seized. Yi Tan Won, founder of the work in Chunan, who had apostatized in 1791 to save his life, stood forth at this time, and died for the faith at Kongju. Six were executed at Yujoo; two at Yangeun, one being the brother of the man Paul who brought the Chinese priest from the border and died for it. That family was practically annihilated by repeated martyrdoms.

In Seoul, six men were beheaded, one of them being a son of a former martyr, and the cousin of a second martyr. Four were arrested in Kwangju, one beheaded and three left in gaol. It is interesting to note how the Christians are all so inter-related by marriage, and also how so many of the martyrs are closely related to others martyred before.

The Chinese priest started to leave the country, but, after arriving at Wiju, decided that it was his duty to return and die with his flock. He thought that possibly his death might stop the persecution. He came back, gave himself up voluntarily, was tried, tortured horribly, taken out on the sands by Nodol, south of the city, and beheaded there, in the most revolting manner. The Government, fearing that the Chinese Emperor might hear about it and raise a fuss, spread the story that he was not a Chinaman, but a Quelpart Island Korean. Later they sent to the Emperor a long defence of their action in order to avoid reprisals.

The death of the priest did not stop the persecution. It even invaded families of the dominating Noron family. "Jossphat" Kim, of that party, was arrested, and beheaded. His family saved themselves by saying that he was an adopted son, and by disowning him. A dozen other nobles, almost as prominent, perished at the same time, and Colombe Kang, and four other women, were beheaded outside the West Gate of Seoul. About thirty other prominent people in the country, at Yujoo, Yangeun and in Chulla, died. Two men, condemned in Seoul, were sent down to Pyengsan and Pongsan Counties, in Whanghai Province, to be beheaded, thereby proclaiming the Gospel for almost the first time in Whanghai. About two hundred less distinguished people in Chulla were arrested, betrayed by the brother of Yoo Hang Kyum. Most of those apostatized. Five were taken back to Seoul, charged with the crime of rebellion, and then taken down to Chulla to be beheaded. All of their property was confiscated, and their families put under the ban. A well known woman named Luthgarde was also beheaded. She left a series of letters exhibiting her faith which would rank well among those of the best women saints of Mediæval Europe.

At this time it was that "Alexander" Hwang Sa Yung wrote his famous or infamous letter to the Pope, urging that the Pontiff send armies or fleets to force the Korean Government to grant religious liberty. Hwang was a Seoul gentleman living outside the West Gate at Aiogai. When the persecution began, he fled to Yeichun, and was kept hidden there in an underground room by some potters. He wrote his letter on silk with sympathetic ink, hoping to send it to Peking. His messenger was seized, and the letter discovered and read. Then he himself was arrested, and beheaded at Hongju. Whether his request that sixty-six thousand soldiers be sent was known to other Christians, or whether it was a purely individual project, we do not know. Certainly it was an unforgivable act of treason against his native land, and he richly deserved his punishment.

The persecution finally ran itself out. How many men actually died during the period, no one will ever know. Hwang Sa Yung, at one time estimated it at three hundred. Another writer said two hundred, but both were martyrized with companions after they made their statements. The total number of arrests must have been far over a thousand. At the end, the Church was in ruins, with every leader gone. Persecution ceased, but the edicts were not recalled, and any magistrate was at liberty to apply them whenever he wished. From time to time, sporadic arrests did occur, just often enough to keep the Christians always apprehensive of their safety.

Those who now assumed the leadership of the Church were "Jean" Chung Yak Yong, Hong Oo Song, son of the martyred "Luke" Hong Nak Min, and "Jean" Yi Ya Chin. The last of these wrote a letter to the Pope, and went himself to Peking to forward it, beseeching help for the Church. The Church in

Peking, however, was itself under terrible persecution just at the time, and the Bishop there could not promise anything. The only gain of that trip was the setting up anew of communications with Peking which had been interrupted. In 1813, there were three more martyrs in Kongju. That year, Jean Yi went again to Peking with the embassy, but received no encouragement as to the sending of a priest. During the years 1811–13, the Gospel spread to the eastern Kangwon and Kyungsang Provinces, and the next persecution fell there in 1815. Here, again, there was a traitor, Chun Chi Soo. It was a time of crop failure and famine. Chun encouraged the satellites of the magistrate in his county to pillage the Christians, pointing out that, as a proscribed sect, they dare not resist. The Christians thought that the men were ordinary robbers, and did resist, so were arrested for rebellion, and were taken in great numbers, the first ones to Kyungju, and later ones to Andong. Many starved to death in the prisons, since the gaolers, who were themselves hungry in the distressing time, stole their food. The persecution spread to Kangwon and Choong Chung Provinces. Seven men were executed at Taiku and one at Wonju.

The persecution of 1815 was unlike that of 1801, since it was wholly religious, while the previous one was partly political. The previous one began with malice aforethought. This happened almost by accident. The traitor, Chun, committed some small crime and was sent to gaol, condemned by the magistrate to starvation. The Christians fed him and kept him alive.

In 1816, the messenger to Peking was Paul Chung, whose father and brother had both been beheaded in 1801. Coming back, he was delayed one day, and escaped arrest, since all of his family were seized the day before. Three were beheaded. At the same time, seven other Christians suffered the death penalty at Haimi near Hongju. For the next five years, things seemed to be fairly quiet. In 1821, there was a terrible scourge of cholera where four hundred thousand people are said to have died. At this time, the leaders of the Church were Paul Chung, the embassy messenger, and Choi Keum Heun, brother of two previous martyrs. Each time that Paul went to Peking, he took with him as servants one or two of the Christians, and they were baptized in Peking and received the Sacrament. These trips could only be made once a year, however, when the regular embassy went, unless there happened to be special embassies of felicitation of some sort.

In 1823, they managed to convert "August" Yoo Yong Sim, one of the interpreters of the embassy, and that made things a bit easier for them. In 1824, they received a promise that, on the following year, a priest would come, but, when they went to the meeting-place beyond the Yalu, no priest was there. New persecutions had broken out in China, and none could be spared. In 1823, the next great persecution broke out in Chulla in the southwest. Many arrests were made, but the King refused to give permission for executions, so the prisoners were left to languish in the gaols. The movement spread to Sangju in Kyungsang Province. Only one place in Choong Chung was touched by it. This persecution differed from the previous ones in that it lasted only three months, and secondly in the fact that the Central Government was not at all interested in it, and thirdly that such multitudes of the prisoners were simply marooned in gaol and left there until brought out for execution at the time of the next public persecution. Lastly, there were a very great number of apostacies, four hundred from among five hundred arrested in one place. It must be remembered, of course, that most of these were new believers. Almost none of them had yet been baptized. None had ever seen a priest. Although they apostatized publicly, they went right on believing in their hearts, and many of them, in later persecutions, suffered martyrdom without complaint.

## Summary of the First Fifty Years

The period 1784–1801 might be called the Period of "Creation and Development," the year 1801, that of "Politics and Religion Mixed," and the period 1802–1832, that of "Continuous Persecution." During all of these periods, the Central Government did not take a very active hand in the persecutions, because it despised the whole group. It did not tolerate them. The edicts of 1801 were not recalled. During all of these fifty years, they had a priest for but seven years, yet, after being again and again almost annihilated, new leaders always took charge, and the work went on. The total of arrests in the fifty years must have been thousands. The total of deaths for the cause were likely at least three hundred, judging from the actual records with names and dates gathered for one-third that number.

From 1801, when the Chinese priest was killed, nearly every year the Koreans begged the Bishop of Peking to send another. Twice they sent letters direct to the Pope. But conditions in China, and, even in the Church in Europe, made it impossible to send any one. In 1827, however, the College of Cardinals wrote the French Mission Étrangères, asking them if they could take up a Mission in Korea. They already had far more work than they could support. All of their Missions were pleading for more means and workers, which they could not give. They wrote to each of their Missions, laying the matter before them, and asking what they should do. Nearly every Mission answered at once that they would submit to the necessary privations to enable the new Mission to be founded, and several men volunteered to be the first to go.

In 1832, the Protestant missionary, Charles Gutzlaff, visited Choong Chung Province in a British ship and distributed many copies of the Scriptures. He met several of the Catholic Christians. Later the books were all brought back to him.

Bruguiere, Bishop of Capse in Siam, was appointed in 1832, and started at once for his field, taking with him a young Chinese student, named "Joseph," who had been in the Penang Theological Seminary. At about the same time, the Cardinals themselves appointed directly a Chinese student named Pacifique Yu, who had just graduated from their seminary at Naples. Bruguiere went by ship to Macao, and then overland in disguise most of the way to North China. He was so eager to go that he insisted upon travelling right through the rainy season, and suffered torments. When he reached North China, he found bitter persecutions going on there, and had many narrow escapes from being arrested. The young priest, Joseph, went ahead for him to Peking to meet the Korean embassy, and later again went on to Manchuria to prepare for him there.

When they met the first embassy, the Koreans were not very cordial to the idea of a French priest coming into the country, as they feared that he would be recognized, and that would start another persecution. The Chinese priest, Pacifique Yu, passed Bruguiere and went on into Korea, in 1833. This man evidently conceived the idea of holding Korea for himself, and of preventing the entrance of the French priests. He selected several young men to be educated for the priesthood, and sent word to the Bishop of Peking asking him to take charge of the young men and train them. He ignored Bruguiere. Bruguiere sent word to the Koreans that he would be there across the Yalu from Wiju at the next embassy time, and ordered them to prepare for his entrance, which they agreed to do.

While Bruguiere was still in Siam, he was intimate with another young priest named Chastan, who asked permission to go with him to Korea. His permission was delayed, so that he could not start with Bruguiere, but he started a bit later to follow him. He was delayed by the persecutions, and ultimately was unable to overtake Bruguiere. While the latter was in Macao, he met a priest named Maubant, who had been assigned to the district of Szuchun in China. Maubant was much attracted by the idea of going to Korea, and applied to his Bishop to be released from his China appointment that he might go. He overtook Bruguiere, and was with him in North China when he started for Wiju.

Bruguiere was almost at the meeting-place, and only a few weeks' time were left, when he was taken sick and died. Word came back to Maubant, and he at once went to the place, buried his friend, and took upon himself the mission of entering Korea. He met the embassy, disguised himself and joined them, and arrived at Wiju late at night. He had to enter the city through the city sewer drain to avoid the frontier guards. He reached Seoul January 26, 1836, the first foreign priest to cross the border. One year later, in 1837, Chastan also entered. Before he came, Maubant had discovered that the Chinese priest, Pacifique Yu, was all bad, that he was living an immoral life, and gathering money by crooked methods. He warned him repeatedly, and, when he refused to repent, he deposed him, and ordered him back to Peking.

The priest tried to organize a party of defence, but he was unable to do so, and departed. The day that Chastan entered Korea, a poor widow, arrested as a Christian, had her legs broken, and her lips torn, and she died under the torture.

The new missionaries began work at once with interpreters. During 1837, they baptized twelve hundred and thirty-seven people and heard two thousand and seventy-eight confessions. As soon as word got back to the Pope of the death of Bruguiere, he appointed, as Bishop, Imbert, also of Siam, a teacher of theology there. Imbert traversed most of China by land, and crossed the border into Korea December 17, 1837. In 1836, Maubant selected and sent to the seminary at Macao three young Koreans to be educated as priests. Bishop Imbert took the same title as Bruguiere had used, " Bishop of Capse."

## PERSECUTION OF 1839

Hardly had the three priests gotten settled, when the great persecution of 1839 broke out. One of the Chunju Yi family, a bitter enemy of the Christians, became Prime Minister. A relative of one of the Christians in Seoul informed about them. The house in which the Bishop had been living was raided, and his Bishop robes were taken. All of the members of the household were arrested and tortured. The head of the house and two young girls in it were beaten until their bones were broken and the marrow flowed out. Forty people were condemned to death. Scarcely any one recanted. They courted death and martyrdom. Many were sent back to the gaols to be further tortured, so as to break their spirit. A few days later, thirty-five more were taken, tortured and condemned to death; several young girls were beaten with the big clubs, had their bones pulled out of their sockets and then were beaten thirteen times with hot irons. These girls, though twenty-five years of age, had vowed themselves to celibacy. The magistrate had them stripped naked and thrown into the gaol of common robbers, but not one of the men would touch them. One sickly man apostatized at first. Later he repented, and besieged the gaol to be taken in. He was given twenty-five blows and died. The judges wonderingly said, " Other prisoners always plead to be allowed to live. Here I ask you to apostatize, and you refuse ! "

The King, in 1839, published a long Edict against the Christians,[14] part of which is as follows,—" King Chung-jong, my predecessor, was a man blessed of Heaven, and yet he was pestered by this Sung Heun who purchased every sort of Western book that he could lay his hands on, calling them the ' Religion of God.' Wholly unauthorized by any use in the past, with all manner of subtlety, and in a way no Sage ever thought of, this cult increased and grew so as to fascinate and deceive the people till it brought upon us a world of barbarians and wild beasts. King Chung-jong, seeing this and fearing what the end might be, severely punished the leaders, but the leaders only, letting the others go free in the hope that their love of life might induce them to turn to a better way. He could not possibly have shown more leniency. Even swine and monsters of the deep, yes, owls and wolves, would have been moved by this to repent, but these people, having lost all conscience, and being incapable of reform, continued until the year Sinyoo (1801), when they were dealt with according to their evil ways. Be careful, I beg of you, my people, my ministers. As a parent teaching a child, or an older brother a younger, I address you. Study how to lead these people away from their place of danger, and those, not wholly dead, urge and counsel. Those who will not listen, let them be destroyed as a warning to the world, so that this evil may never show its head again ! "

Many of those arrested, after being repeatedly beaten, died of the pest in the gaol. One man received one hundred and ten blows of the large club. One woman received three hundred, and since she was not able then to nurse her baby, the baby died. A big reward was offered for the capture of the three French priests. A traitor, Kim Ni Saing, betrayed the Bishop, and he was taken. He was given horrible beatings, and the bending of bones. Six times they tore his legs with blows of the clubs. Eight times he was tortured otherwise. The flesh was torn from his legs with cords, and he was also beaten with the triangular-shaped clubs.

---

[14] *Korea Magazine*, 1917, p. 487.

Two widows, at about the same time, were tortured, one receiving in all three hundred and forty blows, and the other three hundred and ninety. An old lady of sixty-one died of her torture in the prison. One man who had been beaten and had had his cangue jumped on in the gaol, nevertheless, preached to one of his companions in the gaol and won him to the faith. Many sons of the martyrs of 1801 suffered.

Bishop Imbert decided that, if he and his two colleagues were out of the way, the persecution would stop, so he sent word to the other two men to come in and give themselves up. They did so, and all three were again tried with horrible tortures, condemned, and taken out upon the river sands of Yongsan near Seoul. Soldiers played at mimic warfare, stabbing at them from this and that angle until they were almost gone, when their heads were taken off. Their bodies lay exposed on the sands for five days, and then the Christians came secretly at night, and took them away, and buried them on the mountain across the river.

Still the persecution went on, ten being beheaded at once in Seoul, one a son, and one a grandson of previous martyrs. Many palace women were among those seized. One young girl became a Christian, and her own brother gave her poison in the gaol to kill her and avoid the family disgrace. She vomited it up. Then he tried to get the gaoler to strangle her. One man in Wonju was put through the tortures twelve times, receiving two hundred and eighty blows of the large club. He was finally strangled in the prison. Many were burned with hot irons. Hundreds deserted their homes, and all of their possessions, and took refuge back in the mountains. One old lady of sixty-nine received two hundred and thirty blows. One seven-year-old child was beaten and then strangled in the gaol. People began to complain of the many decapitations, so strangulation was quite generally substituted. In Seoul, fifteen were so killed in one day.

At last, the fire burned itself out, and the persecution grew less. Sixty Christians are known to have been beheaded, or, at least, to have died in the prisons from beating, the axe or strangulation. Some people apostatized, but most of them later renewed their vows. Many of these later died for their faith. The greatest number of arrests at this time were in Kangwon Province east of Seoul. There were about one hundred in Chulla and the same in Choong Chung Provinces. No one knows how many were taken at the capital. This persecution was, like that of 1801, a systematic effort of the Central Government to annihilate the Church. The local magistrates were far less interested than they had been at former times. They simply carried out their orders. Unlike the persecution of 1801, there was nothing political whatever about the persecution of 1839. In 1801, most of those who died were of the nobility; in 1839, although many of the nobility suffered, the greater number were from the middle classes. Few women suffered in 1801. Multitudes of them were taken in 1839. One result of this widespread persecution was to make the Gospel known to the farthest corner of the land.

Once more the Church was without leaders, and again a Bishop was appointed, this time Ferreol, also from Siam. He came quite quickly on horseback almost the whole way across China, entered over the Nankow Pass, passed near Peking, and then via Shanhaikwan to Mukden. He was not very well received by the Chinese Christians in Mukden, but went on to Pienmoon, opposite Wiju, to wait for the embassy in the Fall of 1840, but, on account of the persecutions, there were no Christians in the embassy that year, and Ferreol retired to Mongolia to wait for the following year. In 1841, he sent a courier to Pienmoon to meet the embassy, but his courier died on the way. A letter written by Bishop Imbert before his death came through to him, urging his successor to wait a while before trying to come in. It was at about this time that another priest named Maistre became very much interested in Korea. He was staying at Macao.

In 1842, the Opium War of the English and Chinese took place. Some of the French battleships were in Canton, and the Commander planned to go to Korea, and ask about the three priests who had been killed, and also to try to enter into commercial relations with the country. He asked that the two young Korean students in the Macao Seminary be sent with him as interpreters, and they agreed to go. As the students knew only Latin and Chinese, and no French, or very little, Maistre was to go on one ship with one man, and a teacher in the Macao Seminary with the second on another ship. The Opium War ended suddenly, however. The ships were recalled to Europe and everything stopped.

The two students mentioned were those sent by Maubant in 1836. The third had died of disease. These two were Andre Kim and Thomas Choi. Maistre and the two Koreans and a French priest destined for Manchuria service, embarked in a Chinese junk, and, after many hardships, landed in Manchuria. They were seized by the Chinese Customs officials, and would have been put in gaol, except for the cleverness of Andre Kim. They had great hardships travelling through Manchuria, but finally joined Ferreol in Mongolia.

Ferreol, who had originally been appointed simply Coadjutator with Imbert, was consecrated, by the Vicar Apostolic of Manchuria, to be full Bishop, taking the name " Bishop of Bellina." In 1842, he sent Andre Kim to the border to meet the embassy. When it came, they received their first detailed news of the death of the three priests, but were told that it would be impossible for the priest to enter the country that year. Andre Kim decided to try to enter alone, feeling that he could arrange somehow for the Bishop to get in. He crossed in the darkness, and somehow managed to pass the Customs House by concealing himself in a herd of passing cattle. The next day in an inn, however, he was violently accused of being a Chinaman, became frightened, wandered all night in the bitter cold on the mountains, and the next night crossed back into Manchuria and returned to Bishop Ferreol.

In Northeast Korea, on the Tumen River, there used to be the town of Hoong Choong, where one day in the year only, for just a few hours, a fair was held between the Koreans and the Chinese. The Bishop sent Andre Kim there to see if a way could not be opened to enter the country from that side. Kim met the Christians there, but they strongly advised against trying to enter there, since the place was so guarded, so he returned to the Bishop. In 1844, Ferreol went with Andre to meet the embassy. Maistre stayed in Mongolia. The embassy members came, but strongly objected to the Bishop trying to cross the border, since it was being guarded more strongly even than usual, following the death of the three priests. The Bishop then decided to send Andre Kim into the country to see if he could not devise some means of entering. Andre crossed over, and the Bishop returned in a Chinese junk to Macao.

Andre Kim went through to Seoul, arranged for taking a Korean junk across the Yellow Sea, enrolled a crew of farmers, said that he would pilot the boat himself, and set off. They met terrible storms, and the boat was almost lost, but it finally reached the coast, and there met a Chinese junk which towed them to Shanghai. There Kim anchored in the midst of the foreign battle-ships, and asked them to protect him from the Chinese authorities. He got in touch with the Chinese Christians and, through them, sent word to Ferreol. During his long wait at Shanghai, the officials made a good deal of trouble for him, but the foreign ships protected him. There he first met Daveluy.

When Ferreol finally arrived, they arranged for a Chinese junk to tow their Korean junk up the coast to a point opposite Korea, and Ferreol and Daveluy went on board secretly. It took them two months to work on up the coast, because the winds were contrary most of the time. They anchored for weeks in two different harbours with a hundred or so other junks, and the priests had to stay concealed all of the time for fear of being detected and arrested. At last, they started north. They met a terrible storm, and were about to sink. They decided to transfer the priests to the Chinese junk, and hauled up close to do so, when the rope broke. They tried again and again to get connections, but could not. The Chinese junk sailed away, and they were left to the mercy of the waves, being driven hither and thither, and not having the faintest idea whether they were bound for the open Pacific or where they were going. After two days, they drove ashore upon some land, and, to their delight, discovered that it was the Korean island of Quelpart, off the southern coast. They landed, repaired the boat, sailed on up the coast to Kangkyengi, and landed. It was then 1845, just five years since Ferreol first tried to enter the country.

Some months later, arrangements were made for Andre Kim to go with a junk to a place off Whanghai Province to meet Maistre and Thomas Choi, and to send back to China letters to the Bishop, by the Chinese junk that would bring Maistre. Something went wrong. The ship was seized, the crew told about the letters, the Chinese junk was also seized, and the letters taken. Fortunately, Maistre was not on it, or Thomas Choi. Andre Kim and eight of the sailors were arrested. Seven were strangled in the prison. Andre Kim and the last man were executed at Seoul as the French priests had been.

In 1846, Maistre and Thomas Choi made the long trip across to Hoong Choong, to the fair on the northeast coast of Korea, but were arrested by the Chinese authorities and turned back.

### PERSECUTION OF 1846

Again that year a terrible persecution broke out in Korea as a result of the incident of the capture of Andre Kim. There was the same old story of torturings and beatings. This persecution was less virulent, however, than those which had gone before. Many girls who had devoted themselves to celibacy were treated with special severity.

Maistre and Thomas Choi went back to west Manchuria, and, in the Fall of 1846, again tried to enter through Wiju, but the persecutions of that year stopped them, so they went on down to Macao. There they found a French Government expedition of two gunboats about to go to Korea to receive the answer of that Government to the letter left there a year before, demanding an explanation of the killing of the priests. Maistre and Thomas Choi agreed to go along as interpreters. These two boats, the *Gloire* and the *Victorieuse,* went aground off Choong Chung Province on the island of Koonkoto, and were wrecked. The crew took refuge on an island with as much of their gear as they could save. Maistre met several Christians, and talked with them, but the Captain would not let him leave. One small boat sent to Shanghai for help brought back an English ship which took off the crew, but not the equipment. The Korean Government later seized the equipment and used the guns as models for some which it made. Maistre went on back to Shanghai. He had hoped to go back with the ship which was to be sent to retrieve the wreckage, but the various political troubles in France made that expedition impossible.

A few months later, Maistre and Janson crossed in a Chinese junk from Shanghai to Whanghai Province in Korea, hoping to meet a Korean boat which was to be sent to meet them. They missed the boat, and the Chinese Captain became frightened and sailed back to China. Maistre hired another junk, and a Jesuit brother agreed to act as pilot. They planned to go to Koonkoto, and make believe that they were sent to ask about the wreckage of the boats. They crossed over, and, after a great deal of difficulty, found the island. They had long parleys with the local officials, and then, in the night, Maistre and Thomas Choi got away to the shore. The next day, watchers were placed everywhere, and maintained night and day all along the coast, so that they could not then have gotten in. Maistre was at last inside the land, however, after ten long years of striving. Hardly had he gotten to Seoul, and started work, when Bishop Ferreol died of disease, and overwork. In 1854, Janson got into the country via boats off the coast, but was soon taken with some form of insanity, and died.

While the Bishop still lived, he and Daveluy and Maistre were working night and day. In 1855, the report showed 9,040 confessions heard, 516 new baptized, and 13,638 Christians in all. Daveluy started work on a Korean dictionary. He also began to gather original documents and letters regarding all of the former persecutions and martyrdoms. It was from these documents, sent back to Europe, that Dallet's great book was created.

Again a new Bishop was appointed, this time Berneux, who had for eleven years been a missionary in Manchuria. He, with two young men, Pourthe and Petitnicolas, came in a Chinese junk from Shanghai and met a Korean junk off Whanghai Province, and were transferred. The Korean junk sailed right up the Han River to within thirty li of Seoul, where the priests put on mourners' clothing, and walked the rest of the way. Shortly after their arrival, Daveluy was appointed Coadjutator Bishop, taking the title of "Bishop of Acones." A few months later, Maistre also died of disease. In 1858, Feron arrived, and, at the service where Daveluy was constituted Bishop, a Synod was organized with the

Korean priest Thomas Choi and the five French priests. Pourthe was placed in charge of the seminary for young Korean priests, set up secretly far out in the mountains of Kangwon. Later Petitnicolas was associated with him. In 1857, the figures for the Mission were—confessions, 9,381; total Christians, 15,106.

In 1860, the Head of all of the Police in the country conceived the idea that another persecution would please his superiors, so he made many arrests, and filled the gaols. He received no special support in it, and the thing fizzled out. That year, four more missionaries arrived, Joanno, Landre, Ridel and Calais. In that year, Thomas Choi, the only indigenous priest, died. His death was a terrible loss to the whole work, for he carried a district larger and more difficult to work than any of the foreign priests, and apparently was as wise and efficient as Andre Kim, who had been martyred. That year, the figures were 11,114 confessions and 16,700 total believers. It was in 1860 that the Allied battleships besieged the Taku forts near Tientsin, marched to Peking and looted the Summer Palace. All of the Orient was shaken when this news came, and it made a tremendous commotion in Korea. They had believed that the Middle Kingdom was invincible against the world. If China could not withstand the barbarians, who could?

In 1862, there were many political disturbances all through Korea, people rebelling against the petty oppressions of local officials, etc. This was the time of the beginning of the Tonghak Movement. Daveluy was in charge of the Church work in Kyungsang Province at this time, and it was opening up wonderfully. For the first time, believers began to come also from Whanghai Province, especially from the district of Haiju, Pongsan and Pyengsan, the three places where Christians had been martyred. There were a few also from Pyengyang. Bishop Berneux, although sick a large part of the time, personally took charge of this work.[15] It was in 1862 that the King died, and Queen Cho seized the seals of state, and appointed the King who ruled from that time until 1910. She made the father of the young King to be Regent, thereby opening the way for the great

---

[15] *Korean Repository*, 1898, p. 88.

slaughters of 1866, for the Regent was a devout Buddhist, and anti-Christian.

In 1863, Aumaitre arrived, but Joanno and Landre died of disease. That year, the Russians began beating upon the back door of the country up in Northeast Korea, and the Court was greatly worried. In 1864, Bretenieres, Doris, Beaulieu and Huin arrived. A printing press was in operation, and thirteen different books had been published and large editions sent out all over the country. As there had been only sporadic persecutions since 1846, the work had grown greatly. Many of the highest families in the kingdom were Christians, many high officials, and women of the palace, and the nurse of the King and his mother, wife of the Regent, were believers. The Government knew very well that the French priests were in the country, but the capture of Peking had made them very timid as to anything that had to do with foreigners.

A Christian official in the palace presented to the Regent a memorial, suggesting that, in order to escape the pressure of the Russians on the border, they send word to the English and the French, asking them to come and make an alliance. He said that he felt sure that the Bishop could arrange the matter. The Regent seemed for a time to consider the matter favourably. Arrangements for a conference between the Bishop and the Regent were partly made. A Council of State was called, however, and the whole plan was rejected, and, since now the illegal presence in the country of the French priests was officially known, a decree went out to arrest them and all of the Christians, and to annihilate the Church. The Regent may have had some idea of dealing with the priests and the Christians as friends before the Edict, but he certainly did not show any signs of friendship thereafter. His Decree sent out throughout the land reads as follows:

" The barbarians from beyond the seas have violated our borders, and invaded our land. If we do not fight them, we must make treaties with them. Those who favour making treaties are traitors to their home country. Let this be a warning to ten thousand generations. Decree dated in the year ' Pyungin ' (1866)." [16]

---

[16] *Korean Repository*, 1898, p. 247; *Korea Magazine*, 1917, p. 496.

Tablets bearing this Edict were set up in front of the Confucian Temple in Seoul, and by the big bell in the middle of the city and elsewhere.

### FINAL PERSECUTION OF 1866

The satellites of the Court swooped down upon the Christians everywhere, arresting them, looting their houses, binding men, women and children and taking them to gaol. One by one the Bishops and seven of the ten priests were taken, dragged before the highest court in Seoul, submitted to the old familiar tortures of the clubs, the dislocating of bones, and the jabbing in the ribs with the sharp ends of the clubs. In groups, they were taken out and executed, seven of them at Yongsan near Seoul. Daveluy and one other were executed down near Hongju. In his case, the executioner, after striking him once with the axe, stopped and haggled for a time about his fee, before striking the final blow.

No one knows how many Koreans were martyred. The arrests ran into thousands, and no doubt the deaths to many hundreds. Even today, one meets in the territory around Seoul, old people who, in childhood, had members of their families slaughtered. The writer met many such in his early years before 1910. Apparently little or no proof of guilt was asked for. The word of one informer was sufficient. Blood flowed in rivers outside the West Gate of Seoul, and in all of the large centres of the south where there had already been so many martyrdoms. The Regent seemed actually insane in his passionate desire to wipe out the Doctrine root and branch.

All but three of the priests, Ridel, Feron and Calais, were killed. These three stayed in hiding for a short time, and then decided that they must send one of their number for assistance. Ridel went out by boat, and, after great privations, reached Chefoo, and then Shanghai, where he found the French fleet. A short time after, it became still more dangerous for Feron and Calais, so they, also, started out in a small boat, and ultimately got to Chefoo.

The French Admiral, with Ridel as interpreter, came to Korea to demand satisfaction for the killing of the priests. They anchored off the island of Kanghwa, and tried to get in touch with the Government. Failing in that, several of their smaller boats started up the river for the capital. The Koreans made a row of boats across the river to hinder their progress, but a shot or two from the ships cleared the obstruction away. They came up within ten li of the city, but still could not get in contact with any one in authority, so they retired down the river, and looted the island of Kanghwa. The Koreans gathered in one of the ancient fortresses there, and, when a small force of two hundred and sixty French soldiers were sent against them, they disabled or killed about half of them. The French retreated and then sailed away.

The Regent, believing that they had beaten the foreigners, when great China had failed, increased the severity of the persecutions. When his work was done, the Church was practically non-existent. Every leader was gone. Nine of the twelve priests were dead. The young Korean theological students were scattered to the four winds, or dead. The printing press was destroyed, and there was a death penalty for any one who owned one of the books, or to any one daring to call themselves Christian. Christianity in Old Korea practically came to a standstill in 1866. Ten years later, the priests were still trying to somehow get back. Twenty years later, in 1876, the first treaty with a foreign nation was made. In 1884, the Protestants entered the country. Since then the Mission work has been one of the wonders of Modern Missions.

The whole story of Christianity in Old Korea is one of which any nation might be proud. If the " blood of the martyrs is the seed of the Church," it is easy to understand the victories of the Church in modern days. In the preceding lectures, we have given a picture of the various attempts of the people to " explain and understand the Universe, to adjust themselves to Ultimate Reality." They were brave and praiseworthy attempts. The progress in those various experiments is easily evident. Each step was in the right direction. The older cults are becoming moribund, and all seem destined to pass away. Protestants now claim 300,000 believers in the country, and the Catholics almost half of that. The churches are most of them fully self-governing, and self-propagating, and they are on the way at least to becoming self-supporting.

# VIII

## SUMMARY

OUR study is completed. We have surveyed the facts concerning the various separate cults in the land, and their development and doctrines. In closing, let us note again their connections with the lands around about them. Buddhism clearly came from India, through China, to Korea, and then was passed on to Japan. For seventy years, in the sixth century, there was an organic connection maintained there, but since then the two " churches " have developed entirely separately, that in one country becoming the " Creed of Half Japan," while in Korea it has been slipping away. Korea gave Buddhism to Japan, and once gave it back to China when the cult there was almost destroyed.

Confucianism, in essence, came to Korea in 1122 B. C., and, in actuality, in the very early centuries after Christ, and has been pursued all down the centuries most diligently up until that sad " Kaponyun " year of 1895. It was passed on to Japan possibly in the sixth century, lay unnoticed there possibly till the tenth century, and since then, if we may believe Nitobe, has been transformed into Bushido by a fusion with Zen cult ideas, and it has died out there as an organization.

Kwanoo and his spirit hosts swept across the line from China, and he established himself in many centres, but especially in the worship in private homes. Mohammedanism and Japanese Shinto were stopped at the border, and Taoism came across only as an influence and not as a separate cult. Chuntokyo, a synthetic religion with many original features, has grown up inside the land since 1861.

Most original and indigenous of all, Korean Shamanism is seen to be vitally linked up with that of Siberia and that of China, developing itself under the influence of the two strains into some-

thing quite different from either, and wholly different from Japanese Shinto, which looks as though it were purely indigenous, or
came from some other direction.

Lastly Christianity, the most active of all missionary religions,
is seen forcing its way in after a fight of centuries, leaving in its
wake the mangled bodies of its martyrs, but preparing the way for
better things in modern Chosen.

All along the line, the nation is intimately locked up in the bundle
of life with its neighbour countries, receiving and passing on
towards the east most of its religious acquisitions. Curiously, in
spite of the energy and alertness of its eastern neighbour, Japan,
no religious impulses seem ever to have come back from there.

The "Religions of Old Korea" seem destined to pass away to
make room for brighter things. As they are laid aside, the modern
generation will do well to be grateful to those who, in past ages,
toiled to make known the best which they knew in their various
stages of mental and spiritual development. The following little
prayer used to be repeated each year as they offered sacrifices at
the Sajik Shrine, and the present generation might well repeat it
in grateful remembrance and sincere adoration:

> " God indeed did give religion,
> To our ancient land Chosen;
> This is why we offer worship,
> Praying that He give a blessing." [1]

---

[1] *Korea Magazine*, 1917, p. 413.

# APPENDICES

## I

### The Bible of the Chuntokyo, the Tong Kyung Tai Chun

#### Preface and Introduction

At the time when our Teacher preached these words, I worried a good deal lest there be some mistake in them. In the year 1863, he instructed me to get them published, and I tried, but did not succeed. Alas! after 1864, the Great Tribulation came. Our Doctrine fell into disrepute for eighteen years. In 1882, I remembered our Teacher's command, and, after consultation with many friends, I decided to carry out the publishing. We found many errors and omissions in the book, so it was revised in accordance with our remembrance of the Master's teaching, and it was published by the Mokchun Company. This is, therefore, an unabridged edition of the book, and I write these few lines to put at the end of it.

> 1888 Middle Springtime.
> (signed) Choi Si Hyung (Haiwul),
> Head of the Chuntokyo.

How could this great work have been made if the Heavenly Power had not commanded men to do it! Oh, the man! the great Divine Teacher! According to his nature, he was Heaven; according to his flesh, he was man. According to his Divine essence, he was both Heaven and humanity. According to his doctrine, he united together the virtue of Heaven and of mankind. His message to the world is thus revivified. The materials in this book were collected from the libraries of many different men, and with great difficulty edited. When our great Master died, the Doctrine was handed over to the Haiwul Sinsa, who published this book at the command of our late Master, and he has published our religion to all the world.

Since I, his child, received this great authority from the Teacher, I have carried my ordinary responsibilities with anxiety and trepidation of mind. I cannot hope to see such results as our great Teacher saw. I am herewith reprinting this book to help men to refresh their minds, and at the same time to show to all the world the basis of our teaching.

Forty-eighth year since the Foundation.

Third Head of the Order, Son Pyung Heui.

This book is the holy and spiritual Word. If we do not publish it abroad, holiness will be lost from the world. Our Divine Master wrote the book originally, and gave it to his successors. The men of that day recorded what they heard, but there were some errors in it. Our Haiwul Teacher revised it, filling it up and correcting it, but, during the Great Tribulation, it was lost. It was later re-gathered from many sources, but, by comparing with the originals has again been found filled with errors. Therefore, our Wiam Teacher, Son Pyung Heui, has asked me to study the book carefully. If I had kept it as a private study only, I would have sinned against the Divine Master. We have, therefore, gathered funds and are publishing it to all the world.

(signed) Kim Yun Kook.

### THE TONGKYUNG TAICHUN—HISTORY

As we observe the Springs and Autumns as they were from the beginning, and the other powers of Nature, we see that they do not change in their nature, nor in the sequence in which they come. These things are the works of Chun Chu (God) which have been revealed in the world. Ignorant people do not understand that it is by the grace of Chun Chu (God) that the rains come, and the dew, although they are aware of the fact that these things do not come by man's power.

Since the time of the original Five Emperors (of China), there have been many writers who have explained how the sun and moon and stars were made, and how the heavens revolve, so that we know that the heavenly bodies move according to certain fixed laws. Their moving and stopping, rising and falling, is due to the command of Chun Chu (God). They show reverence for and obey the decrees of Chun Chu (God).

Men may become saints also in this way, by studying the Doctrine and virtue, and by practising them. What, then, is our Doctrine? It is from Chun Chu (God). What is virtue? It is Chun Chu's (God's) virtue. Therefore we people may become saints by mastering the Doctrine and virtue. Is it not a joy to know that a mere man may become a real saint? In recent years, however, all of the people of the world have been looking after their own interests only, and they do not obey the truth of Chun Chu, nor the commands of Chun Chu (God). As I meditated upon this, my heart was much troubled, and I did not know what to do. In 1860, news came of the arrival of the foreigners (Roman Catholic priests) in our land; that they had not come to take away our country or our wealth, but that they were erecting churches and preaching their Doctrine. When I heard this, I pondered over it a great deal, and wondered if their Doctrine could be true.

Suddenly, in the fourth month, I was taken sick with a mysterious disease; my heart acted strangely, and I was shaken by chills. No doctor could understand my symptoms, nor could I describe my feelings clearly. One day, as I lay ill, a spirit spoke to me and said, "Do not be afraid. I am He whom the people call 'Sangchei' (God). Do you know me?" I said, "What do you wish, Lord?" He answered, "At the present time, I have no standing among men. I want to send you into the world to teach my Doctrine to the people. Do not doubt, do not doubt." "Shall I teach according to the 'Suhak' (Western Learning—Roman Catholic Doctrine)?" I asked. "No, I have a certain charm (Ryongpoo), which is called 'Sunyak' (spirit medicine). It is shaped like the Taikook (the symbol in the middle of the old Korean flag), or like the Koongkoong (a curved, bow-like figure). Receive it, and heal the diseases of the people. Use it as a prayer, and teach it to the people in my name. If you do this, you will have long life, and virtue, and your virtue will go out to all of the world." Strength was given to me, and I took the paper and swallowed it, and instantly my disease was cured, and I knew that it had been a supernatural sickness.

Afterwards, I tried the medicine upon other sick folks. I found that some were helped, and some were not. I could not understand the reason for this. I watched carefully, and discovered that those who gave full respect and attention to God received benefits, and that others did not. Again and again I tried it. It was evident that results depended upon the faith of the patient. I realized then the reason why our country was in the state in which it was, full of diseases and with no peace from one year's end to another. It was an evil fate put upon us like a curse.

On the other hand, I saw the Western nations. This did not seem to apply to them, for they seemed always to be fighting and always to be victorious. It looked as though the whole world would be gobbled up by them, and we ourselves, too, unless we waked up. I wondered what we could do to protect our country, and help our fellow-men.

Alas! people do not understand what goes on in the world. When I tried to teach them, they closed their minds even more to the truth, and would not obey the Doctrine. This is a terrible thing! The Sages (of Confucianism) are no better than they, for they have no power to correct the evils of the world. I determined to write a few words in order carefully to instruct the people, and to reveal to them the truth. Oh, ye people, carefully note this instruction!

### BASAL THEORY OF OUR TONGHAK RELIGION

The Chuntokyo, Heavenly Way, though it has no visibility or form which may be seen by the human eye, is still a definite Way. The earth has its huge surface and is foursquare. The heavens have their nine stars to light the nine districts, *i. e.*, the whole world (Ed.—here there is a quotation from the Classics illustrating this), and the earth has its eight directions which point out the eight divisions of it. Light follows darkness, and *vice versa*, and the four seasons come in their order while the heavenly bodies do not change in any way. The Eum, and the Yang[1] act always according to their nature, and thousands of things are created by them. Man is the most spiritual being that exists.

We see, then, that there are three grades of existence, Heaven, Earth and Man; and the Five Elements, fire, water, wood, iron, earth. Heaven is the head, Earth the material, and Man is the outgrowth of the Five Elements. The four Seasons, and the time of rain, dew, frost and snow are never transposed. The dew, like people, does not know why it acts as it does. Some say that it acts by the grace of God, others that it is a work of Nature. If we say that it is a work of grace, that is an intangible matter hard to explain; if we say that it is because of Nature, that is not much easier. Why is this? It is because neither of these has been properly defined up till now.

In the year 1860, there was a great tribulation on the earth.[2] The people's minds were all confused and they did not know what to do. There were strange rumours among the people that the foreigners' religion was the thing that had given them victory, and that, by magic, they could do all things, so that no enemy could stand before them on the battlefield. China had fallen, and soon our time would come. Why are the foreigners so powerful? It is because of their religion. That Doctrine is called "Suhak," "Western Learning," and their purpose in life is studying about

---

[1] The Eum and Yang are the Yang and Yin in China. The two opposing elements which by their interaction was supposed by the Orient to have evolved all things. They are visualized by means of the two commas revolving around one another in the centre of the old Korean flag. Sometimes they are said to be the male and female elements in creation.

[2] This was the shock brought to the Orient by the capture of the Taku forts near Tientsin by the allied nations, and the victorious march to Peking.

God. They call their teaching and the whole institution " Seung-kyo," " Holy Doctrine," or " Holy Church." Is it not natural to suppose that they have learned God's appointed times for things, and that they have received the commands of God?

The puzzle was impossible for me to solve. I felt as though old age were coming upon me. My body became chilled. I felt a spirit come, and heard him speak to me, but my eyes could not see nor my ears hear, and my mind was dull. I arose and asked, " What can all of this mean? " An answer came, " My thought about this is the same as your thought, but how can ordinary men know it? They know of Heaven and Earth, but what do they know about spirits? I am spirit, and you are also. Study the Doctrine diligently, and write it in a book. Teach the people, and cause them to live according to the right rules, and I will give you long life." I did study it, and pondered it for a whole year, and then I found the fundamental secret, and I made a prayer formula (or charm) to aid one in receiving the spirit, and also a formula of twenty-one characters to be recited.

In the year 1859, many learned men came to me, and asked me why God sent me into the world. I replied that it was to receive the eternal truth. They asked again, " What is the name of your Doctrine? " I replied, " It is Chuntokyo, the Doctrine of the Heavenly Way." They asked again, " Then, is it any different from Suhak " (Roman Catholicism). I replied, " Yanghak (for-eign teaching) resembles it somewhat, but it is very different. The Western Religion is like a mere rigmarole of prayer sentences, and it has no power. Their purpose is similar to mine, but they do not have the truth." They asked how that was. I answered, " My Doctrine conforms with man's reason. It shows one how to con-trol his mind, think clearly, control his temper, and acquire infor-mation. These foreigners have no logical sequence in their speaking, nor order in their written books, and no decorum in their worship. They only pray for selfish benefits. They have no proper spirit to inspire them in their physical life, and there is no teaching concerning the true God in their system. They have an appearance of it, but no reality. They do not have our sacred Formula; their Doctrine is like that of ' Hu Moo,'[3] and they do not really study to know God. Their differences from us are quite remarkable."

Then they said, " If the Doctrine is similar to theirs, let us call ours also ' Western Doctrine,' ' Suhak.' " I replied, " No, that would not be right. I was born in the Orient, and in the Orient

---

[3] An ancient Chinese religion not much esteemed.

received my Message. The Doctrine is Heaven's Doctrine, but the teaching is Eastern Teaching, Tonghak. They live in the West and we in the East. It is more fitting to call their Doctrine 'Suhak,' and mine 'Tonghak.'"

They asked me again to repeat the Sacred Formula, and I did, as follows:

> "Chi Keui Keum Chi Won Wi Tai Kang
> Si Chun Chu Cho Hwa Chung
> Yung Sei Pool Mang Man Sa Chi."

They asked the meaning, and I said, "I will tell you,—'Chi Keui' means 'God' (or Infinite Energy). Chi means 'infinite' and Keui means energy or force. This God controls everything and orders all things. He (or It) seems to have some sort of form, but I cannot describe it. One cannot see or hear him. It is a sort of atmosphere.

"'Keum Chi' means to 'enter into' the Doctrine (or the Doctrine into me), and means that the spirit or Chi Keui is abiding in me.

"'Won Wi' means to yearn or ask for a thing desired.

"'Tai Kang' means, 'May it generally pour down.'

"'Si' means that the 'Chi Keui' has been 'honourably' escorted into a person by his desire and will, and that he is fitted for his work in life.

"'Chun Chu' means the Lord of Heaven [a] (God).

"'Cho Hwa' means natural power or Nature itself.

"'Chung' means uprightness of mind, or establishing.

"'Yung Sei' means a man's whole life, or forever.

"'Pool Mang' means not to forget.

"'Man Sa' means all things.

"'Chi' means to understand the Doctrine and receive the knowledge. The whole Formula has for its purpose the securing of virtue, and never forgetting it, for it is most powerful, most spiritual and most holy."

They asked again, "If the mind of God is the same thing as the mind of man, why should there be 'good and evil'?"

I replied, "God arranges for man's welfare and for his destiny, so that the saints have the virtues of good spirits and settled convictions. Their virtues put them in harmony with Earth and Heaven. But the common people have wrong spirits and minds without sound convictions. They are not in harmony with

---

[a] This is one of the common names for the personal Christian God. Note that it is always used by Chuntokyo in a slightly different sense, less personal.

Heaven and Earth. Is it not clear, therefore, that their destiny is different?"

They asked again, "Why do the people of the earth not worship God?" I said, "Everybody calls upon God when he is nearing death. That is a proof that the life of man depends upon God. Even the ancient Sages said that all men were made by God. But the people do not as yet clearly understand this."

He asked, "What would happen to a man who cursed your Doctrine?" I said, "He may do as he likes about that." "How is that?" he asked. I said, "My Doctrine is wholly new in the world, and cannot be compared with that of any other age. To those who observe it, it seems at first empty, but later it seems full to overflowing for them. To those who merely hear it, it may seem full, but is empty."

He said, "How about apostates, then?" I said, "Such men are not worth talking about." He asked, "Why?" I said, "We should simply have nothing to do with such men." "Why should men believe and then become apostates?" he asked. I said, "Such a man is like the wind or the grass." He asked, "How can you say that the spirit has come to such a one?" I answered, "The spirit does not choose both the good and the evil." He said, "Then it apparently makes no difference whether he had the spirit or not."

I explained, "In the days of Yo and Soon,[5] all of the people became Yos and Soons. The destiny of the present age seems to be to go around and around, with the world. They bless and they curse, are in God and, then, again, not in Him. If one tries to puzzle this out, he will injure his brain, and it is impossible to understand it anyway. I wish that I could tell you of my own blessed experiences. These other things, all of them, have no relation to me."

O Spirit! what a definite set of requirements, practical and understandable, thou hast given in the Doctrine! Only because we have not fully learned it, we cannot make all of the explanations which we would wish. I can only show the elementary truths to help men to cultivate their bodies, develop their knowledge and renew their minds. All of the endless destinies of Heaven and Earth, and the uttermost truths of the Doctrine are in this book. May all of you men receive it carefully, and build your holy virtue!

### TEACHING FOR EDIFICATION

The teachings of Origin, Form, Truth and Virtue are the basal

---

[5] These are Yao and Shun, the ancient legendary kings of China's Golden Age.

rules of the Chuntokyo, and deep consideration should be given to them, and, from them, men should select what they will do. The Sages received their knowledge without study, and some ancient scholars received theirs only after long meditation. We should study with all our might and get every possible bit of information from our teachers, following the example of these ancient kings.

I was born in the Orient, and at first I wasted much time, so that I almost failed to live up to the record of my family as a scholar, and I almost lapsed down among the lower classes. I look back to the kings who lived in the days of my forefathers. To them my ancestors performed their full duty, even to giving their lives. We are now again in a critical time for royalty. My father did his duty by the King, and did not disgrace his ancestors. He even adopted the name of an ancestor who lived six generations back. Was that not a filial thing to do? At the age of forty, he renounced political ambitions, and spent all of his time writing poetry and travelling about. He was fond of Nature. His home was in Kyungju, and there were beautiful mountains, and fine-looking rocks to the north, and clear lakes to the west. Peach blossoms dropping into the water made it a new world. The blue waters of the river in front of the house resembled the first fishing-place of Tai-Kong, the founder of our Dynasty. The lake near the house would attract Yumkei himself, that famous scholar and naturalist. The house was called " Yongdam," the same name as that of the famous Chinese Sage, Chai Kal Yang. Old age came to him early and could not be averted. I was left an orphan at the age of sixteen.

I had no knowledge at all then, being so young. My father's work was all destroyed and my ancestors shamed thereby. I tried to work for a living, but did not know how. Was it not a pitiful thing? Because of my faulty education, I gave up political ambitions. My estate gradually dwindled away, and made me look anxiously towards the future. At the age of forty, I had no house of my own, no place to shelter me. Then I determined to move my family to Yongdam, my father's former home. That was in the tenth moon of the year 1859. In the fourth moon of 1860, I received the revelation of the Doctrine.

This revelation was most unexpected to me. I had consulted sorceresses and fortune-tellers, and had read of the manner in which people in the ancient times worshipped God in the time of the Three Emperors of China. I mourned over the decadence of the people of my day, and their neglect of the Doctrine. I studied the old Doctrine carefully, and found it all most reasonable. The teaching of Confucius was founded upon one truth, and that of

Buddhism was not far different from it. It is right to examine things old and new if one would learn, and the examination should be made with an open mind. I had not at first any idea of starting a propaganda. I only wanted to know the truth.

In the third moon of 1861, many of my best friends came to me, and persuaded me to establish the Doctrine and teach it to others. I agreed to do so. I had the spirit medicine in my chest, and also the Twenty-One Character Formula for long life. I opened my house to guests. When a group of them assembled, I taught them. They received the teaching well. There were young and old among them. The ancient Sages taught " In Yee Yay Chi " (meekness, truth, decorum, knowledge). I taught particularly self-control and a right spirit.

Just once I offered sacrifice in fulfilling a vow, but after that I freed myself from that forever. The wearing of ceremonial robes, and the rules for putting them on and taking them off interested the Sages very much, but they did not interest me. Eating things beside the road (in the Shamanistic worship of shrines), or folding the hands back of the head (practices of those professing to follow Taoism) are practices of the lower classes, and not worth doing.

Sages do not eat unclean four-footed animals any more than they would expose themselves to taking cold from dampness, nor would I. I do not require celibacy of my followers, because the law of the land does not prohibit marriage. One should never repeat the Sacred Formula while lying upon a bed, for that is sacrilegious. It is our Supreme Law. Is it not a wonderful Doctrine?

When we see a bit of perfect handwriting, we think that it may have been written by the famous writer, Wang Heui. If we see a man reading poetry, we judge that he is a scholar. If a man once repents, he should never again be avaricious, even though he sees the wealth of Suk Soong. If a boy works hard and masters the whole curriculum, he will be changed, and becomes as beautiful as a fairy, and he will never be sick enough to require a doctor. The only way for one to master the Doctrine and receive edification from it is through the individual's own efforts and through his own personality.

If a person depends upon hearsay for my teachings, or even upon written reports, he is apt to get a wrong idea of them. I was worried about this, fearing that many might thus get incorrect ideas, especially those who live at a distance, for it is not easy for them to come to me from afar, and besides I do not care to have too many come for fear of the Government, as it might make trouble for me. Because of this, I have carefully written out this statement, and I hope that you will read it carefully and respect its teachings.

"From faith to works" is the foundation principle of my Doctrine. Outsiders may criticize it, but let them do so. One should teach the truth and let error take care of itself. One should make up his mind after deep consideration, and then stick to his convictions. No matter whether you understand it at first or not, if you will study as I have said, you will soon become accomplished in the Doctrine. Then faith and works will come together. Men say that in order to accomplish things, they must first believe in them, and then they can do them. That is true, and I hope that you will follow that plan.

### What is True and What is Not True (Poem)

Everything in the world from generation to generation has its form and shape. If we judge all things by their appearances as seen with the naked eye, we are apt to make wrong judgments. The reality of things is more difficult to express than is their superficial appearance. I have had parents, and will in the future have descendants. As to the future, one can make certain judgments based upon present experience, but, as to the past, how man was first made and the like, no one can know clearly. If one's thinking is faulty, he may align himself on the side opposite to the truth, for example,—

Chun Wang, Heaven's King (Tangoon?), was said to have been first a man, and then later he became a King. How can one say that this is true, since he had no ancestors? Could one be born without parents? Possibly such things might have happened in the beginning. But the tradition is that he became a teacher and king over the world. Kings are set up by law and teachers through graduations. If there was no king before Chun Wang, whence did he get his laws? If there were no teachers, whence did he get his ceremonial induction into office. It is impossible to say.

Was he born, or did he arise spontaneously? If we say that he was born, we cannot explain how it happened. If we say that he arose spontaneously, we are still more at sea as to how it came about. If we try to reason around in circles like this, we shall lose our ability to make distinctions between what is true and what is not. Now we do know those distinctions. Still, in spite of all, truths concerning the creation are beyond our power to grasp or demonstrate. People imagine that things happen in cycles, but there is no proof of such a thing. Certain things we do know and can demonstrate. The reasons do not change, though we do not know the reason. Water on the mountain-side always acts in the same way. Children know their parents, though no one has introduced them. Is this not so?

How is it that you do not know when a Sage is born into the world, you people? The Milky Way is cleansed every thousand years, and all of the Orient says that, whenever it is cleansed, a Sage is born. Why is that? Is it because the Milky Way knows that a Sage is to be born and changes itself? (The Korean expression for "Milky Way" is "Silvery River.")

See the bull working at the plow. He seems to have some understanding, and a mind and knowledge. If so, why does he toil for men and then die early, while he still has strength to defend himself? See the young crow feed from the mother bird. It knows how to treat its parents with piety. The swallows know their master, and always return to the same house for nesting.

What is not true is very difficult to distinguish, but truth is easily recognized. Whatever conforms to the purpose of the Creator is true; whatever does not so conform, is untrue.

### CHOOKMOON, A SUPPLICATION

I was born in Korea and am abiding among my people. I have received the grace of Heaven and Earth, as well as the virtue of the sun and moon which shine upon me. I did not before know the way of truth, so, for a long time, was sunk into the bitter sea of this world's life. I lost all remembrance. Now I understand the True Doctrine and know that today is a time of holiness. I deeply regret my former sin, and desire to follow Thy guidance, whatever Thou showest me to do, and I promise Thee that I will not forget. In order to understand my mind and the Doctrine, I make clean my place of prayer, and offer Thee this cup of water which I pray Thee to be pleased to take.

### FORMULÆ FOR VARIOUS OCCASIONS

The Formula to be used in receiving the spirit is "Chi Keui Keum Chi Sa Wul Lai." This means "Most Holy Spirit (Infinite Energy), now come in."

The Formula for prayer for long life is, "Si Chun Choo Yung A Chang Saing Moo Koong Man Sa Ji," which means, "God abides in me, and gives me long life, and the ability to know all things."

The Formula to be used in public meetings, "Wi Chun Choo A Chung Yung Sei Pool Mang Man Sa Ji," which means, "God is for me, and considers my circumstances, and forgets not for eternity, so all things will be well with me."

Another Formula for receiving the spirit is, "Chi Keui Keum

Chi Won Wi Tai Kang," which means, " May Infinite Energy (God), which is now abiding in me, be poured out upon all the Universe according to my yearning desire ! "

The balance of the Original Formula is " Si Chun Chu Cho Hwa Chung Yung Sei Pool Mang Man Sa Ji," and means, " Since this Chi Keui abides in me, I am identified with God and of one nature with creation. Should I ever forget this, all the Universe will know it.'

## POEMS OF THE MASTER WHICH REVEAL THE DOCTRINE

### On the Vernal Equinox

Where the spirit of the Doctrine abides,
  Evil cannot come.
The many people of the world
  Do not meet death in the same way.

### An Occasional Poem

Who can know when the ice goes out from the river,
  And the holy birdies begin to sing?
I know not whence my fate is coming.

Another:

  I have received life long commendation
    Which is my eternal destiny.
  And which the holy and virtuous receive.

Another:

  The lake of Yongdam flows,
    Becomes the fountain of all the seas.
  The Spring comes back to Koo-ak mountain
    It is the flower of all the world.

Another:

Whenever I think of the Sacred Formula Words, I know
  That it has conquered all of the evils of the world.

### A Proverb

Broad my Doctrine is but condensed,
  About righteousness, we do not say much.
There is no special truth except what rests upon
  Honesty, Reverence and Faith.

### Poem

I study it in such a way
Then I know something of it.
I am not worried by this world's cares.

### Poem

Every direction and every valley I travelled over;
  Every river and mountain I know.
Every pine and every cedar tree stand among their green;
  Every branch and every leaf, a thousand joinings.

An old stork begat a son.
  He will traverse the world,
Flying to and fro
Will be respected by everyone.

Fate! Fate! has it come or not?
  Time! Time! who understands it?
Holy bird! Holy Bird! Sign for the Sages.
  River, river (Milky Way), sign of wise men to be born.

### Poem

The pretty peach blossoms bloom in the Spring Palace
  And are a joy to all wise men.

### Poem

The height of the Diamond Mountain Peaks
  One step, another step, one sings as he climbs,
Destinies will all be made more clear,
  The more carefully that he meditates.
The various expressions of the Doctrine
  Will grow more like as he goes along.
  There are a thousand blooms
On the branches of a thousand years.
  The moon becomes a mirror
In the midst of the four sea's clouds.

While a man climbs up a tower,
  He is like a stork.
When a horse rides in a boat,
  He is like the heavenly Dragon.

Although men are different from Confucius
  His mind was not unlike theirs.
Altho there may not be a thousand copies of a book,
  The ideas may be as large as though there were.

    It flies up in the skies.
      Is it the red of red flowers?
    It spreads itself over the branches.
      Is it the green of green trees?
    It flies up in the air.
      Is it the whiteness of the snow?
    It flows over the field.
      Is it the clearness of the river?

### Poem

It sails on the waves
  Which should not sweep over the beach.
A man talks quietly on the road.
  It is the beautiful moonlight with the east breeze.
The height of Tai San Mountain.
  When did Confucius climb so high?

### Poem

  The coolness of the breezes came,
    When Too Cham understood his fault.
  The clearness of the river came,
    When Soja spent time with his friends.
  The depth of lake was fine,
    When Yumkei enjoyed his life.
  The deep green of the bamboo shows
    The sincere hearts of the Sages.
  The green of the pine trees is
    A good friend to Spou.
  The brightness of the moon
    Rested lovingly on Taipaik Mountain.

The sound heard by the ears, and the sight seen by the eyes
  Is talked about quietly all down the ages.
A thousand miles is covered with white snow.
  All birds fly to the thousand mountains.
It gets brighter as one goes up the eastern hill.
  Why does the western peak look as it does?

(Note—These last two lines mean, "When Tonghak reveals its brightness, why does Suhak stand in its way?")

### WARNING TO SCHOLARS WHO HURRY THE DOCTRINE TOO MUCH

The destiny of the whole nation (three thousand li of mountains and rivers) depends upon the Doctrine. The fountain is deep and its waters of truth come from far. If I hold my mind intently, I can taste the flavour of it. One can do this if he desires. Turn away, therefore, from dark thoughts, and cultivate a calm, judicial mind. Only as the Doctrine fills your mind, may you have a right attitude. When that happens, the spirit will take possession of you, and you will receive Enlightenment concerning the future. Do not worry about the petty faults of others. Do good to others. This great Doctrine is not for petty matters. Do your best, and it will help you greatly. A great man understands secret things. If he goes on without haste, in time he will accomplish his work and have a long, happy life.

The mind of man is naturally pure, and has no scars upon it. If you cultivate your mind, you can understand virtue, and, if your virtue be increased, it will be identified with the Doctrine. The Doctrine concerns itself with virtue, and not with the man himself. It concerns itself with faith, and not so much with works. It is near and not far off. It may be received by being honest, and not by petitioning for it. Although it seems not true, it is true. Although it may seem far off, it is very near.

### A Secret or a Prophecy

Today many people ask about the Doctrine,
But what do they mean by it?
This is the beginning of the year 1863.
There will be many opportunities to accom-
plish our proper work.
Do not say that it is too late.
Do not worry about the future.

In the new morning, I sing a song,
And wait for a good destiny.
During the last year a spiritual friend
From the northwest came to visit me.
This is my house, I know,
And now is the proper time.
Since the Spring has come
The news may be known.
We may know that the spirit of all the earth
Is very near to us today.
At a certain time that day,
Spirit-minded friends will meet,

But the mysteries of the great Doctrine
    Will never be known by the lowly.


When the South Star falls,
    The Silvery River comes from the north.
The Doctrine becomes as high as Heaven.
    All difficulties pass away.


Through the mirror, I can see for a thousand miles.
    My mind is open when the midnight moon comes out.
Who receives the rain but the people?
    Man's life goes by like the wind.
I want to wash away all of the dust that falls upon me
    So I ride on the stork and go to fairy land.
The moon is bright on clear nights, but has no meaning.
    Good talk and laughter are customs of mankind.
What profit does a man get from all of this world?
    Ask for the Doctrine today. You might receive it.
It has its great truth, but many do not understand it.
    Those who long for it will receive it.
God made all people and He also made the Doctrine.
    Every baby has his own spirit which none may know.
If I study with all my heart without ceasing,
    Everything will be understood, small and great.
I met the Spring holiday on horseback.
    I want to go back home, and do my former work.
It is righteousness, faith, decorum, wisdom
    I like them for my men.
When may I sit down with all of my friends,
    And quietly talk over our best opportunities?
I do not know about the news of the world.
I would like to know whether things are true or not.
    When the weather is overcast on the southern hill,
All of my friends come and gather together,
    But they do not know what is right,
Their names have not been famous.
    What a joy it is to gather ourselves together,
Talk and write, our ideas going deeper!
    Although we had wanted for a long time to do it,
We had not had a chance before,
    We will ever be friends though we now depart,
The deer are lost in the garden of Chin.
    Which party do I belong to?

### Poem

The holy bird has sung in the house of Choo.
　　You might know it.
Although I have not seen all of the worlds,
　　I have known this one.
This makes a man have a great ambition within him,
　　Vain imaginations float in the mind.
A noise of a river I have heard,
　　It was not the Tongchung Lake.
It makes me question whether or not
　　I shall sit down at Ak Yang Noo.
When I think that it is the uttermost thing,
　　It is simply out of sight.
I doubt whether I follow the sun,
　　And can be in the shadow, too.

### Poem

If you do not know whence you can get wisdom,
　　Do not seek far. Study your own mind.
If you do not know where you can get virtue,
　　Think how your own body was made.
If you do not know what the command of God is,
　　Look back to the lights in your own mind.
If you do not know what the Doctrine is,
　　Measure your own faith.
If you do not know what sincerity is,
　　Think whether your mind has lost it.
If you do not know what reverence is,
　　Never cease from piety.
If you do not know what honour is,
　　Just go on living for others and not for self alone.
If you do not know the condition of your own mind,
　　See if your work is for self or others.

### Poem

I do not know whence I can get wisdom,
　　Else I would send my mind there to get it.
I know not where I can get virtue,
　　And cannot ask for it speaking plainly.
I do not know what God's commands are,
　　I know not how to receive His truth.
As I do not know what the Doctrine is,
　　I look out for myself and not for others.

As I do not know what real sincerity is,
    I am contented with knowledge only.
As I do not know what reverence and piety are,
    I am afraid that my mind is sleeping.
As I do not know what fear is,
    I always feel conscious of sin.
As I do not know the condition of my own mind,
    I fear that I have done wrong previously.

### Poem

It is not difficult if I try to overcome it
    Whenever I do meet difficulties.
It is better to keep the mind and spirit
    Mild as the Spring weather.

### Poem of the Night

It is shameful of all these girls
    Who want to spend their lives luxuriously.
Who knows their mind—only the breezes do.
Their faces are covered with white clouds.

The lotus flower dropped down into the water,
    The fishes became butterflies.
The moon shines into the sea,
    The clouds become soil.

The cuckoo sings when the cuckoo flower blooms.
    The holy bird sings where its holy flowers are.
The stork walks on his shadow when he crosses the river.
    The moon loses its light when the clouds chase after it.
The fish become dragons when there are many fish in the lake.
    It is very windy when the wind drives the tiger from the forest.
The wind has a regular path which she travels,
    But loses it when she comes back again.
When a man looks back in front of the moon,
    It is always in front of him.
There is no mark when I walk on smoke crossing the road.
    The clouds are piled on the mountain-top,
But never increase its height a little bit.
    Although there are many mountain folk, they are not all fairies.
Although there are many adults, they are not all soldiers.
    The pebbles on the river bottom count the clouds as they pass.
The butterfly measures the branches of the flowers
    When the wind goes by.

The wind goes down when a man comes into the room.
The mountain falls into the water,
When the boat leaves the bank of the river.
The Spring wind blows in when the flower gate is opened.
The Autumn moon goes when the bamboo fence makes a hole in it.
Though the shadow of a man drops into the water,
His clothing never gets wet.
The looking-glass looks back at the lady, but does not talk.
The half moon over the mountain becomes its comb.
The lotus leaf upon the water becomes its fan.
The smoke locks up the willow tree on the lake.
The lamplight enlarges the hook on the sailing mast of a ship.

*Poem*

Look at the way in which a man uses his pen.
How carefully he also holds his mind.
Of the Five Elements, our country belongs to Wood.
Our people know how to write.
I was born and educated here in the Orient,
Therefore I mention the East, our country, first.
This is not the same as selfishness of mind.
It also does not pertain to writing.
With peaceful mind and spirit, one strokes a letter,
The whole sometimes depends upon a dot.
First of all you prepare your pen brush carefully,
Of ink you must not be stingy.
You can use thick paper and put words on it.
You may write words large and small.
Begin with force and right shapes will come forth,
Which will be lofty as the mountains and strong as rocks.

## II

### THE OKCHU KYUNG—BIBLE OF THE SHAMANS

The Nine Heaven Original Controlling, Thunder Shaking
Chunchon Book.

" King of the thunder shaking spiritual heavens,
Controller of all of the Nine Heavens,

Riding upon nine phoenix birds, he meditates the doctrine,
Laying hold of the Law, he rides upon the Kirin.

He rules the spirits of all of the mountains,
And controls all of the spirits of the thunder.

The Number Three Spirit of the Kapeulpyung cycle meets the
sixth and
Surveys all of the good and evil men in the world.

Chunchon takes away all of their troubles,
  Hence we call him by his precious name,—

The Nine Heaven Original Controlling, Thunder Shaking
  Chunchon."

As we recite the above formula, the Nine Heaven Original Controlling, Thunder Shaking Chunchon is in his Okchung Heaven
(Jade Heaven), seated in the middle of things, surrounded by the
kings of the ten directions of the heavens. This place is the Jade
King Palace, which is called "Eulso Mira Kwan." He is in the
Chakeup Kokmil room. They open a satchel that is like a jewel,
and read the radiant writings therein, and, putting their heads together, they discuss the mysterious meanings. As they deliberate,
all of the other spirits pass quietly around on tiptoe.

Chunchon, sitting peacefully, reads one of the books, and all of
the rulers of the regions, as they hear, raise a shout of acclaim, and
move around in the air. The female spirits scatter flowers all
about them, and then, going back, and taking hold of the hems of
one another's skirts, they dance playfully. All of the spirits then
coming forward, carry in front of them a "Chul" (banner like a
hockey stick with streamers), and behind them they carry an
"Ave" emblem. The banner with the dragon picture and the
chariot drawn by "Nan" birds moves through the air. They
meet on the platform where the letter "Ok" (precious) is written, the platform made of the seven precious things. At that time,
Noisa Hoong (the thunder ruling white-haired old one) comes out
and addresses Chunchon, bowing low to the earth and flushing red.
"You, Chunchon, are most merciful and holy, the father of all
peoples, teacher of the ten thousand spirits! The heavens are now
all assembled in thy presence!"

Chunchon looks into a small box, and reads the precious letters
in it. How mysterious and deep those letters are it is impossible
to estimate. Among them, however, are these,—"The 'Ok'
(precious) Heaven controls all of the other thirty-six heavens,
their inner apartments, and middle courts, the east and west
lighted places, the depths and heights, the four departments and
six places; also the 'yoosa' officials and their departments. All of
this is in order to control the five thunders and the three kingdoms.
Chunchon, being infinitely great, personally surveys all of these
matters. He does not even need to employ all of these agencies."

Chunchon replies, "Noisa Hoong! Because all of you spirits
attained great merit in previous worlds, you have been elevated,
and given positions here with me, and your names are recorded in
the jewel-like palace. Attain still greater merit! In order to do

so, work hard in the thunder office, and in the controlling of fire, thus year by year and day by day your merit will increase and your acts will be revealed. Your nature will become evident and your intelligence bright, and you will be able to witness to the high and the true, and may go upwards on the road of the mysteries. The spirits of this thunder bureau shall work day and night, and, if they do even a little badly, they shall be beaten, and, if really badly, they shall be killed. When the clouds gather or snow comes, they shall not rest. They shall call the dragons and command the crows and compel them to work also, alternately working and resting. Listen carefully to what I say!"

Noisa Hoong, and all of the spirits of the heavens listened with all of their might.

Around the throne of Chunchon was a screen having upon it a picture of nine phoenixes, a regular fog of red. In his hand, he held a gold-covered jewel. A jewel like wind blew, and a satin-like cloud surrounded him. Chunchon was silent for a moment, and then said, " Fifteen hundred æons ago, I had this doctrine in mind, and I went and inquired of my teacher. I pondered much on the matter, and I made inquiry of Taira Wonsi Chunchon. My wish was that in future ages all living beings and the heavenly dragons and spirits, all who should call upon my name, should be freed from sin and come forth; and, even for those who would not call upon my name, I had a desire to save them. Make your minds clean. I will teach you."

Continuing, he said, "All of you heavens and men wish to hear the infinite doctrine. It is very deep and cannot be gotten anywhere else. Since you desire it, this desire itself, even before you hear my words, brings a realization of it. To refrain from all hearing and seeing, that is the true doctrine. Hearing and seeing will pass away, but you remain. You do not really persist, but the truth that was in you persists. What other doctrine is there than that?"

Again he said, " Enter then with faithfulness, and observe it with quietness and act it with meekness. Be faithful even to a foolish extent, quiet as though dumb, meek as a person not quite right in their heads. If you do so, you will forget form, self and even the very forgetting itself. Those entering the doctrine know what it means to have mental action cease; those observing the doctrine know what it is to concentrate; those using the doctrine know the end of all things. When you come to know the end of all things, enlightenment comes. If one knows how to concentrate, his knowledge will be perfect and holy. Knowing the end of all things, he attains great peace. Because he attains this peace, his pure wisdom is perfected. Because his holy wisdom is perfected, wisdom's light arises and the doctrine is further perfected. This is true forgetfulness! True forgetfulness is forgetting even to forget. If one says that there is no forgetting, that is the infinite doctrine. The doctrine rests half between heaven and earth, and neither of them knows it. It is the only infallible feeling, and is also not-feeling."

Again he said, " I wondered how I should exist in this age. On behalf of the heavens and men, I realize now that I must teach this precious doctrine. Those who realize it, I will lead to the bounds of fairy land. The pupils who learn the doctrine will have good fortune. The wind and the earth are not the same. People's heredity is different. ' Keui Oon ' (Energy) is responsible for this. Wisdom and foolishness are not the same. Clearness and confusion are unlike one another. This unlikeness is called ' Soo.' ' Soo ' is used of commands given, or pressure exerted to cause changes. ' Keui ' refers to the infinite Force of Heaven. As to relation between Heaven's commands and ' Keui Soo,' once one attains the true doctrine, he may understand, the cloudy may become clear. Giving commands in connection with the physical world may be foolish and darkening. For example, one might try to change the wind and the earth, but those are under the direction of Heaven and of Earth, and are things which man cannot control. We call them the things of Nature. Giving people knowledge is a thing that is consonant with Nature. The inner beauty of Nature is beyond man's comprehension, the reason for it all cannot be known. However, there is no innate foolishness or lack of clearness in the doctrine."

### ALL OF THE HEAVENS HEARD AND WERE HAPPY

Then Chunchon said, " What I am about to say to you in the Okju Po Kyung, the ' Jade-King-Precious-Saying,' and in the future ages, if you hear my name, make your minds quiet and in meditation repeat this, ' Koochun Eungwon Noisung Pohwa Chunchon Hokil Sunghok Oho Chilsung Hokchun Paiksung Ochik Hwayung Sipang Oonaim Samgei Saching Myungcha Hamteuk Yuwi Sipang Samgei Cheichun Cheiji Ilwul Sungsin Sanchu Chomok Pikoo Choontong Choontong Yakyooji Yakmooji Chulyong Kwisin Moonchei Choongsaing Ilchin Omyung Yuyoo Poolsoonja Koongsoo Hosim Hwawi Mijim.' (Translation—' The Nine Heaven Original Controlling, Thunder Shaking Chunchon! When men call with one voice or with five or seven or a thousand or a hundred, I will appear in the ten different territories, in different metamorphoses, and my mind is revealed in the three kingdoms.

To those calling upon my name, I bring things in accordance with their will. In the ten directions, and in the three kingdoms, all of the heavens and the earth, the sun, moon, stars, mountains, brooks, grass and trees, the flying things, creeping things, the sensitive and the insensitive things, the heavenly dragon spirits—all of these, when they call my name, I hear; those who do not obey, I cut off their heads, and cleave their minds and make them dust and ashes.')"

Chunchon said, " I am the great Saint of the Nine Heavens. Every month on the sixth day and on every day from then to the twentieth which has the syllable ' sin ' in its name, I will survey the heavens, and I will traverse the three kingdoms, and, if there are men who wish to learn the doctrine, who wish to become fairies, who wish to flee the nine mysteries, who wish to come forth from the three sorrows, I will command some intelligent teacher to take them to some house or pavilion where they may dip up water, spread flowers and read this book. If they read it once, fifteen times or a thousand times, I will make their intelligence bright and their strength refreshing, their mind broad and body strong, and will give them all of their desires."

Again Chunchon said, " There are nine spirits in the body. Why should not one call upon them? There is: 1. The Chunsaing, 2. Mooyung, 3. Hyunchoo, 4. Choongchoong, 5. Hyultan, 6. Hoi-hoi, 7. Tanwon, 8. Taiyun, 9. Yungdong. If one calls upon them all, it will be well. There are also three Chung (spirits). Why not call upon them? 1. Taikwang, 2. Samyung, 3. Yoochung. If one calls upon them, he will receive a blessing. There are five sorts of mind all mixed up together and six sorts of pulse, and he has four limbs which are not peaceful, and many joints that are not at peace. For all of these, read this book."

Again he said, " There was a man whose five faculties were dulled and his nine lights darkened. One year, he met the noxious Hyungchoong influences, and all through his life he kept meeting the Kookchun, Kosin, Kwasook, Yangin, Kumpong, Kupsal, Mangsin, Kwimoon, and Kookkyo influences. Wherever he moved, he met dangerous influences. When on the road, he fell into a hole. That man should read this book. He should call the official spirits of the heavens to take away the pains over which the heavens preside; and he should invite the earthly official spirits to try to get rid of the pains due to earthly causes; and the water guardians to get rid of sorrows connected with the waters; he should call the Five Kings and get rid of the sorrow connected with the five sections of the heavens; he should call the Four Saints and get rid of the sorrow connected with the four seasons;

should call the South Star and get rid of all of his original sorrows and the North Star to rid of sorrows connected with that."

Again Chunchon said, " When severe sickness comes, and it does not get well for a long time, and, though one takes the medicine, there is no relief, and one's five faculties fail, and one cannot control his limbs, the reason is that one has sinned before the Five Kings, and the Three Officials, and before the Five Ways, and the Sun and the Moon, and the mountains and the streams, the spirit shrines and ancient ruins, the shrines of the Passes, and other shrines, the village spirits, or the spirits of the well, or the spirits of the kitchen, or some monastery or pagoda, or the thirty-six places in hell, or the seventy-two rulers of hell. Sometimes the sickness comes because of oaths, or not paying prope
remaining enemy to someone for three generations or many æons. If this is so, confess and read this book."

Again Chunchon said, " There are many forms of cursing, the Chunkwan (Heaven official) curse, the Chikwan (Earth official) curse, the Yumwulil (Year-Month-Day) one, and the curses of the four directions. Among these, the great ones are called Kwanpoo and the small ones Koosul. All of these are controlled by the red mouth, white-tongued spirit. When one is on a journey, or rising up, or sitting down, or working, he must know how to escape the curses, else he might meet the Kwanpoo or the Koosul, and he may endure accusations from them and punishments also. If one wishes to avoid all of this and the Kwanpoo and the Koosuls also, let him read this book."

Again Chunchon said, " There are nine districts ruled over by the Earth King, and he has twelve hundred spirits to help him,— Toohoo, Topaik, Tokong, Tomo, Toja, Toson, Taisei, Changkoon, Haksin, Taipaik, Kooryang, Kumpong, Chaoong, Kumsin, Hwah-yul, Sinhwang, Tangmyung, Samsal, Chilsal, Kwangpun, Pyomi, Piryung and Tochin. All of these are earth spirits. Whoever erects a house must be careful not to harm them, else he is apt to get sick and die. Whenever in danger, simply read this book, and the ten thousand spirits will all flee away and one need not fear the Heaven or the Earth, the Eum or the Yang, nor any of the other hundred dangers."

Again he said, " The brides and bridegrooms of earth, when they marry, may incur the ' Hamji ' influence, or the ' Chunkoo,' or the three sorts of punishments, or six sorts of losses may come, their Eum and Yang may be too faint, so that they may have no children. Also one of them may die early or their parents may die. If they wish to avoid all of these things and have children, they should read this book. If they do this correctly, Minister Kamsan of the Nine Heavens will call upon the spirits to use their powers, and sons will be born. If at their birth, there be any noxious ' Taiwul ' influences abroad, or of the ' Samwul,' and if there be any troubles, any evil spirits, or hindering spirits, any severe sorrows, and if the birth itself is difficult, let them read this book, and Wipang Seungmo from the Nine Heavens will come quietly and take care of the matter. When the child is first born, and wrapped in clothing, and Chuntang the spirit king and his fifteen helpers begin to cause trouble, if they will only read this book, all will be peaceful.

"When men live at home, and birds and rats and snakes try to harm them, and the man throws a tile to frighten them; when one offers sacrifices to them, and sees frightful shadows and has bad dreams, and is frightened by thieves, and has a doubt about all men, and at night sounds come from the rafters, and in the daytime, the cows, pigs, etc., get sick, and the family get sick, and friends come around to console, under those circumstances, if they will only read this book, the spirits will all go away and they will have peace."

Chunchon further said, " I will send out as judges carrying my orders Koochun Noikong Spirit General, and the Five-Point Spirit Generals, and the Eight District Spirit Generals, and the Five District Manoi Angels and the Noipoo Chongpyung Angels. They will issue my orders and send out my decrees like fire and wind, . and they will destroy grave shrines, and ancestral tablet shrines and ghosts and familiar spirits. In the last days, there will be many Mootangs, and they will do evil things, and will make useless prayers. Over them, heaven's law will come down to restrain all of the spirits, and to make a record of all evil. It will chain up the ghosts and will bring punishment upon all evil ones. Whenever these things happen, if any one will read this book, they will receive an answer to their prayers."

Chunchon also said, "Though you have the infectious fever of heaven and others, all twenty-five sorts ; or if you have the twenty-four sorts of stomach worms of the heavenly or earthly variety ; or the thirty-six sorts of heavenly or earthly bodily weaknesses, if you will read this book, you will become clean, the worms' poison will pass away, and the weakness will pass also. If one member of a household dies, and then another, and even if whole households are wiped out, or if the spirits in the tombs bring accusations and petitions against one, if these spirits harm one, cause doubts and bring accusations as groups, and unitedly, seizing opportunities and catching up one's sayings, if you will but read this book, right in the moment of death itself, the third heaven above and the nine heavens below will open, call the soul, and will call the Sage, Spirit General White Horse, who will take complete care of you."

Chunchon again said, " If a man has gathered together his baggage for a long journey, and a thief follows him to steal the things; and soldiers trouble him; when on land, leopards and wolves gnash their teeth; when on the water, sharks and sea serpents show their heads; when there are water spirits at the rapids in the river and the waves threaten to engulf and destroy, to seize strong men and kill them, if you but read this book, your life will return to you and you will go peacefully on by land or by water.

" When the sun is burning hot, and the rain does not come, if you but bend your head over this book to read, the showers will fall. When there is too much moisture, or a heavy rainy season rain, if you but read this book, it will all cease. When the fire power is exerted against houses and even against towns, if you but read this book, it will all stop. When the waves come up so that fish pass along where they have no right to be; when the waves engulf people and they are dying, if you read this book, all will be well."

Chunchon said, " If the men wish to escape the Three Troubles and the Nine Plagues, they should sit down quietly at midnight and bow their heads to the North Star Constellation. Above these seven stars, there are three stars separated from one another, two set opposite one another like eyes, and the third placed above them like a lid. The name of that star is Chunkei, Heaven's Bridge. If a man pays attention to that all his life long, he need not fear gaol or any other sort of punishment, and, after death, he need fear no disaster. Among the seven stars themselves, there are two stars called Chonchei, about as big as a wagon wheel. If a man gives attention to those, and meditates upon their shape, he will have long life. If he is diligent in reading this book and in studying the North Stars, he will immediately receive great profit.

" These seven stars taken together are called ' Chunchui ' or ' Heaven's Doorposts.' The central pair are ' Chunkang,' the inside one is called ' Yumtung,' and the other one ' Pakoong.' The twelve Thunders all act as Heaven orders. Chunkang points to the north, and its body is towards the west, and the road that it shows is a lucky one, but its own location is unlucky. There is none like it. If a man pays attention to it, he will live for a thousand generations."

Chunchon said, " If the world grows degenerate, and doctrine becomes darkened, and good actions fail from men, and they are no longer faithful to their King or filial towards parents, and do not show reverence to teachers or elders, or love to their brethren; if they are unfaithful in their marriage relations, and not right towards their friends; if they no longer fear Heaven and Earth, nor the spirits, nor bow to the three lights (sun, moon, stars); if they cease to think highly of the Five Cereals, and, although they have but three bodies, have four mouths (avarice); if they make their scales big and their grain measures small; if they kill and take away life; give but a hundred to others while keeping a thousand for themselves; if they are vile, and adulterous, deceiving and rebellious, the lower spirits will lay hold upon them, and the Taisul Star spirit will send out an order, and the judge, Orai, will first destroy their souls and afterwards punish their bodies and annihilate them. He will despise them, harm them, hate them, and he will drag them through water and after carts. Yet should this evil man read this book, all of his sins will be taken away. Even though he comes under the review of the spirit judge, he will suffer nothing from the water or the cart. If one thinks of the Nine Heaven Original Controlling, Thunder Shaking One, he must bend his head to Him and obey His orders.

" The merits of this book are wonderful. The words were originally spoken by Sin So Ok Chung Chin Chang Saing, the great King. When you receive this book properly, you should reverence it and should offer your vows to Heaven, and also should teach it to others. Wherever this book is, the local site god of that place must protect it and also cause the spirit assemblies of that place to read it. If a man places this book in his house and offers prayers, sweet odours will arise there, and beautiful vapours will enter the rooms, and no trouble can come there. Only blessed and fortunate things can happen there. After death, the man will not see hell. Death, for him, will be simply living again, just stepping over to another place to follow the same gentle teaching.

Chunchon's power must enter into you if you wish all of these things to happen. As you go out and in, sit down and rise up, you should read this book. Respect all men, fear the spirits, and, when meeting troubles, call upon the name of the Nine Heaven Original Controlling, Thunder Shaking Chunchon, and all troubles will pass away."

Noisa Hoong spoke these words of adoration to Chunchon,—

" The supreme Ok Chung Wang (Jade Pure King)
   Governs the thirty-six heavens,
    Rules the Nine Heavens,
      Exists in all of the ten territories.

" With hair unbound, He rides upon a Kirin,
  With bare feet (red), He walks the icy stair,
  With His hands, He grasps the control of the Nine Heavens,
  He shouts and makes the thunders.

" With His wise power,
  He overturns all evil spirits.
  All night long, He helps anxious souls,
  Brings profit to all the living.

" The waves are like the Silvery River,
  His eyes are like the wheel-rims of a thousand moons.
  He vows by worlds not yet existent,
  And we praise Chunchon's doctrine through all ages."

Chunchon said, "Although this book has been given to the world, the men of the world do not as yet know it. The Nine Heaven Departments are under my control, and under me is Messenger Noimoon of the Nine Heavens, he who writes the laws, and Yumpang, the Angel, who assists him. There are four districts—Yangingsa, Chukteisa, Yoowangsa and Pooongsa. In each, there is a minister who has control. All of the spirits praise my government."

As he finished speaking, on the jade stairs, the flowers of Heaven gave praise, the odours of the flowers spread all around, and the kings of the ten realms said that it was good. The Chunnong Spirit and the great official Naipoo and the spirits of the three directions all with joy praised the Nine Heaven Original Controlling, Thunder Shaking Chunchon and received His Okju Kyung book.

### Praise

Ruler of the Nine Heavens, glorious in appearance, revealed in the ten realms, teacher of the nine doctrines, who has read the precious books above the thirty-six heavens. Fifteen hundred years ago, he had majesty and power. With his hands he seized the golden light, and spoke the Okju Kyung. He makes a sound like the thunder, and purifies the minds of men, reveals all wisdom, upsets all evil spirits, oversees the five Departments, and the three realms, is the father of all living things, teacher of the ten thousand spirits, all holy, all merciful, the all high Nine Heaven Original Controlling, Thunder Shaking Chunchon!

*Praise*

The great King, riding upon a Kirin, with a voice of thunder, making all minds to realize, viewing the good and evil in man, bringing profit to all living things, the Nine Heaven Original Controlling, Thunder Shaking Chunchon. Mansei!

## III

### Classic of the Buddhist Rosary—Yumchoo Kyung [8]

In ancient times, there lived a king whose name was Paruri. He spoke to Buddha and said, " My kingdom is small, and, for several years, has been ravaged by pestilence. Grain is scarce, the people are weary, and I am never at ease. The treasury of the Law is deep and wide. I have not had opportunity to cultivate my conduct, but I now wish to understand the Law even in its minutest parts."

Buddha said, " Oh! What a great King! If you wish all of your doubts and perplexities to be destroyed, string together suitably 108 beads. Keep them continually with you, and, with your heart and mind reverentially chant ' Hail Buddha! Hail Dharma! Hail Sangha.' Then slowly take the beads one by one until you will have counted ten and twenty. After you have been able to count twenty myriads, you will be tranquil, not disturbed in mind or body, and there will be complete destruction of all the evil desires of your heart. At the end of the time, when you descend to be born in Yama's place, if you are able to recite the Rosary one hundred myriad times, you will avoid the 108 places (*i. e.*, attain Nirvana), and will attain to the great fruit of everlasting Bliss."

The King said, " I will receive the law."

This Classic of which the above is a translation is in chart form and is placed upon the walls of Buddhist temples in Korea. The date and authorship of it is not known, but it is evidently very old, for it contains many Chinese characters which are now practically obsolete.

According to the Classics, the number of beads in the rosary is always 108, but each bead differs from every other. There are twelve divisions of them. One of the beads is for Sakamuni Buddha; two are for Boddhisattvas; six are for Paramitas; eight are for Guardians; three are for the various Heavens; twenty-eight are for birds and beasts (the constellations); five are for the Five-Point Generals; two are for localities on earth; eighteen for

---

[8] This is copied from an article in the *Korean Repository,* 1895, p. 23.

the avoidance of the Hells; two are for benefactors, and one is for those who carry the rosary with them.

In one of the poems, it is said, "In chanting Buddha, the virtues are many in number. In neglect of this chanting, the faults are like the everlasting desert. The Honourable One of this world (Buddha) has a mouth and words of gold; and releases one from the meshes of the wide net. Now, you can calculate that on repeating the rosary once you will obtain tenfold virtue. If the beads are of lotus seeds, you will obtain blessings a thousandfold. If the beads are of pure crystal, you will obtain blessings ten thousandfold. But, if the beads are made from the Bodhi tree (Ficus Religiosa), even if you only grasp the rosary, the blessings which you obtain will be incalculable."

The Cheisuk Classic says, "When you begin chanting the rosary, repeat 'Om Akcho Svaha' twenty-one times. When you string the beads, after each one, repeat 'Om Mani Padmi Hum' twenty-one times, and, after you have finished, repeat 'Om Vairochana Svaha' twenty-one times. Then recite the following poetry,—

"'The Rosary which I take includes the world of Buddha
Of Emptiness making a cord, and putting all thereon.
The peaceful Sana where non-existence is,
Is the Nest being seen and delivered by Amida.'

When you lay by the rosary, say, ' Oh, the thousand myriads miles of emptiness, the place which is in the midst of the tens of hundred myriads of emptiness, eternal desert, where the true Buddha dwells. There is eternal existence with Tranquil Peace.

"If the small rosary is used every day in the four positions or states (going forth, and remaining at home, sitting or lying down), the user will see the Land of Bliss in his own heart. Amita will be his Guardian and Protector, and, in whatever country he goes, he will find a home." This is the Rosary Classic of which Buddha speaks.

In using the rosary, the devotee repeats the "Hail!" and simply holds each bead until he has counted up to a certain number.

### BIBLIOGRAPHY

1. *Royal Asiatic Society Records,* Korea Branch, 1900–1928, 16 volumes.
2. *Korean Repository Magazine,* 1890–1897.
3. *Korea Review Magazine,* 1901–1906.

4. *Korea Magazine*, 1917–1919.
5. *Poolkyo Yaksa,* by Kwun Sang No.
6. *Poolkyo Tongsa,* by Yi Neung Ha.
7. Edkins, *Chinese Buddhism.*
8. Griffis, *Religions of Japan.*
9. Rockhill, *Life of Buddha.*
10. Armstrong, *Buddhism and Buddhists in Japan.*
11. Reischauer, *Studies in Japanese Buddhism.*
12. Lloyd, *Creed of Half Japan.*
13. Lloyd, *Shinran and His Work.*
14. Starr, *Korean Buddhism.*
15. Richards, *New Testament of Higher Buddhism.*
16. Gordon, *World Healers.*
17. Gordon, *Symbols of the Way.*
18. Rhys David, *Buddhism.*
19. Sven Hedin, *Trans-Himalaya.*
20. Nevius, *China and the Chinese.*
21. Moule, *New China and Old.*
22. Ross, *Corea: Its History, Customs and Manners.*
23. Hackmann, *Buddhism as a Religion.*
24. Griffis, *The Hermit Nation.*
25. Clark, *The Yama Concept "*—thesis in University of Chicago Library.
26. *Encyclopædia of Religion and Ethics,* many articles.
27. Hopkins, *History of Religions.*
28. Menzies, *History of Religions.*
29. Carpenter, *Buddhism and Christianity.*
30. Wright, *Manual of Buddhism.*
31. Parker, *Studies in Chinese Religion.*
32. Douglass, *Confucianism and Taouism.*
33. Erskine, *Japanese Customs.*
34. Anesaki, *The Religious and Social Problems of the Orient.*
35. Pratt, *Pilgrimage of Buddhism.*
36. Dallet, *Histoire de l'Eglise de Coree.*
37. Underwood, *Religions of Eastern Asia.*
38. Bishop, *Korea and Her Neighbours.*
39. *The Korea Bookman Magazine,* 1922–.
40. Hulbert, *History of Korea.*
41. Gale, " History of Korea," in the *Korea Mission Field Magazine.*
42. Jones, *Korea: the Land and the People.*
43. Eitel, *Chinese Buddhism.*
44. DeGroot, *Religion in China.*
45. DeGroot, *The Religious System of China.*

46. Y. T. Pyun, *My Attitude Towards Ancestral Worship.*
47. Hulbert, *Passing of Korea.*
48. Kellogg, *Comparative Religion.*
49. Clodd, *Animism.*
50. Gifford, *Every Day Life in Korea.*
51. Moose, *Village Life in Korea.*
52. Giles, *Civilization of China.*
53. *Presentation of Christianity in Confucian Lands,* Board of Missionary Preparation.
54. Marett, *Threshold of Religion.*
55. Chamberlain, *Things Japanese.*
56. Gale, *Korea in Transition.*
57. McCully, *A Corn of Wheat.*
58. Dubose, *Dragon, Image and Demon.*
59. Murray, *Handbook of Japan.*
60. Beal, *Buddhism in China.*
61. Sumner, *Folkways.*
62. *Oryoon Haingsil,* Korean Confucian book.
63. Hawks-Potts, *A Sketch of Chinese History.*
64. Martin, *Lore of Cathay.*
65. Magazine *Asia* for January, 1928.
66. Knox, *Japanese Life in Town and Country.*
67. Getty, *The Gods of Northern Buddhism.*
68. Peery, *The Gist of Japan.*
69. G. Paik, *History of Missions in Korea.*
70. Monier-Williams, *Brahminism and Hinduism.*
71. Monier-Williams, *Buddhism.*
72. Nevius, *Demon Possession.*
73. Candler, *Unveiling of Lhasa.*
74. Waddell, *Buddhism of Thibet.*
75. Czaplicka, *Aboriginal Siberia.*
76. Boas, *United States Ethnological Survey of Siberia.*
77. Batchellor, *Ainu and Their Folklore.*
78. Mikhailovski, *Shamanism.*
79. Aston, *Shinto.*
80. Tyler, *Primitive Culture.*
81. Troshchanski, *Evolution of the Black Faith.*
82. Banzaroff, *Black Faith.*
83. Jochelson, *The Koryak.*
84. Tangoon Kyo books—
     *Sungkyung Palli.*
     *Kim Yum Paik's Biography.*
85. Chuntokyo books—
     *Chaykei Yoram.*

*Tongkyung Taichun.*
*Chuntokyo Taihun.*
*Chuntokyi Chinun.*
*Kwankam Nok.*
*Chuntokyo Kyochi.*
*Sakwa Yowi.*
*Kyo Oo Chasung.*
86. Shamanistic books—
   *Okchoo Kyung.*
   *Chunsoo Kyung.*
   *Eumpoo Kyung.*

# INDEX

Acolyte, 66, 83
Adam—King Ching, 23, 220
Agriculture, Spirit of, 110, 122, 202
Alexander the Great, 18
Alphabet, Korean, 81, 97
Altars for worship, 103, 110, 215
Altars for ordination, 67
Amida Buddha, 62, 64, 88
Amalgamate sects, 37, 40
Amalgamate religions, 26, 33, 45, 170, 220
Ananda, 18, 50, 61
Anshikao, 25
Animals sacred, 63
Ancestral worship, 19, 26, 98, 99, 112-116, 123, 142, 166
Anyo, 95, 101
Apotropæic rites, 195, 209
Aryan gods, 24, 51
Arhats, 21, 50
Art, Grecian, 20, 59, 62, 221
Art, Korean, 38, 62
Architecture, 46, 99, 133, 156, 179
Asiatic Society, 11
Asceticism, 16, 77, 84
Asoka, 19, 34, 79
Asvagosha, 20, 22, 80
Attitudes of images, 58-64

Bactrian contacts, 20, 221
Bells, famous, 48
Benares, 13, 17
Begging, 30, 41, 77, 78
Birds set free, 29
Bible of Chuntokyo, 145, 258
Bible of Kwankong, 135
Bible of Shamanism, 187, 276
Bible of Tangoonkyo, 140
Bible of Confucianism, 116
Bible of Buddhism, 79-82
Blocks for printing, 35, 45, 80
Boddhisattvas, 21, 50, 54
Bodhi tree, 13, 168
Bone, sacred, 30, 36, 45, 83
Bookcase, revolving, 57
Books, 17, 29, 31, 35, 63, 79-82, 92, 95, 116, 117, 135, 141, 187

Brahmanism, 17-19, 51
Brahman maiden, 54
Burial urns, 57, 74, 75
Buildings, 44, 46, 99, 122, 152, 179-181
Buddha, 45
Buddhist country, 11
Buddhism and Chuntokyo, 145

Calendar, 155
Canon, 35, 79, 85
Caravan routes, 23
Carpenter, 22
Catholics, 145, 146, 224 f.
Cave temples, 57
  Sukoolam, 20, 42, 58, 62, 221
  Rajagriha, 18, 79
Ceylon, 18, 20, 83, 220
Central temple, Buddhist, 40
Ceremonies, Buddhist, 64
  Marriage, 73
  Confucian, 107
  Chuntokyo, 155, 160
Celibacy, 73
Charms, 26, 79, 128, 168
Chamsun—Samadhi, 57, 83, 84
Chinese Christian, 235, 243
  Buddhism, 24
  Priest ignorance, 89
  Japanese War, 150
Chijang Buddha, 54, 62
Chinsa Conference scholar, 105
Cho Kwang Jo, scholar, 98
Choi Chi Won, scholar, 95
Choi Il Taichang, god, 137
Choi Chei Oo, 144-148
Choi Hai Wul, 148-151
Choosing days, 190
Chuntokyo, 66, 86, 120, 155 f., 258
Chunchei ceremonies, 111, 191, 215
Chuhi, or Chuja, 117-120, 169
Classics, 81, 92, 116
Confucius, 15, 91, 100
Confucianism, 26, 29, 35, 38, 40, 51, 95, 99, 121, 122
Confucian temples, 99-104, 107, 123
  County, 103, 104

Confucian college, 41, 99, 100
Councils, 18, 22, 40, 153
Commentaries, 22, 117, 118
College, Buddhist, 41
Commandments, Ten, 66
Concubines, 98, 125
Cosmogony, 138, 167
Crusade, 150
Cremation, 74

Dancing girls, 34, 98
Dates, Buddhist, 27
Death anniversaries, 38, 114, 158
Decorate temples, 32, 53, 180
Dedicate sons, 33
    Images, 64
Demit, 26, 38
Dharmapala, 83
Dharani prayers, 70, 185
Diamond Mountains, 45
Divas, Kings of Buddhism, 17, 47, 68
Divinity attributed, 167
Doctrines, Confucianism, 117-121
    Buddhism, 22, 85-90, 168
    Shamanism, 216-218
    Tangoonkyo, 141-143
    Chuntokyo, 158-169, 258
Dolmens, 57, 143, 181, 202
Dragon worship, 51, 56, 112, 119, 203
Dragon boat of wisdom, 22, 62
Dramas, 48, 76
Dress of sorceress, 182
Drums, 48, 184, 185, 212, 213, 214

Earth spirits, 109, 199
Edicts, 19, 32, 245, 253
Education, 69, 89, 104, 125, 192
Egypt, 19, 73
Endowments, 41, 103, 178
Eight Scenes, Buddhist life, 56
Eternal deity, 21
Eunjin Buddha, 63
Examinations, Buddhist, 35, 38, 96
    Confucian, 95, 100, 104-107

Fahien, 24
Family Shaman, 191, 215, 216
Fairies, 127
Fasting and feasting, 33, 34, 42, 76, 84
Festivals, 75, 76
Five Point General, 197

Five Relations, 92, 117
Fifty-three Buddhas, 56
Five hundred Naheun, 55
Fish, wooden, 48
Fishing tackle, 29
Formulæ Chuntokyo, 86, 145, 155, 172, 263, 268
Fortune-telling, 26, 78, 128
Funerals, 74, 112, 210, 211
Fungsui, 112, 187-210
Future life, 74, 112, 119, 166, 218

Gates of temples, 47
Gautauma, 14, 53
Geomancy, 188
Gestures in prayer, 82
Gifts to temples, 32, 33, 34, 152
Gnostics, 23
Gordon, 11, 22, 48, 58, 62, 64, 77, 81, 221
Gong, brazen, 48
Gods of war, 131-138
Grades in clergy, 69
Grades of living things, 22
Greek culture, 20
Guest-rooms, 48, 231

Hackmann, 14
Haloes, boat shaped, 58
Hananim, 139, 169, 172, 195
Haingkyo temples, 103
Hamel Hendrik, 39
Haiinsa temple, 35, 46, 67, 80
Healing Buddha, 50
Hells, 21, 52, 88
Hermits, 84
Heumijikyo sect, 130
Hideyochi, 32, 38, 132, 224
Hinyana, 20, 79, 82
Hiezan Mountain, 39
History, 11, 93, 132, 144, 175
History books, 92, 96
House gods, 204
Hulbert, 11
Hwatoo formulæ, 83

Iboolam, 221
Ignorance of priests, 89
Ilchinhoi party, 151
Ilkwang Posal, 52, 61
Immaculate conception, 17
Images, 29, 33, 47, 57-64
Imjei sect, 36, 83
Immorality, 125, 217

India Buddhism, 13
India kingdoms, 20, 22
India priests, 28, 31, 83
Invasion of Japanese, 38, 224 f.
Install images, 64
Initiations, 65, 157
Independence Movement, 41, 153

Japanese Buddhism, 27, 85
Japanese nuns, 30
Japanese invasion, 32, 38, 101
Japanese sects, 40, 42
Japanese temples, 47
Japanese priests, 89
Japanese Confucianism, 93, 118, 120-121
Japanese Shinto, 129
Japanese Catholics, 224 f.
Jataka Tales, 17
Jalandhara Council, 22
Janteng teacher, 50, 53
Jizo Bosatsu, 55
Jewish faces, 58, 221
Jewish Passover, 135, 223
Jesuits in Japan, 224

Kakhwangsa temple,
Kamnotan altar, 53
Kakakura Buddha, 58
Kaniska King, 20, 22, 24, 34
Kanghwa altar, 39, 139, 196
Kapilavastu, 14
Kasyap, 18, 50, 61
Kasa robe, 30, 68
Kashmir, 22
Keuija, King, 27, 91, 93
Kishilon book, 20, 80, 81
King Ching, Nestorian, 23
King becomes monk, 29
Killing animals, 29, 33
Kioto Canon, 35, 39
Kings Divas, 47
Kitchen god, 51, 206
Kings of Hell, 52
Kim Yung Kook, Chuntokyo, 151
Kinds, spirits, 194-209
Koot ceremony, 211-214
Koopum pictures, 57
Koryu Kingdom, 27, 32, 36, 66, 85, 89
Kogoryu Kingdom, 27, 95, 128
Kobo Daishi, 23, 45
Kooknak Seikee Heaven, 21
Kumarajiva, 26, 80
Kyungju, 20, 44, 145

Kwanseieum goddess, 33, 49, 58, 60, 62, 64, 88, 168
Kwankong religion, 131

Laban Chonja god, 53, 55
Laotze, see *Taoism*
Legends, 17, 25, 31, 55, 96, 166
Lloyd, 19, 23
Literature of cults, 79, 116, 144
Loshana Buddha, 60
Lotus flowers, 57, 70, 74
Lonely Saint, 53, 55
Lokaraksha, missionary, 25
Lotus Flower Gospel, 21
Luck gods, 205
Lumbini grove, 15

Magic, 26, 78, 176
Magians, 23
Macedonia, 19
Megasthenes, 19
Magadha, 17
Mahaprajapati, 15
Manchuria, Manchus, 13, 32, 39, 45
Malignant spirits, 191, 205, 208
Mahayana Buddhism, 20-22, 79, 82, 88
Marriage, 38, 73
Marananda, 28
Marks of Buddha, 59-61
Mara, evil one, 17
Maya, Buddha mother, 15
Marco Polo, 24
Messiah, Miryuck Buddha, 14, 50, 56, 61, 63, 64
Medallion, 50
Melchisedek, 53
Meukhola, monk, 28, 58, 221
Memorial days, 115, 158
Military monks, 39
Mooti, Meukja, 120, 228
Mootang, sorceress, 181-219
Mohammedanism, 126, 132
Monotheism, primitive, 118, 197
Morality, 107, 216
Moonsoo Posal Buddha, 62, 219
Monasteries, famous, 46
Mountain spirit, 44, 52, 199
Moohak, priest, 36
Monks, great ones, 31, 36, 38, 181, 201
Monks not bow to nobles, 34
Mongol invasion, 32, 35, 45
Motoori, priest, 23, 129
Monuments, 14, 17, 19, 24, 33, 93

Mutilations, 84
Music, 76, 154

Nagarjuna, 21, 166
Naheun Buddhas, 32, 55
Namhan fortress, 39
Nestorians and Stone, 23, 25, 220
National treasures, 29, 41, 48
New Testament of Buddhism, 21
Nine Scenes of Paradise, 57
Nitu writing, 31
Nirvana, 21, 88
North Constellation, 45, 52, 55, 74, 79
Nuns and nunneries, 40, 46

Offerings, 52
Okjukyung, 276
Ordinations, 65, 68, 157, 192
Ornaments, 53
Organization, 40, 82, 152, 193, 219

Paikchei land, 27-29, 45
Pagoda, 29, 32, 35, 36, 57, 110
Palkwai images, 45
Paksoo, sorcerer, 181
Palestine, 32, 199, 222
Palm leaf books, 30, 80
Panyu Yongsun boat, 22, 62
Pansoo, sorcerer, 185, 213
Pantheism, 164-166
Pak Hak Nyun, 13
Patriarchs, 18, 80
Paradise, 21, 88
Parthia, 25
Paraphernalia, 24, 211, 213
Pavilion, 48
Peking temples, 47
Penang temples, 13, 47
Persecutions, 26, 40, 169, 226, 231, 237, 240, 244, 254
Palsang pictures, 56, 81
Plays, 48, 76
Pochunkyo sect, 130
Pongsansi temple, 110
Politics, 170
Portuguese priests, 224
Pootoo urns, 57
Posal Buddhas, 50, 58, 62
Poolkoosa temple, 42
Poverty, 41, 78
Pope, Buddhist, 36, 38
Poolkyo Yaksa book, 13
Poolkyo Tongsa book, 13
Pilgrimages, 25, 30, 36, 84

Pilgrim Progress, 53
Pictures, 20, 32, 50, 53, 54, 62, 101
Plow furrow, 96
Prayers, Chuntokyo, 156-157
    Confucian, 109, 112, 122
    Buddhist, 70-73
    For dead, 53
Primitive monotheism, 119, 197
Printing, 81, 97
Priests, great, 31, 36, 38
Prateyka Buddha, 50
Prayer wheel, 57
Prayer seasons, 72, 75
Preaching, 73
Processions, 65
Priests' names, 67
Pumusa temple, 31, 39
Pupki Buddha, 62

Qualifications, priests, 68

Rain ceremony, 112, 187, 196
Rainy season prayer, 18, 72
Rangoon temples, 13, 47
Review magazine, 11
Repository magazine, 11
Relics, 29, 33
Recruits, priests, 70, 192
Retreats, 18, 72
Rhys David, 14
Road sacrifices, 112
Rosary Classic, 286
Rosary, 71, 158, 168
Royal protection, 46

Sacrifices, 98, 107, 110, 112, 135, 266
Sacred places, 64
Saddharma Pundarika book, 21, 80
Sakamuni Sakayerai, 14
Sakra god, 51, 180
Sajik Shrine, 96, 99, 109
Samadhi prayer, 57, 83
Sam Geui, scholar, 95
Sages, 94
Sanctions, 80, 167
Sanscrit, 22, 30, 49
Sarnath park, 13, 17
Savior Choi Chei Oo, 154, 166
Saree jewels, 17, 57, 75
Scythians, 20
Schisms, 18, 152
Scriptures, Buddhist, 17, 25, 80
Schools, Buddhist, 121
Sects, Buddhist, 30, 37, 41, 81-85
Setbacks, 32, 33, 96

Shamanism, 29, 51, 79, 93, 112, 119, 127, 138, 143, 168, 173
Shamanism, definition, 173
Shaman, definition, 174, 192
Shaman types, 181
Shaman séances, 209-216
Shaman call and preparation, 192
Shaman paraphernalia, 182, 209-216
Shaman spirits, 194
Shaman books, 187
Siberia, 173-176, 180-185
Shinto, Japan, 23, 129
Smiths, Magi, 182, 183
Siddartha, 14
Sianfu, 23
Silla, 27, 29, 33, 45, 72, 94, 95
Sindon, priest, 36
Sinchoongdang picture, 51, 65
Sillongsi Spirit Farmer, 110, 122
Site gods, 110, 199
Sichunkyo sect, 153-155
Sons dedicated, 33
Soonto, priest, 27, 82
Soosoorim King, 28
Signs of Buddha, 50
Sorcery, 92, 173 f.
Spirit worship, 119, 173 f.
Son Pyung Heui, 150-154
Social movements, 170
Special days, 75, 115, 158
Snake worship, 63
Starr, Prof., 12, 81
Stone worship, 63
Statistics, 42, 123, 126, 141, 144
Sukoolam cave, 20, 42, 223
Supreme God, 197
Sulchong, scholar, 31, 95
Sungmoonsa temple, 28
Swastika, 60
Syria churches, 19, 22, 23

Tablets, 102, 108, 112-116, 123, 211
Talismans, 79, 117
Tangoon, 26, 137-143, 142, 206
Tangoonkyo, 137-143
Taiheung Chun temple, 56
Taiseiji Buddha, 60, 90
Taiko, priest, 36
Tang, Land of, 31, 32, 35

Taoism, 26, 29, 45, 51, 53, 127-129, 156, 168, 206, 227
Temples, Kwanoo, 131-137
  Heaven, 110, 122
  Private, 63
  Largest, 45
Tenrikkyo, 144
Ten Commandments, 66
Ten Thousand Buddhas, 56
Ten Kings of Hell, 52, 54
Tendai sect, 30, 53
Thomas, Apostle, 22, 25
Thibet, 25, 28, 49, 84, 127
Three legs stool, 26, 33, 127, 168
Three Kingdoms, 27
Thirty-two forms, 50
Thousand Buddhas, 56
Titsang Buddha, 54
Tree worship, 207
Tombs near temples, 38, 44
Tongtosa temple, 30, 38, 41, 45, 49, 60, 67, 73, 77
Tonghak Movement, 148-151
Trollope, 12, 53, 81
Tribulation, Great, 148, 149
Tushito Heaven, 17

Universities, 32, 44
Urns for burial, 75

Vaishali council, 18
Vairochana Buddha, 23, 61
Vandalism, 38
Vegetarians, 69
Veda Buddha, 50
Vehicles, Buddhist, 20
Visions of Choi Chei Oo, 147
Vows, 34, 67

Wall-gazing Brahman, 81
Water, Sacred, 66, 156, 158, 159
Western Paradise, 21
Wheel of life, 22, 49, 58, 86, 88
White horses, 25, 63, 109
Wheel Kings, 20, 34
White Buddha, 64
Whanung spirit, 138, 206
Women, 42, 78, 128, 154, 182
Worship, Confucian, 107, 111, 112
Wunhyo, priest, 31, 85

For Product Safety Concerns and Information please contact our EU
representative  GPSR@taylorandfrancis.com
Taylor & Francis Verlag GmbH, Kaufingerstraße 24, 80331 München, Germany

www.ingramcontent.com/pod-product-compliance
Lightning Source LLC
Chambersburg PA
CBHW050659280326
41926CB00088B/2408